# Flavor Secrets:
## *Back to the Basics*

# Flavor Secrets:
## *Back to the Basics*

A professional chef's guide to delicious home cooking.

by Lynn M. Miller

Proudly created and printed in the state of Michigan by hard working Michiganders.

© 2009 Lynn M. Miller
Released: November 2009
Second printing: August 2010

Author: Lynn M. Miller

Designer: Jon Fenlon

Printer: Thomson-Shore
7300 West Joy Road
Dexter, MI 48130-9701
www.thomsonshore.com

All book inquiries should be addressed to:
Spitz Press
P.O. Box 725
Bloomfield Hills, MI 48303
Email: spitzpress@gmail.com

ISBN # 978-0-9842249-0-6

For more information, please visit:
www.flavorsecrets.com

*This book is for my family. I especially love you for your patience with all of my monomaniac missions.*

*My husband, Randall Miller*

*My sons, Eric and Aaron Lindauer*

*My daughter-in-law, Christine Lindauer*

*and last but certainly not least,*

*My grandson, Luke*

*Chef Lynn*

Dear Home Cooks,

**I vividly remember** the day after I graduated from culinary school. It was a turning point and I wanted to make sure I remembered and made good use of what I had learned. I had already been teaching cooking classes for several years and I wanted to sort out the most important ideas to pass on to my students who would be cooking at home without professional equipment.

So I sat down and made a list. I wrote down every tip I could think of. Then I went back through my notes from other cooking schools and all of my years of intense hobby cooking and added more. From that moment on, I began designing classes that illustrated the tips and techniques that kicked up flavor and made me a better cook. Over the next few years, I taught them to many others, incorporating my own personal touches. The natural culmination of that experience is this book. Every one of the tips I wrote down is somewhere in this book with an example of how it works.

**So home cooks...** this book is for you. It's chock full of professional tips that really work at home. It's about intensifying flavor and taking the stress out of cooking by planning ahead. It's about mastering the basics and understanding how one recipe can become many other things. It's about how to turn any recipe into something you really love to eat and how to save money doing it. It will help you make simple, beautiful and tasty, yet inexpensive food prepared right at home.

Read on and try some new things. All the major cooking techniques are covered, so things you learn can be applied to every future meal you make. Don't be afraid of mistakes. You will learn from them. Just enjoy yourself and try. You can do it!

*Chef Lynn*

Chef Lynn

# Recipe Table of Contents

**NASTURTIUM** are edible flowers from the mustard family that have a surprisingly sharp and peppery taste. They are easy to grow at home, delicious in salads and sides, and look beautiful as a tasty plate decoration. They also contribute to your daily dose of Vitamin C!

# Chapter One
## *The Main Course*

# Lesson One

## *What's important to know about cooking the main course?*

- **THE MAIN COURSE** has this name because it's the most important part of the meal. That's also why it's listed first in this book. Chefs plan the main course first and then plan the rest of the meal to complement it.

- **FIRST COLLECT AND MEASURE ALL OF YOUR INGREDIENTS.** This way you will have no surprises or missing ingredients. You will be able to concentrate on the methods and as a result the dish will go together much more smoothly.

- **MAJOR COOKING TECHNIQUES** are listed in the chart on the following pages. Once you master them, you can apply them to any food product, including vegetables. In a nutshell, tender cuts are best cooked using quick cooking with high heat. Tougher cuts need longer cooking methods in order to tenderize.

- **TENDERIZATION:** Ways to tenderize meat:

  - Marinate it. (The tougher the product, the longer you need to marinate it.)

  - Pound the raw meat to break up the protein strands.

  - Cut it on the bias to break up the protein strands, before or after cooking.

  - Brine it in a solution that contains acid and/or salt.

- **MARINADES**: Do not store acidic food in containers that contain toxic metals (lead, copper, brass, zinc, antimony and cadmium). It can leach metals from the item and become contaminated. For example, storing tomato sauce in a copper pot or lemonade in a pewter pitcher could lead to a food borne illness. Only food-grade utensils and equipment should be used to prepare and store food.

- **CARAMELIZATION** is a very important but often improperly used word. Technically, this term only applies to sugars. What happens with proteins is actually called the Maillard reaction.

Semantics aside, the result is the same. It's the browning that makes food taste great! Even before braising, first brown your spiced meat, poultry, fish or even vegetables (using a little oil in the pan) on high heat. Browning increases flavor tremendously. Another good reason to do this is that searing kills bacteria lurking on surfaces.

- **SAUTÉ OR GRILL** the side of the food product you will present to your guest. Once it has perfect grill marks or nice, even browning, you can flip it over and finish the underside. This way, you won't overcook it just trying to make it look prettier.

- **TEMPERATURE** is the best way to determine when cooking is complete. In fact, if you ask most chefs how long to cook something, they won't give you a time, but rather will answer, "until it's done." Invest in a good thermometer and check it periodically to be sure it's staying calibrated. The Temperature Appendix at the end of this book serves as a guide for appropriate cooking temperatures. If you overcook food, it makes it dry, tough and hard to chew. Under cooked food is unappealing and can be unsafe. Insert a cooking thermometer into the thickest part of the meat, fish or poultry and wait for the reading to be steady. (Make sure your thermometer is not resting against a bone because bone is porous and will register cooler than the meat.) Have a toothpick ready to plug the hole the thermometer has made as soon as you remove it. This will keep the juices from running out. Juices are tasty and keep the meat moist, so you don't want to lose them.

Watch out for **CARRYOVER COOKING!** When you remove a food from the heat, it is still hot so it continues to cook until it has a chance to cool. To allow for this, a general rule is to remove food from the heat when it reaches 5°F less than the desired end temperature. Then let it sit while it adjusts.

- **BEWARE OF CROSS CONTAMINATION.** For example: If you use a knife and cutting board to cut raw chicken, do not use it for anything else before it is washed and sanitized. You could also assign specific cutting boards to be used only for hazardous foods like chicken. Bacteria can easily be transferred from one product to another. Make sure you thoroughly clean utensils after using them, especially with hazardous products. Marinades and batters can transfer bacteria to other products, so please don't reuse them. Remember to clean your thermometer in between uses. It can easily be a source of cross contamination!

- **BREADING FOOD:** Speaking of batters, if you are breading food to be cooked later on, put it in the refrigerator as quickly as possible and keep it there until you are ready to cook it. Then cook it thoroughly. Coatings act as insulators, so you have to be careful to be sure the food is thoroughly cooked.

- **FOOD SAFETY:** Here's an important quote from the Serve Safe Coursebook: In your refrigerator, "store cooked or ready-to-eat food above raw meat, poultry and fish if these items are stored in the same unit. This will prevent raw product juices from dripping onto the prepared food and causing a food borne illness. It is also recommended that raw meat, poultry and fish be stored in the following top-to-bottom order in the refrigerator: whole fish, whole cuts of beef and pork, ground meats and fish, whole and ground poultry. This order is based upon the required minimum internal cooking temperature of each food."

- **THE WINE** you choose to cook with is important. Find a dry, white or red wine that complements the dish. Most labels will give you hints for the tastes in the wine.

- **FAT IS FLAVOR:** If you don't have much fat, you will need to compensate for it with other strong tastes. For example, two things that really kick up flavor are salt and acid. (Common acids are wine, lemon juice, vinegar and tomatoes.) Add them a little at a time and taste in between so you do not allow any element to become overpowering.

- **FISH:** Whole fish should have firm flesh, normally formed eyes (not dry) and firm scales. Salmon, for example, should smell like fresh cantaloupe. The smell we call "fishy" is ammonia that comes from uratic acid. You can neutralize this by soaking the fish in milk. If the smell is very strong, however, it could mean that the fish is not very fresh.

- **GLAZING:** If your meat or fish looks a little bit dry even though it isn't overcooked, brush on a very light coat of olive oil to give it a nice shine.

- **PORTIONS:** Divide your food into portions or count servings before you plate it. This way you will be sure to have the same amount available for each person.

- **PRESENT A BEAUTIFUL DISH:** As a final note, take a few minutes to make a creative display of your food. Then wipe off the plate rim with a damp, clean kitchen towel. Removing any fingerprints or drips will make the meal you present much more attractive and appealing.

- **REHEATING** works well for most leftover main courses. You can bring it back to its original serving temperature before it will start to overcook.

- **PREPARATION TIME:** No times are listed in these recipes for how long it will take to make a particular dish. This is because the time it will take varies greatly based on the experience and organization skills of each cook. As well, you will get faster and more efficient each time you prepare it. As a general rule, plan about 30 minutes to get out your ingredients and put them together. Add in cooking time and that's about how long it will take you to prepare it. Be sure and read your recipe through before you begin so you can take note of cases where extra time is needed for steps like marinating, brining or resting time. Then set all of your ingredients out in the order you will use them. (This is called mis en place in a professional kitchen.) When you begin, you can efficiently work through each step with everything at your fingertips.

# Cooking Techniques and Their Applications

Learn them and you can apply them to any dish!

For tender cuts of meat: FRYING, GRILLING, POACHING, SMOKING
For tender vegetables: FRYING, GRILLING, BOILING, STEAMING, ROASTING
For tough cuts of meat: BRAISING, ROASTING, SMOKING

| FRYING | GRILLING | POACHING/ BOILING | BRAISING | ROASTING |
|---|---|---|---|---|
| Sauté: High heat in a frying pan with a small amount of oil | Grilling: Direct heat on lower side on a horizontal grill | Shallow Poaching: Cooking in a small amount of liquid between 140°F and 185°F | Braising: Long, slow cooking in liquid, generally between 200°F and 350°F | Roasting: Indirect heat in the oven, with liquid |
| Stir Frying: High heat in a high sided frying pan with a small amount of fat | Broiling: Direct heat on upper side in an oven or broiler | Deep Poaching: Cooking in a lot of liquid between 140°F and 185°F | | Baking: Indirect heat in the oven without liquid |
| Deep Frying: Cooking by immersing in hot oil | | Boiling: Cooking in lots of boiling liquid (212°F and above) | | Poêlé: Indirect heat, roasted in oven with product in butter |
| | | Steaming: Cooking in a covered basket, over liquid that creates steam | | BBQ: Indirect heat in a closed grill (heat is off to the sides) |
| | | | | Smoking: Roasting using indirect heat in a closed oven or grill — Can be cold smoking (under 200°F) or hot smoking (200°F and above) |

Home grown fresh herbs and greens can complement any dish. Here are some that I grow in pots on my patio:

Borage has a lovely cucumber taste. It works in a large variety of dishes, from soups to sauces and fillings.

Golden Thyme is a good source of iron. It's perfect for lamb, tomatoes, eggs, meats, soups and stews.

Oregano is best known in Italian cuisine. It blends well with tomato sauces, fried vegetables, pizza and grilled meat.

Pineapple Sage is great in any meat dish. The colorful flowers even attract hummingbirds and butterflies.

Sweet Basil is the perfect complement for tomato, pepper and cheese dishes.

Watercress gives a wonderful spice flavor to salads and is a great garnish.

# Boot Camp Chicken (Bake)   *Serves 2–4*

This one is for you, Jen — and it's for YOU if you've never cooked anything before. This is the first thing you should try! It's tasty, easy and dependable.

1 whole chicken

Olive oil

1 teaspoon salt

1 teaspoon freshly ground black pepper

1 teaspoon cayenne pepper

1 tablespoon red sweet paprika

1. Preheat oven to 375°F.

2. Wash the chicken and remove anything inside the cavity (plastic envelopes of seasoning or "innards"). Pat the chicken dry with a paper towel and fold the skin around the neck bone to cover it.

3. Using a pastry brush or simply a clean hand, brush the entire chicken lightly with olive oil; then sprinkle it evenly with salt, freshly ground pepper, cayenne pepper and red sweet paprika.

4. Place the chicken breast side down in a baking dish. Put it in the oven for approximately 45 minutes to an hour, depending on the size of the chicken.

5. Chicken is done when it reaches 165°F and when a drumstick pulls away easily from the body of the bird.

6. Remove from the oven and let rest for 10 minutes before cutting. While resting, brush pan juices over the chicken to moisten the outside.

**Chef Lynn's Secrets:**

- Putting your chicken into a hot oven quickly seals in the flavor and keeps the meat moist.

- Let the chicken rest for about 10 minutes before serving to finish cooking. Proteins need a few minutes to seize up so the meat doesn't lose all of its juices during cutting.

- Red sweet paprika turns the skin to a beautiful reddish golden brown that makes the chicken look incredibly delicious!

- Baking with the breast side down keeps them in the juices and helps to keep them moist. The problem with baking a whole chicken is that the dark meat takes longer so the breasts can dry out.

- Add washed, whole potatoes and pearl onions tossed with a little olive oil to the pan with the chicken. Bake as directed and dinner practically makes itself.

**Leftovers?**

- Make a sandwich or top a salad.

- Chop it. Add broth, noodles and spices and you have soup.

- Make Chicken Noodle Casserole (page 114).

# Chicken Stew (Braise) *Serves 8*

This versatile and delicious stew can be eaten by itself with fresh bread, served over a flaky buttermilk biscuit, rice or noodles or as a sumptuous filling for a chicken pot pie.

6 boneless chicken breast halves

½ cup olive oil for frying

3 carrots, peeled and cut into ½-inch pieces

2 stalks celery, peeled and cut into ½-inch pieces

3 cups fresh green beans

3 large yellow onions, cut into julienne strips

3 tablespoons butter

3 tablespoons cake flour

2 cups whole milk

½ cup apple cider

1 cup chicken stock

Salt, freshly ground pepper and lemon juice

## Chef Lynn's Secret:

To caramelize onions, start with high heat. The oil should not be so hot that it smokes, but when you add the onions, you should hear a sizzling sound. Let them sit approximately 2 minutes before stirring. Repeat until they are golden brown. Resist the urge to stir too much because it cools down the pan and then it takes longer! On the other hand, if they brown too quickly and you suspect they are in danger of burning, turn the heat down to medium-high. These delicious onions will have an intense and sweet flavor. Many chefs even add a tablespoon of sugar to enhance the sweetness.

## Leftovers?

- Chilled stew is the perfect filling for a pot pie. Use pie crust for the shell and add sweet, flaky biscuits on the top. Bake and serve.

- Reheat and serve over rice or noodles.

- Save your braising liquid and purée it for your next meal for an awesome gravy.

1. Cook the carrots and green beans separately in water to cover and 1 teaspoon salt until done but slightly crunchy.

2. Cut the chicken breasts into bite-sized pieces. Heat ¼ cup olive oil in a large frying pan and brown (caramelize) the chicken pieces. When about halfway cooked, add the celery and continue to cook until the chicken is done. Remove from the pan and set aside in a large bowl.

3. In the same pan, add the rest of the oil. When hot, throw in the onions and caramelize them. Remove onions from pan and add to the chicken.

4. Still in the same pan, make the béchamel sauce as follows: Melt the butter. Whisk in the flour to the consistency of peanut butter. Cook over low heat for about 3 minutes. Add half the milk and whisk until smooth. Add the cider. Cook for 20 minutes. Add the chicken broth and the rest of the milk slowly, keeping the consistency of the sauce slightly thicker than cake batter. If necessary, you can thin it with more milk or broth. When finished, add the chicken and all vegetables.

5. Spice to taste with salt, pepper and lemon juice.

# Perfection Steak (Grill)   *Serves 1*

Great grill marks will make your steaks look professional. Also, the caramelization (browning) will make them tastier.

8 to 12 oz. beef or veal steak

Olive oil

## Chef Lynn's Secrets:

- Glazing any meat adds both a little moisture and eye appeal. Just before serving, brush lightly (using a pastry brush) with any one of the following: butter (or compound butter: See page 198), chicken broth, BBQ sauce, olive oil, leftover gravy (heated) or apricot jelly (heated).

- In the case of fish, grilling it first with the meaty side down will help it hold together when the cooking process is complete. Use the same technique as for grilling steak but take fish off the heat as soon as it flakes.

- You can put the grill marks on your steaks ahead of time, refrigerate until serving time and finish them in the oven after your guests arrive.

- If you marinate your steaks before grilling, the grill can't be as hot or the marinade will burn.

- Please use a spatula to turn your meat, not tongs because they often tear the meat.

## Leftovers?

- Slice thinly and make a sandwich with mayonnaise, tomato and lettuce.

- Make hash. Chop into slivers and fry in a little butter with potato and onion, diced small.

- Chop and use as a pizza topping.

- Slice very thin and serve with an omelet and a side of horseradish cream.

- Slice thinly and add to a cheese panini.

1. First, choose a steak that is not too thin. Your butcher will be more than happy to cut them to a thickness that you like, so ask for steaks that are ideally an inch and a half or two inches thick. Ideal cuts are beef or veal filet, Porterhouse or New York strip steaks.

2. To make great grill marks, first clean your grill with a wire brush and brush it with olive oil. Then get your grill hot (400°F) . Drop the steak on, slanting it to the right, as if you were making the first stroke of the letter X.

3. Watch the sides of your steak and let it sit until you can see indentations. Carefully lift an edge with a spatula to see if the marks are brown enough. If they are, lift it and reposition it to make the crossing stroke of your X. Let it sit until the marks are equally brown to the first marks. Then flip and finish cooking on the underside. (The first side with the perfect grill marks is the one you will present to your guest.)

4. To get your steaks done to everyone's liking, use a cooking thermometer and consult the temperature guide on page 250.

# Crab Cakes (Sauté) *Makes 12 mini appetizer cakes or 6 main course cakes*

Down size these for a great appetizer!

1 lb. cooked crab meat

½ cup red bell pepper, finely diced

¼ cup celery, finely diced

¼ cup shallot, finely diced

¼ cup fresh chives, chopped small

2 tablespoons lemon juice

½ teaspoon salt

1 teaspoon freshly ground white pepper

¼ cup mayonnaise

¼ cup Italian breadcrumbs

Extra breadcrumbs for forming cakes

Clarified butter for sautéing (page 23)

1. Drain crab and carefully sort through it to extract any shells or hard materials. Try not to break up the crab pieces.

2. Mix the crab with the red pepper, celery, shallot, chives, lemon juice, salt and pepper.

3. Fold in the mayonnaise and ¼ cup breadcrumbs. Mix well.

4. Form into patties and dip them in extra breadcrumbs until they are completely coated. Let sit, refrigerated, for at least 20 minutes and up to 8 hours. (This will help the breading adhere and stay on when you sauté the cakes.)

5. Sauté in hot, clarified butter. Don't crowd your pan! Leave space between the cakes and use two pans if you need to. If necessary, use the spatula to pat them and keep them in shape. Season and serve immediately.

## Chef Lynn's Secrets:

- When you shop for crab, you will find several different grades. Look for whole lump crab for the most attractive and tasty outcome.
- To make nice shapes, turn the cake on its side and roll it like a wheel to smooth the sides.
- Serving these cakes with a colorful sauce will not only enhance the way your dish looks but will also add nutrition and taste. Garnish with chopped fresh herbs that are a different color than the sauce, e.g. parsley or cilantro.
- Sauces that work well are Chive Beurre Blanc (page 219) and Red Pepper Coulis (page 221).
- Always store crab in the refrigerator and use by the "use by" date on the can.

## Leftovers?

- Add a little mayonnaise and use as a filling for hard boiled egg halves.

# Maple Glazed Salmon (Broil)   *Serves 4*

Even those who are not crazy about fish might like this version. It looks moist and attractive and the sweet coating is addictive!

16 oz. salmon, cut into 4 pieces

1 cup maple syrup + extra for glazing

⅓ cup soy sauce

1 teaspoon coarsely ground black pepper

Salt, to taste

1. Place the syrup, soy sauce and pepper in a large plastic bag and mix. Add the salmon, making sure it is completely covered.

2. Marinate in the refrigerator at least overnight and preferably two nights.

3. Broil or sauté just until it flakes. If broiling, keep the fish at least 8 inches from the heat source because it can burn if it gets too hot. It will take about 10 minutes to cook. Don't forget about carryover cooking. Take it out of the oven when it is almost cooked. It will finish cooking as you plate it and carry it to the table.

4. Brush with straight maple syrup, sprinkle with salt and serve. Rice or lemon potatoes (page 94) are good accompaniments.

**Chef Lynn's Secrets:**

- Marinating fish adds moisture and taste to the flesh. The longer you marinate it, the more maple taste it will absorb.

- The mistake most people make with fish is overcooking it because they don't account for carryover cooking. This means that when you remove the hot fish from the oven, it will continue to cook. As soon as the fish pulls apart when lightly raked with a fork, it's done. Take it out of the oven and serve it.

- Beware that the sweet marinade burns easily. I broiled the salmon about 6 minutes, then turned off the heat and closed the door for another 2 minutes to finish cooking.

**Leftovers?**

This salmon will keep well for up to a week.

- Serve for breakfast with scrambled eggs.

- Make an appetizer by spreading a toast point with cream cheese, topping it with a few capers, then the salmon and then a sprinkling of fresh dill.

- Make traditional deviled eggs with egg yolk filling. Cut small oblong pieces of the salmon and stick them in the middle of the mixture. Sprinkle with fresh dill.

# Rack of Lamb (Roast)  *Serves 4*

Tender lamb makes a delicious and beautiful presentation. For rave reviews, carve it at the table or stand the chops up against a mound of mashed potatoes (bones up).

1 rack of lamb (8 ribs)

⅓ cup balsamic glaze (available in most markets)

Salt and freshly ground black or mixed pepper

Fresh thyme

5–6 tablespoons olive oil for rubbing and searing

1. Ask your butcher for a trimmed rack of lamb.

2. Sprinkle the raw meat with salt, mixed pepper and fresh thyme. Put some olive oil on your fingers and rub it in.

3. Heat a large frying pan until very hot. Put about 3 tablespoons olive oil in the pan. Turn the heat down to medium and quickly slide the rack into the pan. Sear it on both sides until crusty and brown. (This will take several minutes on each side.)

4. Transfer the rack to a lightly oiled 9 X 11-inch baking pan and roast in a preheated oven at 425°F until a thermometer inserted into the meat reaches 120°F when inserted into the meat. (It will take approximately 20–25 minutes to cook the meat to medium.)

5. Let the meat rest about 5 minutes before cutting (to finish cooking). Brush lightly with balsamic glaze.

6. Serve each person 2 to 3 chops. Good accompaniments are mashed potatoes and green beans.

**Chef Lynn's Secret:**

If you are searing more than one rack, do not crowd the pan. Sear each one individually. Otherwise, you will drop the temperature of the pan too much and you will not get the desired golden brown finish on the meat.

**Leftovers?**

- Remove meat from the bone, chop it and mix into risotto after the rice is cooked.

- Mix with garlic mayonnaise (aioli) and cooked mushrooms and serve as a topping for sliced tomatoes or grilled eggplant. You can also use this as a stuffing for cooked artichokes.

- Chop and mix with minced shallots and mustard to make a sandwich.

- Chop and mix into a green bean salad.

# Perfection Fish (Sauté or Broil)   *Serves 4*

Many people won't attempt cooking fish at home. Here are two foolproof ways if you keep an eye on it and cook it as instructed.

4 salmon filets or any white fish filet
   (One per person)

Clarified butter (page 23) or olive oil

Salt and mixed pepper

1 fresh lemon

### Chef Lynn's Secrets:

- Don't overcook it! Fish doesn't have much fat or collagen so it will both cook and dry out quickly. How do you know when it's done? Simply, lightly scrape a fork on the top of the filet. When it flakes, it's done. Take it out immediately.

- Sear the side you will be serving to your guest first. Find the perfect color and then flip it to finish cooking. Starting with the flesh side down keeps the fish from curling when you heat it.

### Leftovers?

- Make fish cakes. Mix with finely chopped celery and shallot and a little Dijon mustard. Then sauté them.

- Mix the fish into refried rice.

- Make a sandwich. Mix with mayonnaise just until it holds together. Add finely chopped celery and shallot and place between two slices of great bread with a crisp piece of lettuce.

**TWO DIFFERENT COOKING METHODS:**

1. To broil: Preheat broiler. Spray broiler pan with a nonstick spray. Place fish (skin side down) on the pan. Using a pastry brush, brush lightly with melted clarified butter. Sprinkle liberally with salt and mixed pepper. Place under broiler and cook until lightly browned and fish flakes. Serve with slices of lemon.

— OR —

1. To sauté: Sprinkle the raw fish with salt and mixed pepper. Heat a small frying pan until very hot. Add 3 tablespoons clarified butter.

   *Technique Tip: To keep the fish from sticking, slide the fish (skin side up) into the pan as you slightly shake it. Be careful not to splash the butter out of the pan.*

2. Reduce to medium high heat and cook until golden brown. Using a spatula, carefully flip the fish over and continue cooking just until it flakes.

   *Technique Tip: Squeeze fresh lemon juice into the hot pan, not directly onto the fish. The lemon will "jump" up on the fish and give it that fresh looking "glazed" appearance that you see when you order fish in restaurants.*

3. Serve immediately with extra lemon wedges.

Above: Sautéed tilapia, served with spaghetti squash and fresh tomatoes.

## CLARIFIED BUTTER

Why clarify butter? Removing the milk solids raises the smoke point almost 100°F. In other words, your pan can get hotter (necessary for browning) without burning the butter. Whole butter burns at about 250°F whereas clarified butter burns at about 350°F.

There are two easy methods for clarifying butter.

1. Just melt it at a low temperature and scrape off the white foam. That's it!

2. Melt it at a low temperature then refrigerate it until it solidifies. Then just transfer it to a storage container and pour off the white liquid that collects underneath.

When you have removed the milk solids, what is left is the butter fat, which can even be used to cook for people with a lactose intolerance. Lactose is in the milk solids, which still have a creamy taste. You can save them to use on vegetables or in mashed potatoes.

Do keep the temperature low to melt the butter. If you get it above about 145°F, the proteins will coagulate and the butter will curdle. Don't ask me how I know that.

# Rolled Pork Tenderloin (Roast)    *Serves 4*

Unless they are not pork eaters, there isn't anybody who doesn't like tenderloin! Caramelized onions add moisture, color and interest to this tasty dish.

1 pork tenderloin (about 2 pounds)

2 large yellow onions, sliced into thin strips

2 tablespoons sugar

½ cup Italian breadcrumbs or Pepperidge Farm® Herb Flavored Stuffing, crushed

Salt and mixed pepper, to taste

About ½ cup olive oil

Note: Stuffings are breeding grounds for bacteria, so stuff the tenderloin just before cooking. When you insert your thermometer, make sure it is in the center of the meat and not the stuffing so you get a proper temperature reading. Otherwise, your meat could be under cooked and potentially dangerous.

**Chef Lynn's Secrets:**

• When you pound the meat, use a light touch so you don't tear holes in the tender meat.

• Good accompaniments for this dish are mashed potatoes and corn or cabbage.

**Leftovers?**

• Chop it up, onions and all. Cook some chopped apples in a little apple juice just until they are soft. Add the pork for a minute just to gently reheat and serve as a bed for a juicy chicken breast.

• Chop it up, onions and all. Add dried cherries or fresh diced pineapple, a little mayonnaise and a little mustard. Serve a scoop on top of a lettuce salad.

• Chop it and mix it into cooked cabbage.

1. Preheat your oven to 425°F.

2. In a large frying pan, heat ¼ cup of olive oil. Add the onions and sauté them over medium heat until they are brown. Add 2 tablespoons sugar and stir for a minute. Cool. Mix with the breadcrumbs.

3. Using a sharp knife, slice the pork tenderloin down the middle from end to end. Cut only ¾ of the way through and lay it out flat. Trim the ends and any jagged pieces so the meat forms a rectangle. Scrape off any membrane or white areas.

4. Using the flat side of a meat mallet, pound the meat just enough to even out the thickness of the meat. Then sprinkle it with salt and pepper.

5. Place the onion mixture across the length of the tenderloin, in the center and all the way to the ends.

6. Roll the meat up to enclose the stuffing and tuck in the ends. Place in an oiled baking pan with the cut side down. Brush the outside with olive oil and sprinkle with salt and pepper.

7. Bake in a preheated 425°F oven until the temperature of the meat registers 142°F, approximately 30 minutes. Take it out, brush it lightly with olive oil again and let it rest for at least 5 minutes, until the temperature reaches 145°F.

8. Slice and serve.

## WHAT PAN SHOULD I USE?

**For searing meats**, use a frying pan. They have short sides so that steam can escape and you can get a good sear (browning) on your meat. Too much steam will hold liquid in the pan and cause boiling so your meat won't have enough contact with the heat and won't brown. Be careful not to crowd the pan. Too much food in the pan can also cause boiling because there are too many juices from the meat. Control the heat in the pan so you won't burn your food.

**For roasting in the oven**, use a large pan and leave space around your food. This will allow it to brown evenly.

**For cooking in liquid (braising)**, use a heavy pan with sides and cover it. This will keep the liquid from evaporating and contain it around the food so that it assists flavoring and simmering. Use just enough liquid to surround the meat so that it will flavor the meat and cook it gently.

**For making a reduction**, use a pot with a large surface area — one that is wider than it is tall. Spreading out the liquid exposes more of the surface liquid to the air and it will reduce faster.

**For making stock**, use the opposite. You want the liquid to simmer but not boil away, so use a pot that is taller than it is wide. Less surface area is exposed, so the liquid will not boil away as quickly.

**For melting products** (like chocolate) that can easily burn, use a double boiler. The bottom pot contains water and the top pot sits on top, above the water. This causes a very gentle heating process that insulates delicate products and keeps them from burning. The same is true for baking custard in the oven. You should cook it in a water bath by placing the cooking vessels in larger ones that contain just enough water to come about half way up the sides of the custard containers.

**For steaming**, use 2 pots that are almost exactly like a double boiler, except that the top pot has holes in it to allow the steam from the boiling water to come through and cook (steam) the food. Generally, use a pot that is several inches taller and wider than what you want to cook. If your pot is too large, you can burn your food. If it's too small, it can overflow. Allow also for food that grows in size as it cooks, like rice (which triples in size) and caramel corn sauce (which bubbles up when the soda is added).

# Savory Crêpes with Beef Filling (Fry) *Serves 4 with extra crêpes*

Savory crêpes are easy to make in a small omelet pan. No special equipment necessary!

## For the Crêpes:

1½ cups all purpose flour

2 tablespoons sugar

1½ cups milk

6 large eggs

Clarified butter for frying

½ teaspoon salt

Small amount of olive oil for cooking

## For the Filling:

2 pounds beef tenderloin, sliced very thin

4 tablespoons olive oil

Salt and pepper, to taste

## For the Dijon Sauce:

3 tablespoons shallot, minced

3 tablespoons clarified butter (page 23)

3 tablespoons cake flour

3 tablespoons Dijon mustard

1 teaspoon hot sauce

Any juice left from the meat

1½ cups heavy cream (or milk)

Large pinch of salt

Freshly ground black pepper, to taste

## Method for Crêpes:

1.  Whisk the flour, sugar and salt together. In a separate bowl, mix the milk and eggs together. Then whisk the two mixtures together.

2.  Cover and refrigerate for at least a half an hour to rest.

3.  Heat a teaspoon of olive oil in a small pan. Ladle in a thin mixture of batter, swirling to cover the bottom of the pan only.

4.  Turn the heat down to medium. Cook until tiny bubbles appear and crêpe is brown on the bottom, like you would a pancake.

5.  Flip and brown on the opposite side.

6.  Cool and stack between layers of parchment or waxed paper. Wrap and freeze or fill and serve.

## Filling Method:

1.  Sprinkle salt and pepper on the raw meat and toss it with the olive oil.

2.  Get your grill hot and grill the pieces quickly, only about 30 seconds on each side.

3.  Slice the meat into strips and fill 12 crêpes (3 per person).

4.  Fold the crêpes over and place on oven proof plates, cut side down.

5.  Keep warm in an oven heated to 200°F.

6.  Ladle the sauce over the crêpes and serve.

Above: Savory Crêpes with Beef Filling, pictured with Make Ahead Gravy (page 222).

## Method for the Dijon Sauce:

1. In a one quart saucepan over medium heat, melt one tablespoon butter. Sauté the shallot just until soft. Add the rest of the butter and the cake flour. Turn the heat down to low. Whisk and cook for five minutes.

2. Add the mustard, hot sauce and leftover juice if there is any. Continue to whisk and cook for 15 more minutes to get out the flour taste. While cooking, add in the cream a half cup at a time and whisk in before adding more. If necessary, you can thin with a little more cream at the end.

3. Add salt and pepper to taste. Spoon the sauce over the crêpes and serve.

## Chef Lynn's Secret:

After the initial seasoning of the pan, you may or may not need to add more olive oil. If the crêpes start to stick, simply brush the pan with a very small amount of oil.

## Leftovers?

- Extra filling can be used in all the same ways as leftover steak.

- Crêpes are great for make ahead meals. They can be placed in an airtight container to keep in the refrigerator for up to a week or in the freezer for up to 3 months. You can also freeze the beef. Thaw the beef and crêpes in the refrigerator. Make the sauce fresh and you're done.

# Savory Pork Pie (Bake)  *Serves 6*

**For the Crust:**

1½ cups all purpose flour

⅓ cup Cheddar cheese, grated

½ teaspoon salt

½ cup chilled unsalted butter, cut into pieces

¼ cup (or more) ice water

Cooking spray

1 tablespoon Dijon mustard (to coat crust)

1 egg beaten with 2 tablespoons heavy
    whipping cream (for glazing)

**For the Filling:**

3 tablespoons vegetable oil

2 shallots, minced

1 pound ground regular pork sausage

1 pound ground hot pork sausage

¾ cup cherry tomatoes, finely chopped

3 oz. tomato paste (½ small can)

¼ cup water

½ teaspoon ground cinnamon

½ teaspoon dried savory

¼ teaspoon celery seeds

¼ teaspoon ground cloves

1 teaspoon garlic powder

½ teaspoon salt

½ cup breadcrumbs

1. Preheat oven to 375°F.

2. Mix flour, cheese, salt and butter until the mixture resembles small peas. Add the ice water and mix until a dough ball forms. Wrap in plastic and chill.

3. Prepare the filling by sautéing the shallots in the oil until they are soft and golden. Then add the sausage and cook until no longer pink. Stir in all the rest of the ingredients except for the breadcrumbs and continue to simmer for 10 minutes. Stir the breadcrumbs through and cool.

4. Lightly spray a pie pan with cooking spray. Roll out half the crust into a circle just larger than your pan. Brush the mustard on the bottom of the crust. (This adds flavor and keeps the crust from getting soggy.)

5. Roll out the second circle of dough. Put the filling on top of the bottom crust and cover with second circle of dough. Trim the crusts an inch larger than the pan and fold under. Flute edges, by pinching with your fingers. Brush evenly with egg and whipping cream mixture.

6. Cut slits in the top of the crust (so the steam can vent during baking).

7. Bake until golden brown, about 45 minutes.

8. Serve hot, warm or at room temperature.

Not surprisingly, this hearty dish has its roots in northern country, namely Canada, where it's called Tourtière. This Americanized version is wonderful to serve piping hot in winter, simply with a piece of crusty bread. The pie is shown above with simmered yellow beets, mashed potatoes and baked acorn squash.

## Chef Lynn's Secrets:

- For this savory pie, I love using Jimmy Dean® sausage. Mixing regular and hot labels adds a perfect amount of spiciness. If you don't add in any hot sausage, make sure to add in some pepper to taste.

- When you cut the steam slits in the top of your pie, think about where you will want to slice the finished pie. Make your slits on those lines so that the pieces you serve will have even edges.

## Leftovers?

- Extra pieces of pie can be gently reheated in a 350°F oven for about 20 minutes and served again. The next day, it's even better!

- Keep it for up to a week in the refrigerator. It's even good cold.

- Separate the filling from the crust and put it in the middle of an omelet.

# Slow Poached Halibut (Poach) *Serves 4*

Poaching is slow cooking in liquid, a cooking method that keeps food tender and moist — perfect for fish and especially for fleshy halibut.

4 halibut filets, 4–6 oz. each and equal thickness

2 tablespoons whole butter or olive oil

1 shallot, minced

1 cup fruity white wine

1 quart vegetable stock (or fish or chicken stock)

Salt and mixed pepper, to taste

1. In a large pan with deep sides, sauté the shallot in the butter or oil until soft. Add the wine, stock, salt and pepper.

2. Turn heat down to low and simmer the liquid until it is between 160°F and 180°F. Place fish in stock. If it won't stay under the liquid, you can cover with buttered parchment paper, buttered side down.

3. Simmer about 8 minutes, just until the fish flakes. Remove immediately, sprinkle with salt and mixed pepper and serve.

## Chef Lynn's Secrets:

- When poaching, keep the temperature consistent and between 160°F and 180°F.

- Your filets should be of equal thickness. If one piece (for example a tail piece) has a thinner section, fold it under so the total thickness equals the rest of the fish.

- Serve the fish on a bed of something colorful so that it doesn't look so plain. Fresh or canned tomato sauce, sautéed leek or fennel, caramelized onions or cabbage stewed in chicken broth work well.

- Garnish with something colorful to contrast the paleness of the fish. This could be diced tomato, chopped chives, fresh thyme, tarragon, fennel or even shrimp.

- Equipment Tip: Induction burners are great for poaching because you can set the burner temperature and it will keep it constant. If using a gas burner you will have to watch the temperature manually using a thermometer.

Above: Poached halibut with grilled eggplant, salad and a marigold. Halibut is great for poaching because it has firm flesh that won't easily fall apart.

### Leftovers?

- Leave it whole. Make a sandwich on a bun with horseradish cream, chopped scallions, lettuce and thinly sliced tomato.

- Chop the halibut. Then mix with chopped cooked shrimp, minced cucumber, minced shallot and mayonnaise. Add salt and freshly ground white pepper to taste. Serve as a salad on top of a bed of lettuce.

- Cook mushrooms and onions together. Dice the fish and add it just long enough to heat. Use as a bed for a piece of grilled meat, chicken or vegetables.

# Stovetop Salmon (Smoke)    *Serves 6*

Requires special equipment

6 four oz. pieces of salmon

**Brine Ingredients:**

½ cup granulated sugar

1 packed cup brown sugar

¾ cup kosher salt

¼ cup Kitchen Bouquet® sauce

1 tablespoon fresh lemon juice

½ cup maple syrup

**NOTE:** If you don't have a smoking pan, you can easily make your own. You need a metal roasting pan, a metal rack that fits inside and a cover. The smoking process will discolor the pan, so don't use one where that will bother you. Place the wood chips on the bottom, under the rack. It will get hot, so make sure you have oven mitts on hand.

1. Mix the sugars, salt and Kitchen Bouquet® sauce together. Using your fingers, rub it into the fish meat. Lay the filets meat side down on the mix and use it all. Cover with plastic wrap and refrigerate for 2 hours.

2. Under cold running water, rinse thoroughly.

3. Place on racks, skin side down (not touching each other) and air dry for several hours or overnight to form pellicle (a tacky film on the surface that will hold the smoke flavor).

4. Cover smoker drip tray (if you like) with aluminum foil for easy clean up.

5. Place 2 tablespoons wood chips on tray and salmon on oil sprayed rack.

6. Spice salmon as desired (for example, fresh dill, freshly ground black pepper) and add a squeeze of fresh lemon juice.

7. Cover and smoke on medium heat (preheated burner) for about 20 to 25 minutes for ¾-inch filets. It's done when it flakes. Set your timer!

8. Brush lightly with maple syrup. (This improves the look and keeps it from drying out.)

**IMPORTANT:** You need to have a good exhaust fan in your kitchen to make sure the smoke clears out of the house. (Don't ask me how I know that.)

Above: Stovetop Smoked Salmon with Creamy Parmesan potatoes (page 100) and green beans simmered in chicken broth.

## Leftovers?

- Make an appetizer: Serve small pieces, plated and with a fork. Add a little ball of cream cheese, a few capers and sprinkle it with fresh chopped dill weed.

- Mix with a little horseradish cream and fill the middle of a halved hard boiled egg. Serve as an appetizer or as a side.

- Make a baked potato. Scoop out part of the middle. Drizzle it with melted butter and fill the indentation with chopped salmon. Top with a dollop of horseradish cream and sprinkle with minced leek or shallot.

- Make Smoked Fish Mousse (page 52).

Above: Air drying on racks to form a pellicle.

# Chapter Two
## *Appetizers*

# Lesson Two

## *What's important to know about appetizers?*

Call them appetizers or hors d'oeuvres... They're not just for parties anymore! Don't forget... your family would like some too. Yes, they stave off hunger — they buy you time — but most importantly, they make people feel special. Here are some tips:

- **THINK ABOUT YOUR LEFTOVERS.** You can save money and make economical appetizers by reworking leftovers. For example, a little slice of cold meatloaf with some chutney on top and fresh herb garnish makes a surprisingly good appetizer. Use your imagination!

- **SHOW OFF YOUR PRESENTATION SKILLS.** A pastry bag with a star tip is a simple way to make fillings look fancy. You can use it to swirl filling in hard boiled egg halves and to apply toppings to toast points. You can also use a tip with a plain round opening to fill glasses with pudding or mousse. For this purpose, place the tip low in the glass and start squeezing out the filling. Keep the tip below the surface as you fill to keep air from building up in the mass. This way what you see from the outside will be smooth and won't have any air pockets or lumpy areas.

- **VARY THEIR SIZES.** Use appetizers for sides or garnishes or upsize them and they become a main course. They're so versatile. That's why small plates recently swept the country.

- **HOW MANY TO MAKE?** If you are planning a cocktail party that is scheduled to last for 90 minutes, plan 7–8 appetizers per person. If you have a large variety, you may need to plan on more because people like to try new things. At the beginning of the party, people will eat more. Then you will see a hiatus for about 2 hours, and then you will need more again. Remember to watch how long food sits out. Put out smaller amounts and replenish so that food is always fresh.

If there is no meal, plan 10–12 per person. A cocktail party for three hours in the evening — through the dinner hour — should contain 7 or 8 varieties and include 4 per person per hour. A cocktail hour before a meal should contain 6 per person and 2 to 3 varieties.

- **PLANNING.** Mix it up: raw-cooked, hot-cold, sweet-salty, spicy-bland, etc. Think about different textures, flavors and colors. Have a variety of categories. Include seafood, poultry, meat and a variety of tastes.

- **APPETIZERS SHOULD BE EASY TO EAT.** Ideally, a person should be able to consume them in one bite. They will look more professional if they are all shaped alike, all the same size and if you take the time to line them up or arrange them neatly. You can make them look pretty by using tiny, contrasting garnishes that look and taste good.

- **APPETIZERS SHOULDN'T SLIDE AROUND ON THE PLATE WHEN PASSED.** Movement can wreck your presentation and they can even slide right off. To prevent this, you can make a flat and more stable area on the bottoms of eggs and tomatoes (etc.) by cutting a very tiny slice away. To keep dishes from sliding, you can "glue" them to each other or your tray using mashed potatoes.

- **WITH ALL COURSES,** always remember the first commandment of cooking: Taste everything to check the seasoning before you serve it to your guests.

THE TYPE OF APPETIZERS to choose depends on a lot of things. Ask yourself questions about the event like:

1. Does your group have any dietary restrictions? (Kosher, vegetarian, ethnic, etc.)

2. Is the party being held where spillage is a problem?

3. Will people be standing or sitting? If they are standing, appetizers definitely should be bite-sized. If they are sitting and will have utensils at hand, that's a different story.

4. Are you putting appetizers out on a buffet or will they be passed on trays? If you don't have refrigeration available, you need to plan accordingly. For a buffet, you need appetizers that can safely sit at room temperature for awhile. If they are being served and you have refrigeration available, you can plan more temperature sensitive choices.

5. What will the weather be like? If it's cold outside, you will want to have hot appetizers or tiny soup servings available. If it's hot outside, a refreshing soup like cold gazpacho might be in order.

6. Is the party in the morning, afternoon or evening? People expect different types of food at different times during the day.

7. Appetizers should look good, but they should also be easy to eat. No exploding liquid centers allowed!

# Argentinean Empanadas

*Makes 24 appetizers or 6 entrée portions*

Make these as a hot, tasty appetizer or increase the size and you've got a beautiful entrée!

**For the Filling:**

¼ cup extra virgin olive oil

2 large yellow onions, sliced into thin strips (julienne)

2 pounds ground beef round

4 tablespoons tomato paste

2 tablespoons flour

2 tablespoons paprika

½ cup chicken broth

4 tablespoons seedless golden raisins

3 chopped hard boiled eggs

½ cup chopped green olives

Salt, pepper and oregano to taste

**For the Dough:**

2 cups all purpose flour

1 tablespoon paprika

1 stick (½ cup) cold, unsalted butter

1 small egg

Cold water

1. **For the Filling:** Heat the olive oil and sauté the onions until they are caramel colored. Add the beef and sauté until it's just done.

2. Stir in the tomato paste; then the flour and paprika, then the broth. Stir in the raisins, eggs, olives and spices. Set aside to cool.

3. **Make the Dough:** Mix the flour and paprika together. Cut the butter into small pieces and using your finger tips, work it into the flour until it resembles small peas.

4. Crack the egg into a measuring cup. Add water to make ½ cup. Beat lightly.

5. Make a well in the middle of the mixture and put the egg and water in. Mix it with your hands until it forms a ball.

6. Cover the ball with a thin kitchen towel and let it rest for about ten minutes.

7. Form and fill empanadas. (See box at left). Then bake at 400°F for about 30 minutes.

**TO FORM AND FILL THE EMPANADAS:**
Roll the dough out on a lightly floured surface and cut circles (4-inch circles for appetizers and 10-inch circles for entrees.) Then place the filling on the right half of the circle, leaving an edge all around.

Fold the left half over the filling, stretching slightly as you pull it over. Wet the edges and press together. Press with a fork or crimp the edges with your fingers to form a fluted edge. Place on a lightly sprayed baking sheet and bake.

# Asparagus Mini-Crêpes    *Makes 12 appetizers*

Make your appetizer offerings look professional by taking care to make them all the same size and lining them up on the plate.

4 savory crêpes
  See separate crêpe recipe (page 26) or purchase them in your favorite grocery store. You will normally find them in the dairy aisle.

1 tablespoon salt

12 fresh asparagus spears

1 tub of soft cheese with garlic and/or herbs (Example: Boursin® or Alouette®)

1. Make crêpes and let them cool. Using a 3-inch round cutter, cut three mini-crêpes from each of the larger ones. You should get 3 from each crêpe.

2. In a two quart saucepan, heat one quart of water with 1 tablespoon salt.

3. Cut the tips from the asparagus so they are 4 inches long.

4. When the water begins to boil, add the asparagus (tips only) and cook just until done, about 3 minutes. They should be tender but firm. Immediately plunge them in ice water to stop the cooking. Drain.

5. Spread each mini-crêpe with the cheese, making sure to bring it right to the edge on one side. Place asparagus tip at the opposite side and roll up. Press the edge with the cheese to hold it together and place the finished crêpe open side down on a serving platter.

6. Garnish with something colorful like chopped red pepper.

7. Chill until serving time.

## Chef Lynn's Secret:

- These mini-crêpes can be assembled several hours ahead. Thaw leftover crêpes from your freezer to produce this quick and easy appetizer.

- Very thin strips of smoked salmon (lox) may also be rolled inside of the crêpes.

## Leftovers?

Crêpes can be frozen for up to 3 months. Bits of asparagus stalks can be made into soup. See separate recipe: How to Make Soup Out of Any Vegetable, page 62.

# Chicken Delights    *Makes about 28 appetizers*

These tasty morsels also make a great after school protein snack.

**For Chicken Balls:**

One pound of ground chicken

1 shallot, minced

1 stalk celery, finely diced

1 egg, lightly beaten

1 tablespoon Dijon mustard

2 teaspoons curry powder

3 tablespoons mango chutney

1 tablespoon fresh lemon juice

½ teaspoon salt

½ teaspoon mixed pepper

¾ cup Pepperidge Farm® Herb Stuffing
   crushed into breadcrumbs
   — OR —
   ¾ cup Italian breadcrumbs

½ cup almonds, coarsely ground

Cooking spray

**For Glaze:**

1½ cups mango chutney, puréed

1. Preheat your oven to 400°F.

2. Mix all Chicken Ball ingredients together well.

3. Using your fingers, form the mixture into bite-sized balls and place them on a lightly sprayed baking sheet.

4. Bake until just firm, about 10 minutes. Be careful not to overcook or they will dry out, but make sure they are cooked through.

5. While the bites are baking, purée the chutney. When you take them out of the oven, paint them with the chutney using a pastry brush.

6. Insert serving picks and serve immediately.

**Chef Lynn's Secrets:**

• These little bites can be made ahead. Make the balls and flash freeze them (cooked or uncooked) on cookie sheets. As soon as they are frozen, transfer them to plastic freezer bags and freeze up to 3 months. Return them to cookie sheets to thaw in the fridge. Then proceed with the recipe.

• My favorite chutney is Major Grey®, available in most grocery stores and markets.

• These are also good at room temperature.

Fresh herbs make colorful and tasty garnishes. Here are some more that are easy to grow at home.

Chives are perennial plants and pair well with eggs, fish, shellfish, potato dishes and soups.

Cilantro (or coriander) has a very distinctive taste that people seem to love or hate.

Flat Leaf Parsley: Rinse and squeeze it in a clean cloth after chopping so it will sprinkle nicely.

Marjoram has a sweet, pine and citrus taste that blends well in meat dishes.

Variegated Pineapple Mint adds a scent of both pineapple and mint. Great with fruit dishes.

Spearmint is nice in fruit dishes and desserts for those that like the "other" mint taste.

# Country Pâté  *Makes 1 loaf pan plus 2 medium terrines*

This impressive terrine is not as difficult to make as it looks. The cherries and walnuts give it a lovely sweet and chewy flavor. Make a half-sized batch if you don't want so much.

1 pork tenderloin

Olive oil for searing

2 cups of red wine

5 pounds pork shoulder (called butt)

2 cups shallots, minced

1 cup mixed mushrooms, chopped

½ cup parsley leaves, minced

3 garlic cloves, minced

2 tablespoons salt

½ teaspoon pink salt number 1
   (available in sausage supply shops)

4 tablespoons McCormick® mixed pepper

4 cups dried cherries, chopped in half

3 cups walnuts, coarsely chopped

1¼ cups cake flour

4 eggs

½ cup Grand Marnier

1 cup heavy cream

30 thin slices smoked prosciutto

1.  Chop the pork tenderloin into ¼-inch pieces.

2.  Heat olive oil in a large frying pan and quickly sear the pieces. They do not have to be cooked completely. Do not crowd the pan so you get a good sear. If there is too much meat in the pan, it will boil instead of brown.

3.  Place tenderloin pieces in the refrigerator to cool.

4.  Add the red wine to the hot pan and stir in any little bits on the bottom of the pan. (This is called deglazing.) Simmer the wine until it becomes thick and jelly-like, about 10 minutes. (Note: As it becomes thicker it will cook faster, so be careful not to burn it or to cook it all away.) Using a spatula, move the jelly to a small container and cool it in the refrigerator.

5.  Grind ⅔ of the pork shoulder coarsely and ⅓ finely.

6.  Place all raw pork in a large bowl and add in the cooked pork, shallots, mushrooms, spices, salts, cherries and walnuts without mixing.

7.  In a separate bowl, mix flour, eggs, liquor and cream. Add to the pork and mix it all together.

8.  In a small, hot frying pan, fry a small piece of the meat mixture just until cooked through and taste it to check the spices. Adjust them if necessary.

9.  Line terrine molds (or loaf pans if you don't have any) with smoked (or regular) prosciutto. Let the ends hang over the sides.

10. Press the meat mixture into the pan and fold prosciutto ends over the meat.

11. Bake in a hot water bath until the temperature of the meat reaches 140°F.

12. Remove from the oven and let sit at least 15 minutes so the temperature rises to 145°F (carryover cooking).

13. Cut a piece of cardboard to fit inside the terrine and cover it with tin foil. Place it on top of the meat and weight it with a full soda pop can or something equally as heavy. Cool the weighted terrine overnight in the refrigerator. Serve cold.

**Chef Lynn's Secrets:**

- Keep all ingredients as cold as possible at all times. Chill equipment and if possible, grind and mix in a cold environment (such as your garage in winter). If you are not careful about this, the fat in the meat can separate and compromise the texture of your terrine.

- Terrines can be wrapped tightly and frozen until ready for use (up to three months). Thaw under refrigeration before serving.

- If you don't have real terrine molds, you can use a loaf pan and cover it with aluminum foil before cooking.

# Grape Leaves My Way   *Makes about 24 filled leaves*

These are not your traditional grape leaves, but rather a hearty version that smacks of tender meat, toasty pine nuts and tomato.

½ cup pine nuts, toasted

1 cup short grain rice

¼ cup olive oil

1 medium yellow onion, finely chopped

1 pound ground pork

1 pound ground beef

½ cup fresh dill, chopped very small

½ cup tomato paste

Salt and pepper

2 jars grape leaves in brine

 (Or fresh leaves that have been dropped into boiling water for 10 seconds and cooled on absorbent paper towels)

**PINE NUTS** are the edible, shelled seeds from pine trees. They are a source of protein and fiber and are used in many dishes, from pesto and cookies to coffee and couscous.

Pine nuts go rancid quickly, but will keep up to 9 months in the freezer.

Store all nuts in airtight containers in the freezer for maximum freshness.

1. Preheat your oven to 400°F. Place the pine nuts on a cookie sheet and toast for about 7 minutes, until lightly brown.

2. Heat 2 cups of water until it starts to boil. Add the rice, cover and reduce heat to simmer for 20 minutes.

3. In a separate pan, heat the olive oil and sauté the onion until soft. Add the pork and beef and cook until no longer pink.

4. Add the rice to the pork mixture as well as the dill, pine nuts and tomato paste. Continue to simmer about 10 minutes to blend the ingredients.

5. Taste and add salt and pepper as you like.

6. Drain the grape leaves and place them on your counter. One at a time, make a V-cut to remove the thick part of the stem. Pull the V-cut together so that one side overlaps the other. Place 1 tablespoon of filling on the leaf and roll up, folding the ends in as you go.

7. Place the filled grape leaves in the top of a steamer over lightly simmering water for 20 minutes to soften the leaves.

8. Serve or freeze in airtight containers for up to 3 months.

Above: Fresh grape leaves, blanched and stuffed with meat and pre-cooked rice can be a meal in themselves.

### Chef Lynn's Secrets:

- Using fresh dill in this recipe is essential. In this case, dried spice just does not produce the same taste result.

- Toasting the nuts increases their flavor. You can either place them on a cookie sheet and put them in a 425° F oven for about 7 minutes or you can sauté them in a hot, dry frying pan. The nuts are done when they are lightly browned.

- You can make and steam the grape leaves, then wrap tightly and freeze up to 3 months. Thaw in the refrigerator and serve.

- If you can get some fresh grape leaves, this is the best! Just steam them in the top of a double boiler for a few minutes to soften them before beginning. Yum!!

# Manchego Triangles    *Makes 36*

Here are two different fillings for this hot appetizer so that you can please everyone! One is for the meat eaters and the other is for the vegetarians. Choose one or make both.

**FOR BOTH FILLINGS:**

1 pound Filo dough

1 cup melted butter

**FILLING NUMBER ONE:**

1 egg, beaten

1 pound Manchego cheese, grated

Pinch of salt

**FILLING NUMBER TWO:**

½ cup + 2 tablespoons olive oil

2 cloves garlic, minced

½ yellow onion, small dice

5 green onions, sliced

1¼ pounds ground pork or sausage

¼ cup red wine

Optional: ½ cup fresh parsley, minced

½ cup tomato paste

1 teaspoon curry powder

1 tablespoon dried oregano

1 tablespoon basil

2 teaspoons rosemary

½ teaspoon chili powder

1 egg, slightly beaten

⅓ cup Parmesan cheese

Optional coating: 1 cup sesame seeds

**TO PREPARE FILLING NUMBER ONE:**

1. Grate the cheese and mix it with the other ingredients.

**TO PREPARE FILLING NUMBER TWO:**

1. Melt the 2 tablespoons olive oil in a large skillet over medium heat. Add the green onion, yellow onion and garlic and sauté 3 to 4 minutes.

2. Stir in ground meat and cook until no longer pink.

3. Pour in the wine and simmer 2 to 3 minutes. Reduce heat to medium low and add the parsley, tomato paste, curry powder, oregano, basil, rosemary and chili powder. Simmer 15 minutes.

4. Drain off any fat. Cool. Blend in the beaten egg and Parmesan cheese.

**TO PREPARE THE TRIANGLES (BOTH FILLINGS):**

1. Lay a sheet of Filo dough on the counter. Brush lightly with melted butter. Lay another sheet on top and again brush lightly with melted butter. Repeat until you have 3 layers.

2. Cut the layered dough into 3 strips.

3. Place 1 tablespoon of filling on the bottom of each strip and roll it up like a flag. If desired, sprinkle on sesame seeds and press lightly.

4. Bake at 350°F, 25 to 30 minutes or until lightly browned.

5. Serve hot.

Above: Nothing is more tempting than hot cheese. Manchego has great melting properties. I like to stuff the triangles so full that some oozes out and gets crispy.

## Chef Lynn's Secrets:

- The triangles can be flash (quickly) frozen on cookie sheets and then packed in freezer bags before baking. Preheat oven and bake directly from the freezer. Baking time will be a little longer.

- For me, the quintessential pairing with Manchego is Quince jam, now widely available in markets that carry specialty cheeses. For an addition to an after dinner cheese tray, add a teaspoon of quince in the center of your Manchego cheese triangles.

- Keep unused dough covered with a slightly damp towel at all times or it will dry out and become impossible to work with.

- If the dough tears, don't panic. Just put another piece over it and keep going. With so many layers, you will never miss it and it will all hold together just fine at the end.

**Note:** Manchego is a hard, Spanish whole milk sheep cheese. It has a sophisticated and slightly salty taste. It's also my favorite cheese in the world.

# Sausage with Tomato Chutney    *Serves 6*

*Surprisingly, cinnamon and meat make a wonderful combination. See if your guests can guess the ingredients!*

4 Roma tomatoes, skinned, seeded and finely chopped

2 tablespoons shallots, minced finely

3 teaspoons granulated sugar

½ teaspoon cinnamon

½ teaspoon salt

¼ teaspoon freshly ground black pepper

½ teaspoon freshly squeezed lemon juice

2 tablespoons extra virgin olive oil

3 large sausages, Chorizo or your favorite spicy ones

3 small red or yellow potatoes

Salt and pepper to taste

Fresh chives or basil, chopped tiny for garnish

Cooking spray

**First, prepare the chutney:**

1. In a glass or plastic bowl, mix together the tomatoes, shallots, sugar, cinnamon, salt, pepper and lemon juice.

2. Cover the bowl and refrigerate for 12 to 24 hours so that the flavors blend.

**Prepare the potatoes:**

3. Preheat the oven to 400°F.

4. Toss the potatoes with 1 tablespoon olive oil. Sprinkle with salt and pepper. Place them on a lightly sprayed baking sheet.

5. Bake for 5 minutes. Remove from oven. Let cool on baking sheet.

6. Slice potatoes into ⅛-inch circles.

**Cook the sausage:**

7. Heat 1 tablespoon olive oil. and cook the sausages in a nonstick frying pan until done. Cool and slice into ⅛-inch pieces.

**Assemble the appetizers:**

8. Stack with the potato as the bottom layer. Top it with a teaspoon of the chutney, then the sausage. Garnish with chopped chives or basil. Serve with a fork.

**Chef Lynn's Secret:**

To easily skin and seed the tomatoes, bring a pot of water to a boil. Using a sharp knife, make a small X on the end of the tomato, opposite the stem. Plunge the tomatoes in the hot water for 20–30 seconds, until the skin starts to peel away. Remove and immediately drop into ice water to stop the cooking. Don't leave them in the hot water because the tomato will cook and become mushy. You want the flesh to stay firm. When cool, you can slide the skins right off and then quarter, seed and chop them.

# Perfection Toast Points  *Serves 16 (2 toasts per person)*

Perfectly browned toast points in all shapes and sizes make a wonderful base for many different toppings.

8 pieces Pepperidge Farm® sandwich bread
(white or wheat)

Clarified butter

1. Preheat your oven to 400°F.

2. Using a sharp knife that is longer than the bread, cut crusts from the bread. Then cut each piece diagonally.

3. Using a pastry brush, paint both sides of the bread completely with clarified butter. (Do not soak.)

4. Place bread on an ungreased baking sheet.

5. Bake approximately 7 minutes, until the underside is toasted. Flip over.

6. Bake approximately 2 minutes more. Both sides should be a beautiful light golden brown color.

7. Cool and use or store at room temperature, uncovered, for one day.

**Chef Lynn's Secrets:**

- Make these fresh the day you plan to serve them.

- For sharp, straight edges, cut bread when it is slightly frozen.

- To keep toasts from becoming soggy, create a moisture barrier by applying a layer of butter or other "sealant" before adding toppings. This will also help the appetizer to stay together and not fall apart as it is both carried around and eaten.

- Instead of baking, toast points, croutons and crumbs can all be sautéed in a hot frying pan. Use the clarified butter as instructed and the look of the "toasting" is very similar.

- To clarify butter, simply melt it and scrape off the white foam that rises to the top. These are the milk solids. Removing them raises the smoke point of the butter so you can expose it to higher temperatures without burning.

**Leftovers?**

- Chop the unbaked crusts into small cubes.

- Toss lightly with clarified butter and bake exactly like the toast points to make beautiful croutons that will keep for weeks in your pantry.

- Crush them with the side of a knife or process them in your kitchen machine if you need breadcrumbs.

# Quiche Bites   *Makes 48 bite-sized appetizers*

These little protein and vegetable bites stave off hunger and also make healthy after school snacks. Size them to muffin shapes and they make an interesting side dish.

2 cups asparagus chopped small or 2 handfuls fresh spinach (2 cups packed)

½ cup vegetable stock

1 shallot

1 tablespoon olive oil

½ cup minced red pepper (about ½ pepper) + more for garnish if desired

¼ cup ham or prosciutto, diced tiny

½ cup coarsely grated Parmesan cheese

1 tablespoon yellow mustard

½ teaspoon garlic powder

1 dash hot sauce (Tabasco®)

½ teaspoon salt

½ teaspoon freshly ground black pepper

8 large eggs

¼ cup half and half (or cream or milk)

Cooking spray

### Chef Lynn's Secrets:

When spraying your baking pans, hold them over the sink to catch any droplets that miss the pan. Even a little cooking spray on most floors can turn them into instant skating rinks!

- A container with a pour spout — even a measuring pitcher — is handy for filling muffin cups cleanly.

- You can freeze the Quiche Bites in freezer bags or an airtight container for up to 3 months. Gently reheat or microwave to serve.

1. Preheat your oven to 350°F.

2. Spray muffin cups with cooking spray.

3. Wash the asparagus or spinach and trim ends. Chop into small pieces.

4. In a medium sized frying pan on high heat, heat the vegetable stock. When it just begins to boil, add the vegetables and simmer about two minutes for spinach and 3 minutes for asparagus. (In the case of spinach, the stock will all be absorbed.) Asparagus should be just cooked through and still slightly firm. Cool.

5. Mince the shallot. Heat 1 tablespoon olive oil in a medium sized frying pan over medium heat. Sauté the shallot just until it's soft, about 2 minutes.

6. Mix the vegetables, shallot, red pepper, prosciutto (or ham), Parmesan, mustard, hot sauce and salt and pepper well.

7. In a mixing bowl, whisk the eggs until they are very well blended and the color is even — no white spots. Add ¼ cup half and half and whisk again. Add the vegetable mixture and stir well. Fill mini muffin cups.

8. Bake until just set, 18–20 minute. (You can check to make sure they are done by inserting a toothpick into the center of one bite. It should come out clean.

9. Cool in the pan. Loosen edges with a sharp knife and then remove to transfer to serving plates.

# Mini Grill Toasts  *Serves 4 (2 appetizers per person)*

Hot cheese, shaved ham and olives... What's not to love?

8 slices Pepperidge Farm® thin sliced sandwich bread (white or wheat)

4 oz. shaved ham, cut into ¼ inch strips

8 green olives, sliced thin

8 oz. Brie cheese

1. Place the 8 slices of bread on your counter in groups of two — as if each one represents a sandwich.

2. Cut the rind from the Brie and cut thin slices of cheese. Place one ounce of cheese on every slice.

3. Divide the ham into four equal parts and place one part on each of four slices.

4. Top with equal parts olive slices and then another bread slice with only cheese on it.

5. Heat a panini grill. Brush the grill with olive oil and place the sandwiches inside. Grill just until the cheese is melted and there are medium brown stripes on the bread.

6. Remove and cool for two minutes. Using a very sharp knife, trim the crusts from the bread and slice them diagonally.

7. Serve hot.

**Other great combinations:**

- Mini-Reubens (pastrami & sauerkraut on rye bread)

- BBQ shredded chicken and Cheddar cheese,

- Roast beef and Swiss cheese... The sky is the limit!

**Chef Lynn's Secrets:**

- Use this basic recipe as a spring board for your imagination. Re-create any great sandwich in mini form and you will have a crowd pleasing appetizer. (If you use meat, put a slice of cheese on each side of the meat so that the sandwich will stick together.) Be sure to serve this one with a napkin!

- For precise cuts, use a very sharp knife and clean it after each cut.

# Smoked Fish Mousse    *Makes 2 cups*

This delicious mousse is always a party pleaser!

¼ cup shallots, minced

3 green onions, cleaned and trimmed

1 pound smoked fish
   (salmon, white fish or mackerel)

½ cup unsalted butter, room temperature

½ cup sour cream or crème fraîche

½ cup cream cheese

2 tablespoons fresh lemon juice

3 teaspoons hot sauce

1 teaspoon white pepper

1 teaspoon salt

Toast Points (See recipe, page 49)
   or French baguette

Fresh chopped dill for garnish

1. Place the shallots and onions in a food processor and chop them using the cutting blade.

2. Carefully check the fish for bones and then add it to the shallots. Pulse 3 or 4 times.

3. Add the butter, sour cream, cream cheese, lemon juice, hot sauce, white pepper and salt. Mix well.

4. Taste and adjust seasonings if necessary.

5. Spread on toast points (page 49 and pictured below) or thinly sliced French baguette.

6. Garnish with chopped fresh dill.

**Chef Lynn's Secret:**

Any kind of smoked or lightly cooked fish works great in this recipe.

**Leftovers?**

- Use the mousse as a filling inside halves of hard boiled eggs or stalks of peeled celery. Garnish and you've got another great looking appetizer.

- Put a spoonful and a little garnish on top of a 4 to 6 oz. piece of sautéed fish and serve as a main course.

# Stuffed Eggs     *Serves 4*

4 eggs

½ shallot, minced very finely

¼ cup celery, minced

1 small can (4 oz.) tuna fish

2 teaspoons mustard

¼ cup mayonnaise

1 teaspoon champagne vinegar

Salt and white pepper to taste

Garnishes: fresh chopped chives or red pepper, diced finely

## Chef Lynn's Secrets:

- Lowering the eggs into the already heated water helps to keep the pesky green "ring" from developing around the yolks in your hard boiled eggs.

- If you plan ahead and cook your eggs one day before peeling them, they will peel much easier. The fresher the eggs, the harder to peel.

- Throw away any eggs that rise to the surface when placed in water. They are old enough to have accumulated air inside the shell and may be bad. Watch the "use by" date on the carton.

- Keep your eggs from sliding around on the plate by slicing a very thin, straight edge on the bottom to make a flat resting place that stabilizes them.

1. Prepare the hard boiled eggs: Fill a one quart saucepan ⅔ full with water and heat it to a full rolling boil. Using a large spoon, lower the eggs into the water. Set a timer for ten minutes. Drain and cool the eggs.

2. Peel the eggs, cut them in half and carefully remove the yolks.

3. Mix together the shallot, celery, tuna, mustard, mayonnaise, vinegar, salt and pepper. Taste and decide if you need more spices.

4. Fill the centers of the white of the boiled egg with about a teaspoon of the mixture and garnish with fresh chopped chive or tiny diced red pepper.

**Other Fillings:** This is a wonderful and creative way to use leftovers! Here are some ideas, but you can easily invent your own. Mix in just enough of the sauce or mayo so that you are able to form spoonfuls of the mixture and remember to add salt and pepper or other spices and fresh herbs that you especially like. Use the amounts above as a guide and consider using the following:

- Diced roast beef, meat loaf, chicken or pork mixed with BBQ sauce.

- Diced chicken mixed with minced red pepper chutney.

- Diced crab or shrimp mixed with horseradish cream.

- Fill halves with Smoked Fish Mousse, (page 52).

- Mix cooked yolks with mayonnaise, mustard and cream cheese.

# Chapter Three

## *Soups & Salads*

# Lesson Three

## *What's important to know about soups and salads?*

- **TURN LEFTOVER VEGETABLES INTO A DELICIOUS MEAL COURSE.** Soup is a great venue for that! Rather than throwing even a small amount away, why not create a healthy dish that becomes an extra course for your next meal? Take a good look at the recipe for how to make soup out of any vegetable and I bet you will almost always find something in your vegetable drawer that you can make soup out of.

- **SOUPS CAN EASILY BE MAKE AHEAD MEALS.** Soups are filling and therefore great for dieters! They can be frozen in individual portions and prepared quickly. Not only are they nutritious and good for you, they require slow eating, which gives your brain time to realize that your stomach is full.

- **INTENSIFY FLAVORS WHENEVER POSSIBLE.** You can do this by removing the liquid in the vegetables through roasting in the oven. Squash and tomatoes are especially good candidates for roasting. Nuts also have increased flavor if they are toasted until they are light brown. (400°F oven for about 7 minutes. The extra taste is worth taking the time.)

- **LAYER INGREDIENTS.** You can make the taste of your soups more sophisticated by layering the ingredients. Let's say you are making squash soup. Instead of choosing one squash, choose two – for example, acorn and butternut. Roast them to intensify the flavor and then mix them together so the soup flavor isn't identifiable as one or the other. If you are putting wine in your soup, use a couple of different kinds. Use several different spices and last, make your soup ahead when you can. It will be even better the second day because the flavors will have had time to settle down and meld together.

- **THICKENERS:** If your soup is too thin, you can thicken it by adding beans, lentils or some diced potato. Simmer it until the additional ingredient is cooked and then purée it. You can also add some more of your main ingredient at the same time and the extra vegetables will absorb some of the liquid to make it thicker. Simply simmering your soup will also thicken it because some of the liquid in it will evaporate. (Just note that this method can take awhile.)

  You can also make a slurry of equal parts of flour (especially cake flour because it is the starchiest), Arrowroot or Minute Tapioca® and an equal part of water, milk or wine. The best slurries, however, are made of a liquid that also has some taste, like broth or wine. Use white wine for light soups (and sauces for that matter) and red wine for dark soups.

- **"BE A SMART COOK, NOT A GREASY COOK":** as one of my former instructors used to say. Mounting butter means adding just a little butter at the end, just before you serve the soup. Whisk it in quickly and it forms a beautiful glaze on the top of the soup. The subtle, rich butter taste comes through without adding a lot of calories.

- **WATCH OUT FOR BACTERIA.** Be careful about cooling your soups. Failure to cool food properly is one of the biggest causes of food borne illness. Bacteria grow really well between the temperatures of 41°F and 135°F (5°C and 57°C). This range is called the temperature danger zone and your food products — any of them — should not be in this range for more than 4 hours (and this is cumulative!) or you should throw it out. This is long enough for organisms to grow that can make you sick. When people cool soup at home, they sometimes exceed this limit. After you make your soup, try to cool it as quickly as possible. You can do this several ways:

  – Put it in a bowl of ice water.

  – Stir it.

  – Divide it into more shallow containers, set them in ice baths and stir them.

  – Account for the extra liquid when you are making the soup and add ice directly into the soup.

Never put a container of hot soup in the refrigerator! The heat can cause the refrigerator to warm up, putting all the other food you have in there in jeopardy. Your refrigerator should be lower than 41°F and your freezer should be at 0°F. Do not set your soup pot in the garage in the winter in cold climates and assume that it's cold enough out there. Keep a thermometer out there to be sure if you want to do this. The outside temperature has to be below freezing for quite awhile before your garage is cold enough to be used as a refrigerator.

And a last note, every so often check your thermometer to be sure it is calibrated. Dropping them on the floor, for example, can change the readings. Each thermometer should come with instructions for how to do this.

- **FOR SALADS, FRESH, CRISP INGREDIENTS ARE ESSENTIAL.** Whenever you eat anything raw, it should be clean and crispy with uncompromised color. The best way to achieve this is to buy salad ingredients as close to serving time as possible, keep them cold and wash them in cold water as close to serving time as possible. Spin them dry or blot them with a paper towel to remove excess water.

Nothing looks or tastes worse than a warm salad with wilted greens. If you need to prep ahead, you can wash and mix them hours before the meal, but then return them to the refrigerator until just before you are ready to serve them.

- **SEASONAL INGREDIENTS** and vine ripening are crucial for taste. Especially in cold climates, there is a world of difference between an imported tomato in December and a vine ripened tomato that you pick out of your garden in August.

- **DRESSING:** Don't douse salads with lots of dressing! A little goes a long way. Let crispy, fresh greens speak for themselves. They have lots of flavor.

- **PRESENTATION** means a lot. Spending the time to fluff and arrange your salads will make them look a lot more professional. Think about using contrasting garnishes that add taste, texture and color.

# Cream of Pea Soup  *Makes 2 quarts*

I've been making this soup for 30 years and it has never lost its appeal.

1 large yellow onion, diced large

1 clove garlic, chopped (optional)

4 tablespoons olive oil

2 carrots, diced large

2 stalks celery, diced large

1 large potato, peeled and diced large

3 cups frozen green peas

Chicken stock (approximately 1 quart)

1 cup whipping cream or half and half

1. Sauté the onion (and if you are using it, the garlic) in the olive oil until they are soft.

2. Add all the other vegetables except the peas and continue to sauté until they are slightly browned and partially cooked.

3. Add the frozen peas and continue to cook for one minute.

4. Add just enough chicken stock to cover the mix. Continue to cook until all vegetables are tender, about 20 minutes.

5. Purée and chill. Add the cream at serving time (or for a healthier version, don't) and serve at room temperature or slightly chilled. This soup is good at any temperature.

**Chef Lynn's Secrets:**

- Using frozen peas for this soup is just fine, but if you make this soup when you can get fresh peas you won't believe the lovely difference in flavor.

- Serve it cold in the summertime and hot in the winter time.

# Butternut Squash Soup with Orange  *Makes 2 quarts*

The orange flavor in this soup is a delightful surprise.

Approximately 2 pounds of
 butternut squash

1 large yellow onion

4 pieces bacon

4 tablespoons olive oil

3 tablespoons turmeric

1½ cups orange juice

Approximately 1 quart chicken broth

Salt and mixed pepper, to taste

Large pinch of cayenne pepper

2 tablespoons fresh lemon juice

1 pint heavy cream

1. With a sharp knife, make two slashes (steam vents) in each squash. Place the squash in a microwave safe dish and cook on high for 15 to 20 minutes. Cool.

2. While the squash is cooling, place the olive oil in a 4-quart saucepan. Add the onion and bacon and sauté over medium heat until both are soft.

3. Turn the heat off and peel and seed the soft squash. Cut into large cubes and place the squash in the pan with the bacon and onion.

4. Add the turmeric, orange juice and just enough chicken broth just to cover the squash. Cook over low heat for about 20 minutes.

5. Cool slightly and purée the mixture.

6. Taste and season with salt, peppers and lemon juice.

7. Add cream and serve or cool and refrigerate.

## Chef Lynn's Secrets:

- You can cut calories in this soup by substituting half and half, whole milk or by totally omitting the cream.

- You can also omit the turmeric. It's there primarily for color. The disadvantage of turmeric is that it is difficult to remove stains from tablecloths.

- You can purée the soup in a stand alone blender, a food processor or right in the pot with an immersion blender

- The soup will keep a week in a covered container in the refrigerator or up to 3 months in the freezer.

# Minestrone    *Serves 6*

Soup doesn't get any healthier than this!

1½ cups macaroni

2 yellow onions, peeled and chopped into small dice

2 stalks celery, peeled and trimmed

1 leek, trimmed and cleaned

2 large carrots, peeled and trimmed

1 large potato, peeled

2 handfuls green beans, trimmed

1 small yellow squash

1 small zucchini

2 fresh tomatoes, peeled and cored

1 six oz. can tomato paste

1 fourteen oz. can diced tomatoes

1 cup dry white wine

Vegetable or chicken stock

Salt, pepper, cayenne pepper

Optional garnish: finely grated Parmesan cheese

1. Bring 2 quarts water and 1 tablespoon salt to a boil and cook the macaroni about 7 minutes, until just done. Drain. Set aside.

2. Dice all of the vegetables and the potato into bite-sized pieces.

3. Sauté the onion until golden brown. Add the other vegetables and sauté until all are just tender.

4. Stir in the tomato paste. Then add the diced tomatoes and the cooked macaroni.

5. Add white wine and stir through.

6. Add stock and stir through.

7. Season to taste with spices and serve hot.

8. Optional: Pass finely grated Parmesan cheese for those who like it for garnish.

**Chef Lynn's Secret:**

Celery is stringy and is much more pleasant to eat if it is peeled. Just use a regular potato peeler to do the job before you dice it.

# Roasted Tomato-Basil Soup   *Serves 4*

This soup is delicious all year round.

2 cups roasted tomatoes
   (See recipe, page 83)

4 tablespoons olive oil

2 shallots, minced

2 cups chicken broth

2 fresh or grilled red peppers
   (To grill them, see technique, page 82.)

10 large fresh basil leaves

½ cup whipping cream

Salt and mixed pepper

1. Heat the olive oil in a small frying pan. Sauté the shallot until soft. Transfer to a medium sized saucepan.

2. Chop the tomatoes and add them to the onions. Add the chicken broth and grilled pepper.

3. Chop the fresh basil. Reserve some for garnish and add the rest to the soup. Simmer on low heat for twenty minutes.

4. Stir in the whipping cream.

5. Pulverize using either a kitchen machine or immersion blender. Purée until smooth or leave it a bit chunky — as you wish.

6. Add salt and pepper. Taste and adjust seasonings.

7. Ladle into soup bowls and garnish with remaining chopped basil.

**Chef Lynn's Secret:**

You can also make this soup with fresh tomatoes, but roasting them reduces the moisture in the tomatoes and intensifies the rich tomato flavor. So make it fresh in late summer when the tomatoes are vine ripened and bursting with flavor. Then roast them in winter and spring when tomatoes are imported and need some flavor help.

# Soup: How to Make It out of Any Vegetable     *Serves 4*

An attractive way to serve soups is in three small terrines, or small, but tall glasses. Serving it this way as a main lunch course provides interesting variety and fun.

2 large onions, diced large (2-inch pieces)

4 tablespoons olive oil

4 stalks celery, peeled and diced large

2 carrots, diced large

2 pounds main vegetable
   (asparagus, squash, corn, tomatoes etc.)

2 quarts chicken stock

Salt, to taste (about 1 tablespoon)

Lemon juice, to taste (about ¼ cup)

Tabasco® sauce, to taste (about 5 drops)

**Thickening agents:**

Add 1 or 2 potatoes

Mix 2 tablespoons cornstarch, arrowroot or cake flour with just enough water to make a thick paste. Add it to the liquid and cook until it thickens.

**Optional flavors:** 1 to 2 cups heavy cream, 1 cup orange juice, ¼ cup bacon fried soft, ½ cup brown sugar, apple juice or an apple.

You can roast the vegetables to intensify the flavor or not. In the case of squash soup, mix different kinds of squash and vary the cooking techniques. The combination of the different tastes builds great flavor.

1. Sauté the onions and celery over medium heat with the olive oil until they are juicy and start to get soft. Do not let them get brown. (This is called sweating.) Add the carrots and let simmer until soft. Add the main vegetable and enough of the chicken stock just to cover the vegetables. Let it simmer for approximately 30 minutes.

2. If you would like your soup to be thicker and would like to add potatoes, add them with the vegetables. Otherwise, you can thicken the soup after you purée it, by making a slurry of cornstarch, cake flour or arrowroot mixed with water as indicated.

3. Season with all of the seasoning ingredients. Cool and purée with an immersion blender or food processor.

4. If you want to make a cream soup, add the heavy cream and the half and half. Simmer ten more minutes.

5. To serve, if you like, you can add texture with additional cooked and cut up vegetables.

**Chef Lynn's Secrets:**

- Some people get various grades of food poisoning from homemade soup because they don't cool it quickly enough. Cooked food is only safe between 41°F and 135°F for four hours. After that, you ned to throw it out. Set your pot in an ice bath to speed up the cooling process.

- Choose spices and ingredients that will help you achieve your color goals as well as enhancing the taste. For example, turmeric makes squash soup a nice color and tomato paste enhances the color of fresh tomato soup.

- Garnish ideas: Choose something that tastes good with your main vegetable and is a contrasting color. For example, tiny bits of red pepper, chopped fresh herbs, coarsely grated Parmesan, or a small amount of flavored oil.

# Arugula Salad with Tangy Lemon Dressing  *Serves 4*

The peppery taste of arugula is a perfect counterpoint to pizza, lasagna or ravioli. It also pairs well with Carpaccio.

## For the Salad:

4 cups fresh arugula leaves

2 cups shaved or coarsely grated Parmesan cheese

2 cups Italian black olives, pitted

1 cup toasted pine nuts

## For the Dressing:

½ shallot, peeled

1 clove garlic, peeled

⅓ cup rice wine vinegar

⅔ cup extra virgin olive oil

4 tablespoons fresh lemon juice

1 tablespoon Dijon mustard

1 teaspoon sugar

Salt and white pepper, to taste

## Chef Lynn's Secrets:

- You can always recognize Arugula by its "oak leaf" shape. I love it for its unusual peppery flavor.

- You can easily change this salad to offer some variety. Delete the olives and try one of these combinations:

- Change the pine nuts to walnuts and the Parmesan to Goat or a blue cheese like Stilton® or Gorgonzola.

- Add slices of pears and change the nuts to pecans. In this case, you can keep the Parmesan or also change the cheese to a blue cheese.

- Add slices of fresh avocado to the salad as is.

- Top any of these salads with a sliced chicken breast and you have a main course instead of a side.

## To make the salad:

1. Preheat your oven to 400°F and toast the pine nuts on a cookie sheet for about 7 minutes. You will know when they are done by their enhanced nutty smell. They should also turn a golden brown. Cool.

2. Wash and spin the arugula leaves or pat them dry with a clean paper towel. Place in individual serving bowls or on a large platter.

3. Top with the cooled nuts, olives, cheese and dressing.

## To make the salad dressing:

1. With your food processor blade running, drop in the shallot and garlic clove. Using a spatula, scrape down the sides.

2. Add the rice vinegar, olive oil, lemon juice, mustard, sugar, salt and pepper. Process for one minute. Taste and adjust seasonings if necessary.

3. Transfer to serving bottle (cruet) and pass at the meal so each person can add the amount they would like on their salads.

# Michigan Salad  *Serves 4*

Here's a tribute to my home state. This salad can be found in almost any restaurant in every Michigan neighborhood.

**For the Salad Dressing:**

6 tablespoons lemon oil

2 tablespoons champagne vinegar

Pinch each of salt and pepper

**For the Salad:**

6 cups mixed baby greens

1 cup caramelized walnuts

1 cup Michigan dried cherries

1 Granny Smith apple, cut into very fine strips

¼ cup shredded red bell pepper

1. First, make the dressing. Whisk the lemon oil, vinegar, salt and pepper together by hand. Set aside.

2. Wash the greens in cold water and spin it or pat it dry with paper towels. Toss it lightly but thoroughly with the dressing. Mound the lettuce in the middle of large serving bowls or plates.

3. Sprinkle the walnuts and cherries on the salads.

4. Top with the apple and then a bit of the pepper for color.

**Chef Lynn's Secret:**

A mandolin is an indispensable tool in every professional kitchen. These range from a large French version that costs around $150 to a plastic Japanese version that costs around $40. The plastic version is actually easier to handle and can be put in the dishwasher. I have both and almost always use the smaller plastic one! With it, you can quickly and easily make perfect julienne and other cuts to make your vegetable presentations look professional and appealing.

# Pecan-Rice Salad   *Serves 8*

Here's a great "make ahead" dish for a dinner party. It will last up to 7 days in the refrigerator, improving its flavor as the week goes by.

2 cups long grain brown rice, washed

2 cups wild rice, washed

1 cup red bell pepper, diced small

1 cup yellow bell pepper, diced small

1 cup pecan pieces, chopped

1½ cups dried cherries

½ teaspoon salt

¼ teaspoon pepper

½ teaspoon cayenne pepper

1 tablespoon champagne vinegar

⅛ cup raspberry or cherry vinaigrette

Optional: fresh cilantro, chopped small

1. Place 4 cups water in a 2-quart pot. Bring to a boil. Add brown rice. Cover and reduce heat to low. Cook for 20 minutes; then remove from heat and cool.

2. Place 4 cups water in a 2-quart pot. Bring to a boil. Add wild rice. Cover and reduce heat to low. Cook for 40 minutes; then remove from heat and cool.

3. While the rice is cooking, chop peppers into small dice.

4. Chop pecan pieces and cherries to about the same size as the rice kernels.

5. Combine the rice, bell peppers, pecans, dried cherries, salt, peppers, vinegar and vinaigrette and mix well. Chill for several hours (or more) to blend flavors. Garnish with cilantro at serving time.

**Chef Lynn's Secret:**

Washing rice removes its chalky looking caulk and increases its luster. Place the rice in a sieve. Lower the sieve into a pot of water and swish it around using your hand. Lift the sieve out, replace the water and repeat two more times.

# Cucumber Salad   *Serves 6–8*

This recipe came to me from a grand southern lady in every sense of the word. It's traditional in southern states.

2 English cucumbers

1 tablespoon salt

1 shallot, minced

½ cup champagne vinegar

1 tablespoon olive oil

1 tablespoon sugar

2 tablespoons water

2 tablespoons caraway seeds

⅓ teaspoon freshly ground pepper

2 teaspoons hot sauce (Tabasco® or Red Devil®)

1. Wash the cucumbers. Slice them very thin and place the slices in a glass bowl. Sprinkle with the salt and toss. Let them stand at room temperature for one hour. Drain off any water.

2. Mix the rest of the ingredients together and pour the mixture over the cucumbers. Again, toss.

3. Check your seasonings to see if anything needs to be adjusted.

4. Chill at least 2 hours before serving.

**Chef Lynn's Secrets:**

English cucumbers are long, thin and usually individually wrapped. I like to use them because they have little or no seeds and a very mild skin that you don't have to remove. Leaving them on is a good way to add some fiber to your meal.

**Leftovers?**

Use as a filling in a sandwich, with or without meat.

Make toast points (page 49). Spread them with cream cheese and top with chopped and well drained cucumber salad.

Fresh Greens for Salad or Garnish:

**Arugula** is also called rocket, and adds a distinct peppery taste to salads.

**Mustard greens** add a sharp, peppery taste as garnishes, or to salads or sandwiches. The mustard aftertaste is delightful.

**Red and green butter lettuce** have mild, pretty leaves that add color and crispiness to any sandwich or salad. Also wonderful simply as an edible plate garnish.

**Dandelion greens** add interesting garnish to dishes, but the taste is relatively bitter, so don't use too much in salads. Look for small, young ones for the best taste.

The flavor of **Leek** is something between garlic and onion. You can always substitute it for onion if you are looking for a smoother, milder taste.

**Wirsing** (also called Savoy) cabbage is the wrinkly one. It has a lovely, mild flavor.

# Potato Salad    *Serves 12*

The subtle tastes of a variety of ingredients are what make this salad irresistible.

3 pounds potatoes (if possible, mixed types)

8 hard boiled eggs, chopped

⅓ cup leek and 1 red bell pepper, chopped small

3 stalks celery, chopped very small

12 oz. fresh green peas

1½ cups mayonnaise

2 tablespoons prepared mustard

2 teaspoons salt

1 teaspoon ground pepper

Juice of 1 lemon

2 cups Parmesan cheese, coarsely grated

Garnish: Ground red paprika and 4 tablespoons chopped chives

**Variations:**

1. Substitute one pound of cooked pasta for the potatoes.

2. Add one pound of cooked chicken to either version.

1. Peel and cut the potatoes into bite sized pieces (This reduces cooking time and ensures more even cooking). Place them in a 4-quart pot and cover them with water. Add a large pinch of salt. Bring to a boil and cook just until you can easily slide a fork into one (4 or 5 minutes). They should still be firm (Remember that they will continue to cook as they cool. Be careful not to overcook them because your salad will be mushy). Drain the potatoes in a colander and pour cold water over them to cool them faster. Spread out on a cookie sheet to finish cooling and to dry out just a bit.

2. Cook the eggs: Rinse out your pot and fill it ⅔ with fresh water. Bring it to a boil. Using a large spoon, lower the eggs into the water. Cook for 10 minutes. Pour into a colander to drain and let the eggs cool. (This method of cooking will keep that pesky green ring from forming around the yolks.) Peel and chop the eggs.

3. Chop the leek, pepper and celery into small dice.

4. Cook the peas: Bring 4 cups water and a large pinch of salt to a boil in a saucepan. Add the peas and bring the water back to a boil. Reduce heat to low and simmer for 15 minutes. Drain and rinse with cold water. Remove any loose shells.

5. Add the rest of the ingredients and using a spatula, carefully fold together. Taste and adjust seasonings.

6. Chill at least 2 hours before serving.

7. Garnish by sprinkling with ground red paprika and/or chopped chives.

Above: No picnic is complete without good old American potato salad. Here's a sophisticated version that is sure to please.

## Chef Lynn's Secrets:

- Potato Salad is a good one for using up odds and ends of things. I even like to mix up the potatoes for a more sophisticated flavor. For example, you could use a mix of Yukon Golds, Peruvian purple potatoes and red potatoes. Use one or all – whatever you have! Yukon Golds are especially nice because of their attractive yellow color.

- Try and use fresh peas if you can. This is one case where fresh makes an extreme difference. They add ten degrees of delicious!

- Make sure that you stay within the "use by" date on the end of the carton, but fresh eggs don't peel as easily as older ones. When you pour the eggs into the colander, some of them should crack. This will allow air to get under the shell and make them easier to peel. Peel them under cold running water and the shells should slide off easily.

### How to clean a leek:
(pictured on page 67)

Most people waste a full cup of leek by cutting it straight across where the white end meets the green leaves. Cut it on an angle instead. There is more good stuff in there! Peel off the outer layer and slit the leek up the middle. Spread it between your fingers and wash it thoroughly under running cold water.

The mild taste of leek is preferable to onion in this salad, which can be strong and overpowering.

# Roasted Beet and Goat Cheese Salad     *Serves 6*

Making use of the beet's greens is both a healthy and cost saving technique.

3 large red beets with greens

3 large yellow beets with greens

1 cup vinaigrette, page 228

12 oz. goat cheese, softened

3 tablespoons whipping cream

2 cups ground pistachios

4 tablespoons minced shallot

Approximately 1 cup chicken or vegetable
broth or cooking the greens

One head butter lettuce

18 cherry tomatoes

Salt and freshly ground pepper, to taste

**Chef Lynn's Secret:**

Prepare the beets, spinach and cheese ahead
of time — even the day before. Then all you
have to do at the last minute is to slice the
lettuce and tomatoes and build the circles.

1. Trim and peel the beets. Wrap them in foil
   and roast them in a preheated 375°F oven
   for about 45 minutes, until tender. Cool and
   set aside.

2. While the beets are roasting, make your
   choice of vinaigrette dressing (page 228).
   Place the dressing in a squeeze bottle and
   refrigerate.

3. Mix the goat cheese with the cream and
   shallots. Form into 6 discs and dip in
   the ground pistachios. Set aside in the
   refrigerator.

4. Make a chiffonade* of one set of the beet
   greens. Heat the chicken broth in a 2-quart
   saucepan. Add the greens and cook about
   5 minutes until they are completely wilted.
   Set aside in the refrigerator.

5. At serving time, chiffonade the butter
   lettuce and place it on plates. Halve the
   tomatoes and sprinkle them with salt and
   pepper. Place them on top of the butter
   lettuce and drizzle the vinaigrette on top.

6. Slice the yellow beets and chop the red
   beets. Drain the greens and toss them with
   the vinaigrette. Make a circle on the serving
   plate using the yellow beet slices. Top the
   circle with  the greens and then the goat
   cheese. Top that with the red beets and
   sprinkle with salt and pepper.

*Chiffonade = Rolling the leaves up from the side
   into a stick shape and then making very small
   slices from end to end.

# Green Bean and Asiago Salad   *Serves 4*

Any aged cheese works well in this salad.

1 pound French green beans

2 tomatoes, skinned and diced small

½ cup slivered almonds

1 small shallot, minced (2 to 3 tablespoons)

¾ cup Asiago (or other hard cheese)
   coarsely grated

½ teaspoon salt

½ teaspoon freshly ground black pepper

Optional: 1 teaspoon garlic powder added to
   the vinaigrette

Dijon Mustard Vinaigrette (See separate
   recipe, page 228, without cream)

## Chef Lynn's Secrets:

- To check to see if your beans are done,
  fish one out using a slotted spoon and
  taste it. It should still be firm but should
  not have a "green" or "raw" taste.

- "French" green beans (or haricot vert)
  are very tender, thin green beans. Not to
  worry! You can leave the little "tails" on
  the ends.

- Parmesan or any other hard cheese can
  be substituted for the Manchego without
  compromising the taste.

1. Preheat your oven to 400°F.

2. Fill a large bowl with ice water and have
   it ready.

3. Wash and trim the beans and slice them on
   an angle into bite-sized pieces.

4. Bring a pot of water mixed with 1
   tablespoon salt to a boil. Drop the beans in
   all at once and cook until just done but still
   firm, about 3 to 4 minutes. Remove with a
   slotted spoon and immediately plunge into
   ice water. Leave for one minute and then
   remove with a slotted spoon. Leave the hot
   water on the burner and the ice water in
   the bowl.

5. Using a very sharp knife, cut a small X in
   the bottom of each tomato. Plunge into the
   boiling water for about 20 seconds, just
   until the skin begins to curl. Remove with
   the slotted spoon and plunge into the ice
   water to stop the tomato from cooking.
   Drain and pull the tomato skins off. Chop
   the tomatoes.

6. Place the almonds on a cookie sheet. Bake
   in the oven until the nuts are golden brown
   and smell toasted, about 7 minutes. Remove
   from oven and cool.

7. Mix the beans with the nuts, tomatoes,
   shallot and cheese. Sprinkle with salt and
   pepper.

8. Toss with ¼ cup vinaigrette (or more
   to taste) and chill until serving time.
   Check spices and serve cold or at room
   temperature.

# Chapter Four
# *Vegetables*

# Lesson Four

## *What's important to know about vegetables?*

- **MEAL TIMING:** In my cooking classes, I have found the meal timing — getting everything done at the same time — is very stressful for people. Understanding how to blanch vegetables ahead can really help.

  Blanching is easy, it allows you to prepare vegetables ahead of time and pops their beautiful color so they look fresh and appealing. **To blanche:** Bring a large pot of water mixed with 1 tablespoon salt to a boil. Put the vegetables in the water and cook them until they are just done but still firm. In most cases, this will be only a couple of minutes. The best way to know when they are done is to fish one out with a slotted spoon and taste one. It should not have any raw or "green" taste, but should still have a little crunch. Remove the vegetables with a slotted spoon and immediately plunge them into ice water to stop the cooking. As soon as they are cool, drain them. Then just cover and refrigerate until serving time. At serving time, reheat in a frying pan for a couple of minutes in a little stock, juice, cider or even just 2 tablespoons of butter — just enough to glaze them but not enough to add a lot of calories. This is a simple reheat and if you do it quickly, it will not cause anything to be overcooked.

- **HOW MUCH TO MAKE?** To solve this problem, I imagine the servings as I pick out the vegetables at the store. For example, a small handful of beans is one serving, so 6 handfuls is 6 servings.

- **WHICH ONES TO MAKE?** When planning sides of anything, including vegetables, think about your main course and what will pair well with it. If you have meat or poultry, think about what the animal eats. That will always pair well.

- **KEEP THEM LOOKING FRESH:** To keep air sensitive vegetables (such as avocados) from turning brown, immerse them in acidulated water. This is water that is 50–75% juice. (The acid is citric acid and will not flavor it because it isn't in there long enough.) So for example, mix half water and half pineapple juice for this purpose. Or, squirt fresh lemon juice directly on the flesh.

- **MAKING THEM AHEAD HELPS WITH MEAL TIMING:** Vegetables can be blanched in salted water in the morning and held in the refrigerator all day. (Drop into boiling water and 1 tablespoon salt per 2 quarts and cook just until done. Then plunge into ice water to stop the cooking. Remove as soon as they are cool and refrigerate loosely covered. (You will also notice that the color is brighter and more attractive.) At serving time, simply heat in a frying pan with one or two teaspoons of butter or oil. Then serve immediately.

  Why the salt? It definitely kicks up the flavor of the vegetables. Just be sure to add it at the beginning. If the water is already boiling, the salt will give the water bubbles more surface area and will cause it to pop and sputter, which can make a mess or worse, splatter and burn your skin.

- **PREPARING VEGETABLES:** When preparing a lot of vegetables, you can save time by setting up your own assembly line. Wash them all, then trim them all, then peel them all. Then clean your cutting board once, wash them again and chop them all into pieces.

- **CHOPPING SAFETY:** First, make sure you have really sharp knives. At best, learn to sharpen your own. I sharpen mine weekly using a simple whetstone sprinkled with water. (You can sprinkle your whetstone with water or mineral oil. Just don't mix it. For example, if you start with water, continue with water, etc.) Hold the blade of the knife at a 20 degree angle and lightly press with your other hand as you slide the knife across the stone. If your whetstone has different grades, start with the coarsest one first and work your way to the finest. Finish by drawing your blade across a knife steel (long, thin piece of steel with a handle) a few times at the same angle. This last step takes off the fine burrs and straightens the knife. That's all there is to it.

Second — and this is the reason most people cut themselves — you need to stabilize what you are cutting. If your cutting board doesn't have rubber feet that grip well, place a wet towel under your cutting board to hold it in place. Make sure your knife and what you are cutting are dry, and start by making a cut on the bottom to create a flat place for what you are cutting to rest. If you do this, you will have a very secure start. When you cut, hold the vegetable with your fingers folded back and tuck your thumb into your fingers. With your cutting hand, angle the knife blade away from your left hand. There are lots of videos online that show safe cutting techniques. It's worth watching one to save yourself the headache. Definitely don't hold what you are cutting up in the air! Always cut down toward a hard surface.

- **SLICING AND CHOPPING:** Mandolins are wonderful cutting tools. A French mandolin can cost $150 but an equally effective plastic version can be purchased in Japanese specialty stores for about $40. The clean cut matchstick and julienne pieces that you can make will make a tasty garnish or stir fry and will elevate your work by leaps and bounds. Take the time to learn how to use one, but with all sharp instruments, be careful! The razor sharp blades on mandolins can be wicked. Use the guards and hold your hand out straight as you move the guard with the palm of your hand.

- **STORING FRESH VEGETABLES:** Store most vegetables in the refrigerator, but avocados, bananas, pears and tomatoes ripen best at room temperature. In general, you don't need to wash them until you are ready to prepare them because moisture helps mold to grow.

Store whole citrus fruit, hard-rind squash, eggplant, and root vegetables — like potatoes, sweet potatoes, rutabagas and onions — in a cool, dry and well ventilated place, preferably between 60°F and 70°F. Refrigerate anything else — especially melons. Keep onions separate or they can flavor other things.

Store canned goods and other dry food between 50°F and 70°F, but note that even canned food spoils over time. At higher temperatures, they will go bad more quickly and acidic food, like canned tomatoes, does not last as long as food low in acid.

- **RIPENING FRESH TOMATOES:** Keep your tomatoes at room temperature and not in the sunlight. To speed up ripening, place them in a closed paper bag, ideally with a riper tomato. As tomatoes age, they naturally release ethylene gas, which in turn causes the ripening. Enclosing them concentrates the gas on the fruit. If you want to slow down ripening, keep the riper tomatoes separate from the green or unripened ones.

- **WASH YOUR VEGETABLES** thoroughly at the time of serving — not before or you can speed up spoilage. Also be sure to cut away any brown and damaged spots.

- **THE COLOR OF A BELL PEPPER:** tells you how ripe it is. They all start out green, then proceed to turn yellow, then orange and then red. The longer it's on the vine, the sweeter the pepper, so red peppers are the sweetest.

- **SALT:** There are an unbelievable number of salts on the market and there is no best answer to which kind to use. I use simply kosher salt available at any grocery store on the planet. It's a couple of dollars for 3 pounds. The coarse granules dissolve more slowly than those in fine salt, so if you sprinkle it on just before serving, the taste on your tongue is right up front and it beautifully enhances your dish.

# Braised Fennel   *Serves 4*

Fennel is sometimes called anise. In this recipe, its licorice taste is complemented by the addition of sweet juice.

1 fennel bulb

2 tablespoons lemon extra virgin olive oil

$2/3$ cup orange juice

Salt and freshly ground pepper, to taste

1.  Preheat your oven to 350°F.

2.  Wash the fennel bulb. Trim away stalk ends and any brown spots. Leave a thin slice to hold the fennel together. Cut the bulb into four even pieces.

3.  Heat the lemon oil in a small frying pan. Add the fennel and brown (caramelize) on all sides.

4.  Place the bulb pieces in a small oven proof casserole. Use a casserole just large enough to hold the pieces. Pour in the orange juice. Sprinkle lightly with salt and freshly ground pepper.

5.  Bake until soft, about 60 minutes. Spoon the juice over the fennel several times during baking.

6.  Serve hot or cold as a side dish. Braising is a good way to cook vegetables because they absorb a lot of flavor from the cooking liquid and retain their moisture. Brussel sprouts and Cipollini onions are also good candidates. Just follow the same instructions above.

**Chef Lynn's Secrets:**

*   When the fennel is cooked, pour off any juice and simmer it in a pan on the stove until it starts getting thick. Spoon this over the fennel as a sauce to add even more citrus flavor.

*   You can also do the braising on the stovetop. Just use a small heavy bottomed pan and cook it over low heat until it's done. It will cook in about half the time required in the oven.

*   An interesting way to serve fennel is as a salad with blue cheese and pears.

# Vegetable Casserole   *Serves 6*

Here's a great way to make your vegetable dish ahead of time.

3 cups carrots (about 6), peeled and sliced very thin

1½ cups cauliflower, sliced thin

1½ cups broccoli, sliced thin

4 tablespoons Minute Tapioca®

2 cups orange juice

¼ cup Dijon mustard

Salt and freshly ground pepper, Approximately ¼ teaspoon each

1 teaspoon ground nutmeg

Cooking spray or butter for greasing the pan

1½ cups chicken broth

½ cup Parmesan cheese, coarsely grated

1. Preheat your oven to 350°F. Butter or spray a small casserole pan.

2. Wash and trim all vegetables as indicated. Mix them together and place them in a buttered baking dish.

3. In a bowl, whisk the Minute Tapioca®, orange juice, mustard, chicken broth and spices.

4. Pour the liquid mixture evenly over the vegetables.

5. Bake for about 45 minutes, until the vegetables are cooked through and the top is very lightly browned. Halfway through cooking, use a spatula to press the vegetables down into the broth.

6. Spoon into individual serving cups. Sprinkle with Parmesan cheese. Serve hot.

## Chef Lynn's Secrets:

1. This casserole is even better if you make it ahead. It gives it time to settle down and congeal. Just gently reheat in a 350°F oven for about 15 minutes and serve.

2. Easily turn this dish into a gratin by topping it with buttered breadcrumbs and/or cheese.

3. This colorful and filling vegetable casserole can easily be used as an entrée for a lone vegetarian in your group when the main course is meat. Also remember to substitute vegetable broth for the chicken broth.

# Cabbage Balls  *Makes about 10*

I learned the method for this delicious side at the Ritz-Escoffier School in Paris, but its ingredients have changed over the years. You can include the sausage or leave it out. It's your choice.

1 medium sized head of Savoy cabbage (also called Wirsing)

1 medium yellow onion, minced

1 stalk celery, peeled and diced small

1 large carrot, diced small

1 medium sized turnip, diced small

1 leek, diced small

2 cups regular ground sausage

2 cups spicy ground sausage

1 egg

6 oz. tomato paste

½ cup bread crumbs

Salt and pepper

½ teaspoon tarragon, chervil and parsley

1.  In a large frying pan, sauté the onion until soft and golden.

2.  Add the celery, carrot, turnip and leek and continue to cook until they are soft.

3.  Add the sausages and continue to fry until it is just cooked through.

4.  Add the tomato paste, salt and pepper. Set the pan aside to cool.

5.  Fill a 6-quart pot ⅔ full of water and heat it to boiling. While it is heating, remove any discolored leaves from the cabbage and throw them away. With the point of a knife, cut as much as you can of the thick, white core out of the bottom of the cabbage.

6.  Plunge the cabbage in the boiling water. As the leaves start to soften, pull them off with tongs and set them aside on a platter to cool.

7.  In the cooled frying pan that contains the meat mixture, stir in the egg and bread crumbs. Add salt, pepper and spices to taste.

8.  Fill each leaf by first laying it on a cutting board and making a V-shaped cut to remove any thick parts of the stem. Fold the V together, which will round the leaf. Fill the center with stuffing and wrap the leaf around it to make a ball that totally encloses the filling. Press together inside your fist to remove excess liquid and keep the ball tight and/or place the ball in the middle of a kitchen towel and swing it in a circle to compress it.

9.  Steam for about 20 minutes. Serve hot. If you have demi-glace on hand, you can heat it and spoon it over them at serving time.

Cabbage balls make a fun dish for cooking dinner parties. Make the filling ahead and let your guests fill and twirl them in the towels to prepare them for steaming.

### Chef Lynn's Secrets:

- These cabbage balls are great hot or as a cold leftover the next day. If served hot, you can also drizzle them at serving time with your favorite gravy or a little Demi glace. They make an impressive presentation.

- Try using just ¼ pound of bacon instead of the sausages for a hint of meat taste. Or make them totally vegetarian. Suit yourself! They are delicious in every preparation.

- This dish can be made a day ahead and gently reheated. They can also be wrapped tightly and frozen (before steaming) for up to 3 months.

- Leftover cabbage? Slice it into fine strips, heat it, spice it and use it as a bed for a piece of sautéed chicken or meat.

# Cauliflower Purée     *Serves 4*

This is a good starch alternative for mashed potatoes because it looks and tastes almost like them. People will ask you what you put in the "mashed potatoes" to make them taste so good!

1 head cauliflower

3 cups vegetable or chicken broth

2 tablespoons whole butter

2 tablespoons half and half

1 teaspoon salt

1 teaspoon white pepper

1. Trim the leaves and cut away the thick part of the stem of the cauliflower. Separate the florets.

2. In a 4-quart saucepan on high heat, bring the broth and 1 teaspoon salt to a boil. Add the florets and reduce the heat to medium low.

3. Simmer the cauliflower until very tender, about 8 minutes. Drain, reserving the liquid.

4. Add 2 tablespoons whole butter, 2 tablespoons half and half, 1 teaspoon salt and ½ teaspoon white pepper. Mix and purée the mixture. Taste to see if you need to adjust the spices.

5. Serve hot.

**Variation:** Use ½ head of cauliflower and 4 carrots.

**Chef Lynn's Secrets:**

- Replacing potatoes with puréed cauliflower once in awhile is a great way to cut the starch in a meal without suffering. Some people will not even know they are not eating potatoes.

- Note: The amount of cream you will need will depend on the size of the cauliflower head. You can also thin it with vegetable or chicken stock to cut calories, but if you thin it with cream it will taste more like mashed potatoes. (For those who are lactose intolerant, just use chicken broth for thinning.)

- OK, so I went overboard on the lettuce in the photo at the right, but how else am I going to show you something that has no color?

# Eggplant Three Ways    *Serves 4 — Choose 1, 2 or 3 ways!*

It's as easy as 1–2–3. Serve any method alone or all three together.

1 large purple eggplant

About 1 cup extra virgin olive oil

Salt and pepper to taste

1 small egg, beaten

1 cup Italian breadcrumbs

¼ cup Parmesan cheese, coarsely grated

Parmesan cheese for garnish

### Chef Lynn's Secrets:

- There was a time when eggplant was so bitter you had to salt it and let it stand for the salt to change the taste before you could cook and eat it. Luckily, varieties have changed over the years to become much more palatable, so this step is no longer necessary. We salt now simply for taste.

- Brush olive oil lightly on the slices and circles and toss some with the dice. As an alternative for the dice, you can mix in ⅓ cup of your favorite tomato sauce.

1. First cut a very thin slice from the smallest end of the eggplant and discard it. Then cut four ¼-inch circles.

2. Turn the eggplant and cut the rest of it into ¼-inch lengthwise slices and cut all but two of these slices into lengthwise strips. Then cut across these strips to make ¼-inch dice. Place dice (about 3 cups) in a bowl and toss it with ¼ cup olive oil and a sprinkling of salt and pepper.

3. Brush the circles and the long flat pieces heavily with olive oil. Sprinkle with salt and pepper.

4. First grill the large pieces: Lay the two flat pieces on an angle on a hot grill and then reduce the heat to medium. When you see nice grill marks, use a metal spatula to move the pieces to the left at an angle that makes an X with your first position. Continue to grill until you see grill marks in the other direction. Flip over and continue grilling until done but still firm. Remove from heat and cool. Cut into strips and place on serving dish.

5. Next, fry the round pieces: Dip the round pieces first into beaten egg and then into Italian breadcrumbs. Heat 2 tablespoons olive oil in a medium frying pan (10-inch). Fry over medium high heat until the breadcrumbs are light brown and crispy. Flip and repeat. Transfer to serving dish.

6. Last, simmer the diced eggplant: Add the diced eggplant to the same frying pan and cook about 2 minutes until it softens. Add ¼ cup coarsely grated Parmesan cheese and cook, stirring one minute more. Garnish with cheese and serve.

# Grilled Bell Peppers + Variations    *Serves 6*

Grilled peppers are delicious in any form — by themselves, with oil and spices or as an ingredient in another dish.

4 whole bell peppers — any color

Olive oil for brushing grill

**Chef Lynn's Secret:**

- Once you have grilled the peppers and removed the black skin and seeds, they will hold their flavor and keep up to a week in the refrigerator. They don't, however, freeze well as this compromises their texture.

- An ideal grilling temperature is between 375° and 400°F. A flat, round surface thermometer is ideal for setting on a grill if you want to check. If you don't have one, you can check by flicking a little water on it. The water should sizzle, but the grill should not be smoking.

1. Clean your grill with a wire brush and using a clean rag, lightly brush it with olive oil. Heat the grill and get it very hot.

2. Remove any labels from the peppers, cut the stem close to the pepper and wash it.

3. Lay the peppers on the hot grill and let them sit until the skin becomes totally black. Using tongs, move the peppers to each side, top and bottom, until the skin is completely black and the pepper is starting to ooze and collapse. (This will take about 30 minutes in total.)

4. Place the peppers in a heavy plastic bag or a paper bag and let them cool about 20 minutes.

5. Remove the peppers from the bag and peel away the black skin with your fingers. Do not rinse them under water or you will rinse away flavor.

6. Slit the pepper and scrape out the pod and seeds with your fingers. Trim the pieces into the desired size or simply strips.

7. Use in a recipe as is or as a side dish.

**Variations:**

**Marinated Peppers:** Cut grilled pepper strips and sprinkle them with a good quality extra virgin olive oil, a good quality balsamic vinegar, salt and pepper and fresh chopped basil or chives. Marinate overnight in the refrigerator and serve the next day as a delicious side dish.

**Grilled Pepper Tortilla (Pictured at left):** On an oven proof baking dish, top large tortilla chips with strips of marinated peppers for more interesting nachos. Add a little of your favorite grated cheese and melt the cheese in the oven just before serving. Garnish shown is chives.

# Oven Baked Tomatoes  *Serves 4 as a side dish*

Tomatoes are a lovely and colorful addition to any presentation. When baked, their concentrated flavor is almost unbelievable. No matter how you use them, they will be tasty and appealing.

4 Roma tomatoes, if possible vine ripened

3 tablespoons flavored olive oil

Salt and freshly ground black or
  mixed pepper

1. Preheat your oven to 300°F.

2. Cut the tomatoes in half, lengthwise.

3. Brush cut sides with the olive oil and sprinkle with salt and pepper.

4. Place on a rack, cut sides down.

5. Bake for approximately one hour.

6. Turn the oven off and leave the door closed for another hour.

7. Remove tomatoes from the oven and cool.

8. Store in a covered container in the refrigerator. Tomatoes will keep for 7 days.

### Chef Lynn's Secrets:

- Baked cherry tomatoes have a completely different look and make an interesting and tasty salad topping. They can be tossed in the oil and spices and simply spread out on a baking sheet. Bake at 300°F for one hour, turn the oven off and leave them for thirty minutes longer in the warm oven. Cool.

- Use your favorite kind of flavored or plain extra virgin olive oil. Or for a delicious kick, use the leftover oil from your favorite jar of sun-dried tomatoes, artichokes or olives.

- Romas or oblong tomatoes are very flavorful and can be sliced or chopped and used on top of pasta dishes or in soups, salads and sauces.

### Leftovers?

- Make Tomato-Basil Soup, page 61

# Peperonata   *Serves 4*

Peperonata has everything… It's easy, lovely, low calorie, delicious, versatile and filling!

6 medium yellow onions

2 red bell peppers

1 green bell pepper

1 yellow bell pepper

¼ cup olive oil

A sprinkling of salt

Freshly ground black pepper

Pinch of cayenne pepper

## Chef Lynn's Secrets:

- Make the Peperonata the day before and refrigerate it overnight to develop more flavors.

- As you cook the vegetables, you can stir them by simply sliding the pan back and forth on the burner. Caramelizing the vegetables (slightly browning them) makes them taste toasty and kicks up the flavor in this dish. So resist the urge to stir! When you do, you cool down the mixture and keep it from staying hot enough to toast. Watch the onions. They should turn a beautiful, golden brown color.

- You can stir these by sliding the pan back and forth on the burner.

- Peperonata makes a wonderful side dish or a great topping for steak, chicken or fish.

- Making it ahead gives the flavors time to intensify and it tastes even better.

1. Cut the onions and peppers into thin strips. These are called "julienne" strips.

2. In a large frying pan, heat ¼ cup olive oil. You can tell when the pan is hot enough by flicking a few drops of water into the pan. Use a very small amount and stand back. The water should cause the pan to sizzle.

3. Drop the onions and peppers into the pan. If your pan is hot enough, they should sizzle.

4. Stir every three or four minutes, letting the vegetables slightly brown, but be careful not to burn them. The volume will reduce by about half as they soften.

5. Turn the heat down to medium and continue to cook for 30 minutes or until all vegetables are soft. Turn off the heat and cool in the same pan.

6. Season with salt and pepper, to your taste and a pinch of cayenne pepper.

7. If you have any leftovers, Peperonata will keep well in a covered container in the refrigerator for about three days.

# Roasted and Grilled Vegetable Primer

Here's a little different take on vegetable preparation.

Roasting and Barbecuing Vegetables is done in an uncovered casserole pan in the oven or inside a closed grill. It concentrates flavor by reducing the moisture. You can roast or barbecue any vegetable. You just have to be careful not to overcook it and dry it out too much. Lightly brush the vegetable with olive oil, sprinkle with salt (or garlic salt) and freshly ground pepper and roast at 350°F just until you can easily pierce the vegetable with a fork. Here are some that work well:

- Asparagus: 10–15 minutes

- Beets (Wrapped in foil): 45 minutes

- Carrots: 20 minutes

- Peppers (Whole, stuffed): 60 minutes

- Potatoes: 60 minutes

- White and sweet potatoes and yams: 60 minutes

- Squash (Slash skin several times so that it doesn't burst when it gets hot): 60 minutes

- Tomatoes (Whole or halved): 20 minutes

- Turnip: (Wrapped in foil): 45-60 minutes

Grilling Vegetables is done on a grill, over direct heat. Clean and brush the grill with olive oil. Lightly brush the vegetables with olive oil and spice them with salt (or garlic salt) and freshly ground pepper. Use high heat and work to get nice cross hatched caramelization (browning) marks whenever possible. At the beginning, while the vegetable is still its firmest, make the marks. Then flip it over and finish cooking. Present the first side to your guest. Grill pieces and strips of vegetables just a few minutes on each side. Corn and potatoes will take about 20 minutes. Here are some vegetables that work well with this quick cooking technique:

- Asparagus & carrots (Whole or strips)

- Corn on the cob (Wrapped in foil)

- Peppers (Pieces in a basket)

- Potatoes (Pieces in a basket)

- Summer squash (Strips)

- Tomatoes & zucchini (Pieces)

- Sweet potatoes & yams (Pieces)

## Chef Lynn's Secrets:

- Roasted vegetables are great as a base for soup or sauces. They add a rich depth of flavor.

- Times given are for whole vegetables. If you slice or chop them, the times will be much less.

- This is a good place to use your flavored olive oils. With grilled vegetables, garlic, lemon and mustard oils are especially nice.

- If you want to grill pieces of vegetables, you can do this by using a wire basket on the grill. This way, you don't have to worry about the pieces falling through the grates.

- Although the florets are more tender, don't forget the broccoli stalks. Simply slice them thinly and on an angle before cooking for an attractive and tasty side dish.

# Simply Healthy Spaghetti Squash  *Serves 6*

Spaghetti squash is so named because it breaks apart and looks exactly like golden spaghetti noodles when its meat is removed from the shell.

1 whole spaghetti squash

Flavored oil (lime, tangerine or lemon)

Salt and McCormick® Mixed Pepper

1. Preheat your oven to 350°F.

2. Using a sharp knife, make a slash in the top of the squash (so it won't burst). Place in a baking dish and bake approximately one hour, until a fork can be easily inserted through the skin.

3. Remove the squash from the oven and split in two. Cool until you can comfortably handle it, approximately 15 minutes.

4. Using a large spoon, scoop out seeds and discard.

5. Scoop out the squash and place in a mixing bowl. Mix with flavored oil; then transfer to serving bowl. Sprinkle liberally with salt and McCormick® Mixed Pepper and serve.

## Chef Lynn's Secrets:

- Spaghetti squash has a bland taste by itself, but the flavored oil and spices in this recipe perk it up so it becomes an interesting and delicious side dish.

- Squash can be prepared several days ahead. Cover with plastic wrap and refrigerate. Simply bring it to room temperature before serving.

## Leftovers?

- Turn it into soup following the How To Make Soup Out of Any Vegetable recipe. (Add another type of squash to so you have a mix and better flavor.)

- Bring it to room temperature and use it as a great looking garnish on top of a piece of grilled meat, chicken or fish.

# Spicy Carrots with Almonds    *Serves 4 as a side dish*

Try these with a great steak and cauliflower purée instead of potatoes.

5 large carrots

2 cups vegetable or chicken broth

½ red pepper, chopped

½ teaspoon salt

½ teaspoon pepper

½ teaspoon hot sauce or Sambol Oelek

1 teaspoon nutmeg

¼ cup sliced almonds

1. Trim and peel the carrots. Cut them into 1-inch slices.

2. In a 2-quart saucepan, bring 2 cups vegetable or chicken broth to a boil. Add the carrots and red pepper. Reduce heat to medium-low.

3. Simmer the vegetables until very tender, about 12 minutes. Drain, reserving the cooking liquid for future use.

4. Purée the carrots. Then add in the hot sauce, nutmeg, pepper and sliced almonds.

5. Stir in enough vegetable stock to make a smooth purée, about 3 tablespoons.

6. Serve hot.

**Chef Lynn's Secrets:**

- You can thin the purée with any number of things. For a creamier texture, use milk, cream or half and half. You can also use wine or juice, for example orange or lemon juice, to add an interesting citrus flavor.

- This is a great diet dish. Spicy dishes make you feel "full" quicker and their tastes linger longer.

- If you goof and your carrots are a little too "soupy", dump them out on a paper towel. Let the towel absorb the excess moisture until you can scoop the carrots and they hold their shape.

- The cooking liquid can be saved for up to 7 days. Use it in any recipe that calls for broth.

# Stir Fry Vegetable Table

Using the list below, you can create your own stir fry. See where your vegetables of choice are listed on the table. Add them in the order they are listed, starting with the longer cooking vegetables and moving to those with the least cooking time.

| | |
|---|---|
| **LONGER COOKING TIME:** | Broccoli florets (Sliced if large)<br><br>Carrots (Peeled and sliced into pieces or strips)<br><br>Cauliflower florets (Sliced into pieces)<br><br>Green beans (Trimmed and sliced into 1-inch pieces)<br><br>Onions (Peeled and diced or cut into strips)<br><br>Shallot (Peeled and diced or cut into strips) |
| **MEDIUM COOKING TIME:** | Asparagus (Thick) (Thorns removed and cut into 1-inch pieces)<br><br>Celery (Peeled and cut into 1-inch pieces)<br><br>Snow peas (Trimmed and cut into 1-inch strips)<br><br>Summer squash (Trimmed and cut into 1-inch pieces)<br><br>Sweet bell pepper (Trimmed and cut into 1-inch strips)<br><br>Zucchini (Trimmed and cut into 1-inch strips) |
| **VERY LITTLE COOKING TIME:** | Asparagus (Thin)<br><br>Bok Choy (Shredded)<br><br>Cabbage (Green, Napa or Wirsing, shredded)<br><br>Greens (From beets, Swiss chard etc. – shredded)<br><br>Spinach (Chopped) |
| **ADD JUST TO HEAT:** | Chop Suey vegetables (Canned)<br><br>Mung beans (Canned)<br><br>Sprouts<br><br>Tofu (Cut into small squares)<br><br>Water Chestnuts (Sliced or chopped) |

# Stir Fry Vegetables with Peanut Sauce *Serves 4 as a main course*

Stir frying is easy and fun. Make this dish (pictured on page 93) your own by including your favorite vegetables.

2 cups Jasmine rice

3 cups vegetable stock

2 tablespoons butter

2 cups thin green onions, washed, trimmed and cut into strips

2 cups carrots, washed, peeled and sliced thinly on an angle

2 cups red bell pepper, washed and cut into thin, 1-inch strips

6–8 cups young asparagus, washed, thorns peeled and cut into 1-inch strips

4 cups Wirsing (the wrinkly one) cabbage, shredded

1 cup water chestnuts, drained and sliced into thin strips

¼ cup olive oil (Can be flavored with lemon)

Salt and pepper, to taste

**For the sauce:**

3 cloves garlic, minced very fine or 2 teaspoons garlic powder

¼ cup soy sauce

⅛ cup sugar

¼ cup honey

1¼ cup maple syrup

½ tablespoon sesame oil

⅛ cup hoisin

¼ cup peanut butter

1 tablespoon fresh lemon juice

1. **Prepare the rice:** Using a strainer, wash it thoroughly in water. Bring 3 cups vegetable stock and 2 tablespoons butter to a boil. Add the rice. Cover and reduce heat to low. Cook for 20 minutes without opening.

2. Prepare the vegetables as indicated and place them in bowls next to your cook top in the order they are listed.

3. **Make the sauce** by combining the first 7 sauce ingredients in a 2-quart saucepan. Heat the liquid until it just begins to boil. Remove from the heat and add the peanut butter and lemon juice. Taste and adjust the seasonings as necessary.

4. Heat the olive oil in a wok or chef's pan.

5. Sauté the green onions and then as each begins to cook, add the other vegetables in the order listed. Let each one soften before adding the next. When the last one is cooked, add the sauce. Continue to cook about 2 minutes on low heat to thoroughly heat the sauce, and serve over the rice.

**Chef Lynn's Secrets:**

- Look for young, thin vegetables for stir fry. Cut them on an angle whenever possible. It's a simple trick that makes a much prettier presentation.

- This stir fry sauce can be used separately as a dipping sauce for porous vegetables, tempura, sushi, or whatever you can dream up. I would add one green onion, sliced very thin and crosswise at an angle to add a little taste and make it pretty.

# Chapter Five
## *Potatoes, Rice & Grain*

# Lesson Five

## *What's important to know about potatoes, rice and grain?*

- **STARCHES ARE ESSENTIAL AND VERSATILE VEGETABLES**. They taste great plain. They taste great with sauces. They taste great with condiments like butter and sour cream. They are the perfect "bed" for other parts of the meal. They also can slide into the background and be a supporting cast for thickening soup and adding depth of flavor.

- **GARNISH:** It's easy to garnish starches because their color is neutral. Anything with color makes an outstanding contrast. Always look at the entrée and contrast colors with it, so the colors of the whole dish work together.

- **USE CAUTION WHEN ADDING LIQUID.** Starches have a tremendous capacity to absorb liquid, but they too can be given too much. It's better to err on the low side and add more so you don't end up, for example, with a soupy dish.

- **USE CAUTION WHEN ADDING SALT TO BOILING WATER.** Adding salt adds flavor when cooking potatoes or blanching vegetables in water, but you need to add it at the beginning, before the water is boiling. Here's the reason:

  When water is heated to the boiling point, the dissolved gases in the water start to come out. It's just like opening a bottle of champagne. When you release the pressure by pulling the cork out, the pressure needs to equalize or dissipate. It has dissolved carbonation that has to come out, but it can only come out so fast. The same thing happens when water boils and turns to steam. The gases come up from the bottom because that's where it's the hottest. When you add salt, the gases grab onto the surface area of the salt and it provides more opportunities for the gases to form and release. This happens very quickly, so it will almost explode. You see this in popping and sputtering. If your pan is really full, water can spill over the sides or fly onto your skin and burn.

- **IF YOU BOIL POTATOES** for 4 or 5 minutes and cool them before deep frying them, it will seal the pores of the potatoes and stop them from absorbing so much oil.

- **KEEP RAW AND COOKED POTATOES COVERED.** Potatoes will turn black if exposed to the air. When you peel them, submerge them in water or other liquids as quickly as possible. They can also discolor after cooking, so keep them covered.

- **STORE POTATOES** in a cool, dark place. Light encourages the development of solanine, a toxin that can cause nerve damage. You would have to eat a LOT of potatoes for it to hurt you, but it's best if you see a small amount of green, that you simply cut it out. Sprouting is also an indicator of the presence of solanine, so if you see a large amount of green or if your potatoes are sprouting, throw them out.

- **RICE:** If a recipe calls for a certain type of rice, there is probably a reason. Rice is classified as short, medium or long. Different rice has different starch contents and therefore behave differently when they are cooked in liquids. For example, Arborio rice works well in risotto because it has a high starch content and the dish is supposed to hold together and be a bit sticky. If you try and make risotto with Jasmine rice, which has a lower starch content, it will not hold together. Jasmine rice is more suited to pilaf, where the rice is not supposed to stick together.

- **COOL RICE QUICKLY.** Many people don't realize it, but cooked rice is on the list of danger foods for bacteria. Do not leave it at room temperature or it can develop a toxin. Cool it quickly and store it in the refrigerator. If you set out a buffet, it should not be at room temperature for more than four hours. Note that this time is cumulative, so if you are using leftover rice, think about the total time it has been sitting out.

- **RICE** will roughly double in volume, so allow for that in choosing the size of your cooking pot. For every cup of medium or long grain rice, add 1 ½ cups of cooking liquid. For short grain rice, you will need about 2 cups of cooking liquid for every cup of rice. That "liquid" is traditionally water, but I prefer to cook it, whenever possible, in something that adds flavor. Examples of that would be any type of broth or bullion. Just choose a liquid that will complement whatever you are serving the rice with and think about the color it will give to the rice. Beef stock, for example, will give the rice a dark color, whereas vegetable stock will cause it to remain light.

- **COOKING RICE:** You don't need a fancy rice cooker! See the recipe for Perfection Rice, page 104. If you do this, your rice will come out perfect every time.

- **STORE RICE, UNCOOKED** in a cool, dry place (50° to 70°F) for up to a year.

- **WHEN CHOOSING FOOD PRODUCTS TO USE,** especially those with long storage times (like dried goods), it's best to use the FIFO or FIRST IN-FIRST OUT method. You will have less waste if you store new purchases behind previous ones and use them in that order. Otherwise, it's easy to lose track of which ones have passed their "use by" dates.

- **GRAINS** are grasses. When eaten whole, they provide protein, vitamins, minerals, carbohydrates, and fats. Rice, barley, oats, wheat and Quinoa are examples.

Rice makes a complementary and delicious bed for Stir Fry Vegetables.

Ricers are available in many styles and price ranges. Using one practically guarantees creamy mashed potatoes.

# Lemon Chive Potatoes  *Serves 6*

These potatoes make a pretty side dish. All you have to do is to pile them in a bowl!

2 pounds Yukon Gold potatoes

1 tablespoon salt

Water

¼ cup extra virgin olive oil

4 tablespoons butter, cut into 4 pieces

½ cup yogurt

Zest and juice of one lemon

⅛ cup chives

Salt and pepper to taste

**Chef Lynn's Secrets:**

- If you don't have a ricer, mash the cooked potatoes well using a fork.

- In the summer time, make these potatoes ahead and serve them slightly chilled.

- They pair well with chilled pink salmon for a meal that requires no cooking at serving time. I would also pair them with lamb or cold chicken.

- Use more chives if you have them and really like them.

1. Peel and cut the potatoes into large pieces.

2. Place the potatoes in a one quart saucepan and cover them with water. Add 1 tablespoon salt. Bring the water to a boil and cook the potatoes until you can easily cut through them with a fork about 20 minutes.

3. Place the butter in a heat proof mixing bowl.

4. Drain the potatoes. Then rice the potatoes on top of the butter so that it melts. Cool.

5. Add the rest of the ingredients and whisk until thoroughly blended.

6. Cover and store in the refrigerator until serving time.

7. Remove from refrigerator ½ hour before serving just to take the chill off or if you like, heat them. Don't worry about heating them though. The beauty of these potatoes is that they are great cold!

# Baked and Hasselback Potatoes    *Serves 4*

This lovely potato dish comes originally from Scandanavia.

4 Yukon Gold potatoes, washed and peeled

½ cup white or Italian breadcrumbs

¼ cup grated Parmesan cheese

1 tablespoon melted butter

Olive oil, to drizzle

Sprinkling of sweet paprika, salt and pepper

**Chef Lynn's Secret:**

Alternatively, wash the potatoes well and don't peel them. The skin is delicious, so why not take advantage of the wonderful nutrients in the potato peel?

1. Cut a very small slice from the bottom of each potato to stabilize it in the pan and keep it from sliding around.

2. Make slices across each potato, about ¼ inch apart. Do not cut all the way through the potato. (Some people put a chopstick on each side of the potato to keep from cutting all the way through.)

3. Using the blade in a food processor, mix breadcrumbs, butter, cheese and seasonings.

4. Drizzle potatoes lightly with oil and sprinkle them with salt and pepper. Then fan each one individually and dip it into the crumb mixture.

5. Place potatoes in a baking dish. Cover with foil and bake at 375°F for about 45 minutes. You should be able to test one with a fork and insert it easily.

6. Remove foil and bake about 15 more minutes, or until the crumbs are slightly browned.

**Simple Baked Potato:** Wash and rub each potato with 1 tablespoon of butter. Sprinkle with salt and pepper and wrap the potato in foil. Bake at 375°F for about an hour.

# Basic Risotto + Possibilities! *Serves 6*

Turn this into a hearty vegetarian main course simply by substituting vegetable stock for the chicken stock.

3 cups Arborio rice, washed three times

1 large yellow onion, diced small

5 tablespoons olive oil

2 cups dry white wine

Large pinch of saffron

Approximately 48 ounces chicken stock, heated

½ cup Parmesan cheese, grated

3 tablespoons whole butter

Salt and white pepper, to taste

Pinch of cayenne pepper

1. In a large frying pan, heat the olive oil. Add the onions and cook over medium heat until they are soft and golden.

2. Add the rice and stir until slightly toasted, about four minutes.

3. Add ½ cup white wine and the saffron and cook for several minutes.

4. Add the chicken stock a cup at a time, letting it completely absorb each time before you add more. Stir often.

6. Continue cooking the rice and ladling in the stock until the risotto is creamy and thoroughly cooked.

7. Stir in the Parmesan, butter, spices and serve.

NOTE: You can easily change this up. A vegetable that can be grated (like carrot) can be added in raw in the last five minutes of cooking time. The color and taste add a lot.

Pieces of cooked vegetable (or meat) can be stirred through at the end and whole strips of cooked vegetables or meat can also simply be laid on top of the risotto for a main course.

## Chef Lynn's Secrets:

- Why Arborio rice? Arborio is a particular type of rice that is grown in the Po Valley in Italy. The reason we use it for risotto is that it has a very high starch content. It absorbs a lot of liquid and becomes very creamy.

- Saffron is a spice that is the dried stigma (center spoke) of a type of crocus flower that grows primarily in the Philippines. Per pound, it is the most expensive spice in the world. Luckily you only need a pinch!

- Stick to white wine when making this dish because red wine will give it a gray, unattractive color. You could, however, use beef stock instead of chicken or vegetable and in that case, you could use red wine. The dish will be dark and will pair well with red meat.

## Chef Lynn's Secrets:

- Do take time to wash the rice. It will give your finished dish more luster.

- Heating the liquids will cut your cooking time from 45 to about 20 minutes.

- You can make this 75% of the way in the morning, refrigerate, and quickly finish just before serving.

- For a spectacular presentation, make a layered "ring" of different flavors and/or colors of risotto. Fill well buttered (shallow) individual or pan rings. Unmold an hour before serving time to bring them to room temperature. Serve plain or fill centers with hot vegetables. You can even fill each person's ring with their personal favorite!

- Asian stores are great places to look for inexpensive but unusual and attractive serving dishes.

## Leftovers?

### Make Risotto Balls:

1. Cut a piece of fontina or Cheddar (or other cheese with good melting qualities) into a ¼-inch square. Press left-over risotto around the cheese into the shape of a ball, completely covering the cheese.

2. Dip in egg, then breadcrumbs and rest for 20 minutes on a parchment covered sheet tray.

3. Deep fry and serve immediately.

# Cheese Gnocchi   *Serves 6*

Gnocchi can be served as a side dish or a main vegetarian course. They're also a definite kid pleaser!

1 pound russet potatoes (1 large)

4 oz. whole butter (1 stick)

½ cup Parmesan (or other hard cheese), grated

1 egg yolk

½ cup all purpose flour

1 quart chicken (or vegetable) broth

1 quart water

3 cups of your favorite tomato sauce or use Fresh Tomato Sauce (page 224)

Approximately 1 cup grated Parmesan cheese for sprinkling over the tops

Optional: fresh basil chiffonade (page 238)

1. Bring 1 quart water and 1 teaspoon salt to a rolling boil. Add the potatoes and cook until very soft.

2. Place the butter and cheese in a heat proof bowl. Drain the potatoes well and then press through a vegetable mill directly on top of the butter and cheese to melt them. Cool the potatoes. Then add the egg and flour. Mix well.

3. Roll balls of a scant teaspoon of dough lightly in flour. Press them lightly with the tines of a fork to form little cylinders with ridges in them. Place on a floured platter and let them air dry while you prepare the rest of the meal.

4. Heat 1 quart chicken broth mixed with 1 quart water to a full boiling boil. Drop in the gnocchi and cook about 10 minutes or until done.

5. Spoon ½ cup of your favorite tomato sauce over the top of each serving and sprinkle with more grated Parmesan cheese.

**Chef Lynn's Secrets:**

- If you are making a lot of gnocchi, you can accomplish it quickly by tightly stretching a piece of kitchen twine across the top of a pot of boiling liquid and securing it to the handles. Fill a pastry bag with the gnocchi batter and pipe it directly into the boiling water, cutting each piece off by pressing the tip against the string.

- Gnocchi can be made well in advance. Flash freeze it on cookie sheets and then transfer to freezer bags. It will keep for up to 3 months.

# Couscous  *Serves 4*

Israeli couscous, picture on the right below, is larger than normal couscous and its appearance can resemble caviar.

1 cup couscous (quick cooking)

1 cup broth (vegetable or chicken both work well)

Salt and white pepper, to taste

Pinch of cayenne pepper

### Chef Lynn's Secrets:

- Most couscous is made from semolina (the starchy part of the wheat kernel) and therefore is more similar to pasta than rice or grains. It's eaten in many different cultures, so quick cooking versions of it are available in virtually all markets.

- Israeli couscous is larger and a little different product – actually baked wheat. I prize it for its looks. It appears like lovely caviar when paired with fish.

- Water can be used to prepare both types of couscous. Using broth, however, is tastier. Beef broth can be used, but remember that the color of the finished product will be dark.

- Couscous is relatively bland tasting. You can, however, easily make a lovely dish by simply mixing in one cup (or more if you like) of any combination of cooked vegetables (diced small) or raw vegetables (diced tiny) at the end of the preparation. This way they will be perfectly cooked and will retain their own fresh taste. Here are some suggestions:

  – Sautéed or caramelized onion

  – Sautéed bell pepper — any color

  – Any roasted or grilled vegetable, including squash

  – Chopped pine nuts, almonds, peanuts or any other nut

- Top your creation with some strips of braised meat, poultry or fish and you've got a beautiful and hearty main course.

### FOR REGULAR COUSCOUS:

1.  Bring the broth to a boil.

2.  Add the couscous and spices.

3.  Put the cover on the pan for 5 minutes.

4.  Serve hot or cold.

### FOR ISRAELI COUSCOUS:

1 cup couscous

3 tablespoons olive oil

1½ cups broth (vegetable or chicken)

Salt and pepper, to taste

### Method:

1.  Over medium high heat, in a two quart saucepan, heat the oil. Add the couscous and spices and stir to thoroughly mix.

2.  Add the broth and mix again. Turn the flame to low and simmer for 12–15 minutes.

3.  Cover and let it sit untouched for 5 minutes.

4.  Serve hot or cold.

# Creamy Mashed Potatoes + Great Variations   *Serves 4*

My favorite version of this recipe is to use half white and half sweet potatoes with the addition of Parmesan cheese.

2½ pounds baking potatoes

2 tablespoons salt

¼ cup whole butter

Approximately ⅔ to ¾ cup whipping cream or half and half or any type of milk

1 teaspoon salt and 1 teaspoon white pepper for seasoning

### Chef Lynn's Secrets:

- The amount of cream you add will vary slightly depending on which flavoring you choose, so add the flavoring first and then the cream a little at a time until you get the consistency you are looking for. (Exceptions to this are the herbs, which you can stir in at serving time.) Choose a flavoring that complements your main course.

- If you do not have a ricer, use a fork and mash your potatoes really well. Do not use a food processor as it will destroy the consistency of the potatoes. Whisk them by hand or with a mixer on medium speed.

- Make your potatoes fancy by piping them using a pastry bag and a round or star tip.

### Leftovers?

- Form into patties, dip them in whipped egg and then breadcrumbs and fry them in clarified butter until the outside is crispy.

1. Peel the potatoes and place them in boiling water with 2 tablespoons salt. The real secret to creamy mashed potatoes is to cook them until they fall apart when pierced with a fork, about 20 minutes after your water starts to boil. Some people would say until they are almost overcooked. Drain.

2. Put the butter in a large bowl. Force the potatoes through a vegetable mill or ricer and into the bowl on top of the butter so it melts.

3. Whisk in the milk a little at a time until you get a creamy but not runny consistency.

4. Season with salt and pepper, to taste. Potatoes can be made a day ahead, covered and refrigerated. Reheat at 350°F for about 20 minutes.

### Delicious Variations:

Adding some flavoring to your mashed potatoes always gets an "Aaah!" from the crowd and usually a request for the recipe. Here are some matches made in heaven that you can stir in as soon as your potatoes are mashed.

You can mix and match them as well. Here are some ideas:

- 4 tablespoons Parmesan or other cheese
- 4 tablespoons fresh herbs
- 2 tablespoons truffle oil
- ¼ cup minced shallot
- 2 tablespoons prepared horseradish

I also recommend you add 1 teaspoon lemon juice with any filling to bring out the flavor and then mix in the cream to the correct consistency.

# Potato and Turnip Gratin  *Serves 4*

Here's another make ahead magic trick. Prepare the dish in the morning, well before you plan to serve it or even a full day ahead. It will hold beautifully and reheat well.

4 cups Russet potatoes, peeled and sliced thinly

1 cup peeled and shredded turnips

2 purple Peruvian potatoes, peeled and sliced thinly

½ cup cake flour

Approximately 4 cups whipping cream

3 tablespoons butter

Salt and pepper, to taste

½ cup Parmesan cheese, coarsely grated

### Chef Lynn's Secrets:

- Turnips are round root vegetables that are white with some purple on the outside. They add a sweetness and more sophisticated taste to the potatoes.

- Purple Peruvian potatoes have medium starch content and are good for baking. They look just like regular potatoes except for their color. If you can't find them, just increase the amount of white potatoes. They are included here for color and interest.

1. Preheat your oven to 350°F.

2. In a large mixing bowl, mix the potatoes and the shredded turnip.

3. Mix in the cake flour.

4. Place in a generously buttered 9 X 11-inch baking pan or four individual serving pans.

5. Pour the cream over. The cream should just reach the top of the potato mixture.

6. Bake for 45 minutes. Sprinkle with Parmesan cheese.

7. Turn the oven off, keep the door closed and leave them in the oven 15 minutes more.

8. Serve or set aside in the refrigerator when cooled (covered) and gently reheat at serving time.

### Variations:

1. Replace the turnips with carrots.

2. Replace the turnips with leek and parsnip.

3. Replace the turnips with any combination of the above.

4. For a little "bite", add 1 tablespoon Dijon Mustard or 1 teaspoon Sambol Oelek* to any of the above.

*SAMBOL OELEK is an Indonesian paste made from hot chilies, found in most upscale markets.

# Orange and White Potato Puffs  *Serves 8*

Sweet potatoes and yams actually have different family names, but both are tubers and so similar in taste that the difference is not worth worrying about. They are often even mis-labeled by grocers!

**FOR THE WHITE PUFFS:**

1 large white potato

⅓ cup butter

½ cup cold water

1 teaspoon salt

¾ cup all purpose flour

Large pinch of nutmeg, freshly grated
     if possible

2 small eggs

**FOR THE ORANGE PUFFS:**

1 large sweet potato or yam

1 teaspoon salt

⅓ cup butter

½ cup cold water

¾ cup all purpose flour

2 small eggs

Large pinch of nutmeg, freshly grated
     if possible

1½ quarts corn oil

Salt for sprinkling finished puffs

1.  Peel and dice the potatoes into 1 inch cubes. Keep the two types of potatoes separate. Place the white potato in one saucepan and the sweet potato in another, with enough water to cover and 1 teaspoon salt. On high heat, boil the potatoes until they are very done and falling apart (about 20 minutes). Drain, place in a low sided dish and mash with a fork. Cool or cover and refrigerate until you are ready to proceed.

2.  Then follow the rest of the steps separately for the white and sweet potatoes so you end up with mixtures that are two different colors:

    a.  Heat the butter and water until the butter is melted.

    b.  Using a wooden spoon, beat in the potatoes, flour and nutmeg until the dough pulls away from the sides of the pan and is very thick. Cool for a few minutes and beat in the eggs.

    c.  Set aside and repeat for the sweet potatoes.

    d.  Heat the corn oil in a heavy bottomed pan. When the oil is hot (325°), drop heaping teaspoonfuls into the oil and deep fry until golden brown. I usually hold the spoon in one hand and slide the mixture off with the index finger of the opposite hand and into the hot grease. Drop it carefully so that it doesn't splash.

    e.  Deep fry until golden brown, about 3 minutes.

    f.  Remove the browned puffs with a slotted spoon and place them on paper towels to absorb any grease. Lightly sprinkle

immediately with salt. Remember that the hot puffs will continue to cook after you remove them from the oil (carryover cooking), so take them out just before they are as brown as you would like them.

Once the puffs dry, the salt won't stick. Instead of white salt, you can also use bacon salt, celery salt or garlic salt or a mix for a tasty flair.

g.  Serve hot.

### Chef Lynn's Secrets:

- This is the classic French recipe for Pommes Dauphine, tweaked a little bit. It's OK if your potatoes are not creamy after mashing. A little texture in the puffs is fine. I really like to mix up tastes and sometimes throw in some turnips or Peruvian purple potatoes. If you want to make them into little cylinders (like tater tots), add flour a little at a time until they hold their shape.

- When you heat your oil, you know it's hot enough if you drop in a teaspoon of dough and it sizzles and rises to the top. Keep the temperature up or your puffs will separate and fall apart. As always, be very careful when working with hot oil!

# Perfection Rice   *Serves 6–8*

Follow these steps and your rice will be perfect every time.

1 tablespoon butter

1 medium shallot, minced finely

2 cups Jasmine rice

3½ cups chicken stock, broth or water

¼ cup butter

Salt and white pepper

1. Using a strainer, wash the rice thoroughly.

2. Over low heat, melt 1 tablespoon butter in a 2-quart saucepan.

3. Add the shallot and cook until soft, about 2 minutes.

4. Add the stock, broth or water. Turn heat to high and bring to a boil.

5. Add the rice and cover. Turn heat to low. Cook for 20 minutes. Don't take the cover off during cooking.

6. Stir in ¼ cup butter, salt and pepper and serve.

7. Optional: To spice up your rice, mix in ¼ cup of one of the following:

   • Dried cherries

   • Toasted pine nuts (375°F for about 7 minutes)

   • Chopped fresh green onion

   • Parmesan cheese

**Chef Lynn's Secrets:**

• The type of rice you use makes a big difference. If you are cooking wild rice for example, it requires a different amount of liquid and has different cooking time. Wild rice needs a 2:1 water to rice ratio. In other words, for 1 cup of rice use 2 cups of liquid and cook it about 10 minutes longer as well.

• With lighter colored foods, it's best to stick with white pepper. Black or mixed pepper can look like dirt.

**Leftovers?**

• Make refried rice by frying the rice in butter or olive oil and vegetables. (See separate recipe.)

# Sweet Potatoes with Sweet Sauce (or Yams)    *Serves 4*

Think about this one as a side at Thanksgiving. You can make it ahead and it reheats beautifully.

2 large sweet potatoes or yams

½ cup unsalted butter

½ cup granulated sugar

½ cup brown sugar

2 teaspoons rum extract

1 tablespoon fresh lemon juice

½ cup mango chutney

½ teaspoon nutmeg

1 teaspoon each cinnamon and ground cloves

**Chef Lynn's Secrets:**

- What's the difference? Many grocers don't know the difference so sweet potatoes and yams are often mis-named when presented to the public. They do have different species names, but both are tubers and the appearance and taste are so similar that it doesn't pay to worry about it. Cooking methods and uses are exactly the same.

- If kept in a cool place, all potatoes will keep for months before cooking.

1. Preheat your oven to 350°F.

2. Wash the sweet potatoes. Peel them and cut them into ¼-inch slices or chunks. Place them in a Dutch oven.

3. In a small saucepan, melt the butter.

4. Mix the granulated (white) sugar, brown sugar, extract, lemon juice, chutney and spices with the butter until it is well blended.

5. Pour the liquid over the yams and stir so that all are coated.

6. Bake about 1½ hours, until the sweet potatoes are cooked through. Cool in the sauce until you can easily handle the pan.

7. Move the sweet potatoes to a serving dish.

8. Pour the sauce into a small saucepan and boil until thick and syrupy, about 4 minutes. Pour the hot, thickened sauce back over the sweet potatoes and serve.

**Variation:** Sweet potatoes and yams can also be baked or mashed just like white potatoes. To bake them, wrap them in foil and bake in a 350°F oven for about an hour. You can also serve them with the same condiments — sour cream, onion and bacon — or just plain with a little butter. To mash them, boil the potatoes in salted water until very soft. Mash or press through a vegetable press. Add butter and if you like, brown sugar. (See recipe for white potatoes.)

# Quinoa  *Serves 4 (Yields 2 cups)*

Here's an easy dish to prepare when you want to offer something really different. If you need to get some roughage into your diet, this is a great way to do it.

1 cup Quinoa

2 cups broth (vegetable or chicken) or water

Salt and pepper, to taste

## Chef Lynn's Secrets:

- Here's something different to try out. Quinoa is the seed of the goose foot plant and ranges in color from almost white to black. An attractive side, it's a grain that has been cultivated in South America for over 6,000 years.

- Quinoa is a great vegetarian dish because it is a source of complete protein, provides fiber and is gluten free. (Some companies even use it to make gluten free pasta.) It contains all 9 amino acids and is chock full of vitamins and minerals. You will find it in a box usually near the rice in your local grocery store.

- As simple to make as couscous, it is also on the bland side if served alone. You can easily enhance it by following the suggestions for couscous on page 99.

- Or make a cold Quinoa salad for a picnic: Combine 4 cups of cooked Quinoa with:

  – 1 stalk celery, diced small

  – ½ large shallot, diced small

  – ½ large red pepper, diced small and 1 carrot, peeled and diced small.

- Dressing: Standard Vinaigrette: Whisk together:

  ¼ cup champagne vinegar

  ½ cup lemon flavored olive oil

  Use just enough of the dressing to moisten the mixture. Sprinkle with salt, white pepper and add a pinch of cayenne pepper.

1. Using a mesh strainer, rinse the Quinoa under running water to get rid of any impurities.

2. Place it and the liquid (broth or water) in a 2-quart saucepan.

3. Bring to a boil. Reduce the heat and simmer uncovered for about 15 minutes.

4. Cover and let sit for 5 minutes or reduce heat and simmer for another 10 minutes. It will absorb all of the liquid.

5. Sprinkle with salt, pepper and add a pinch of cayenne pepper. Serve hot or cold.

## Why white pepper?

In light colored dishes, black pepper can look, to some people, like grains of dirt or sand. White pepper adds the flavor without the distracting color. If this doesn't bother you, then black pepper is fine.

# Refried Rice    *Serves 6*

Easily change this to your personal taste by adding different vegetables.

4 cups cooked long grain rice
(white or brown)

¼ cup olive oil

3 scallions or ½ cup onions or shallot

2 cups fresh corn

1 cup fresh peas

1 teaspoon each salt and freshly
ground pepper

½ teaspoon cayenne pepper

¼ cup soy, teriyaki or vegetable stir fry
sauce (purchased)

**Optional:** 1 cup chicken, ham, bacon,
beef or sausage, chopped

1. Heat the olive oil in a large frying pan or on a griddle. (You may need to add a little more later on if the mixture starts sticking.) Sauté the onion until soft, stirring it often with a spatula.

2. Add the rice and continue to cook for several minutes. Add the corn, peas, sausage or meat (if you are using it) and spices. Flip the mixture often and sauté until the ingredients are lightly browned.

3. Add your choice of sauce and mix thoroughly. Cook for several minutes more, until the sauce is very hot.

4. Serve hot.

## Chef Lynn's Secrets:

- Everything in this dish could be a leftover from dishes made within a few days.

- Frozen peas work fine. Just toss them in frozen. You can change up the vegetables and include anything you have available that works together.

- Wild rice is also good and provides more fiber.

# Chapter Six
## *Pasta & Eggs*

# Lesson Six

## *What's important to know about pasta and eggs?*

What's important to know about Pasta:

- **NUTRITION:** Pasta is not just pasta anymore! So many new products are on the market now that pasta can contribute so much more than simple starch to the daily diet. You can find whole grain pastas, gluten free pastas, pastas with or without eggs and pastas that are fortified with extra fiber and nutrition. Today, there is something available to fit almost anyone's diet.

- **HOW MUCH TO MAKE?** Generally, 8 ounces of pasta will make about 4 cups of cooked pasta.

- **GIVE IT A REST!** If you make your own pasta, let the raw dough rest at least 30 minutes before you cook it. When you work the dough, the glutens tighten up. They need time to relax in order to tenderize once again.

- **USE A LITTLE SALT IN THE COOKING WATER.** Putting a little salt in the water when you cook pasta will enhance its flavor. Better yet, cook it in all or half and half broth and water. You can use chicken, beef or vegetable stock or broth. The pasta will absorb any flavors that you can expose it to.

- **STIR THE PASTA WHEN YOU PUT IT IN THE WATER.** This simple stir should keep the pasta from sticking.

- **WATCH YOUR COOKING TIME.** Pasta is like everything else. Overcook it and you wreck it. In the case of pasta, it becomes gummy, not to mention unattractive and bland tasting. Dried pasta generally takes 7 to 8 minutes to cook after it is placed in boiling liquid. Fresh pasta, however, requires much less time. It can be as little as 3 minutes, depending on the shape and size of the pasta. If you keep an eye on it, you will see it change to a uniform color and that's when it's done. Fish one out and taste it to be sure.

- **RINSING** after cooking is not necessary if you are using your pasta right away. It takes some time before the pasta will stick together. If you want to hold it awhile before using it in your dish, you can toss it with several tablespoons of olive oil to keep it from sticking together. Cooling it quickly also helps. You can do this by spreading it out on a cookie sheet or other large surface so it isn't piled together.

- **SOAK UP THE SAUCE.** The purpose of ridges, waves and curls in pasta is to create more surface area to soak up the sauce. Pastas that have them can stand up to heavier and chunkier sauces. Pastas with holes in them can also take a heavier sauce. Use delicate sauces for tiny or thin pastas so you don't smother them.

- **TO REHEAT PASTA:** If you have plain pasta (with no sauce), bring a pot of water to a boil. Just put the pasta in and leave it for one minute for each 4 ounces of pasta. Drain as usual and serve.

- **FREEZING** in an airtight container works well with dishes that contain sauce. You can also freeze individual cooked shapes, but they don't reheat as well.

- **STORE** dried pasta for up to a year in a cool, dry place between 50°F and 70°F.

What's important to know about eggs:

- **EGGS ARE NUTRITIOUS.** For only pennies and 75 calories, you get 13 essential nutrients in each egg you consume.

- **CHECK OUT DIFFERENT KINDS OF EGGS.** Chicken eggs are the most commonly used eggs, but tiny quail eggs or larger duck or goose eggs can also be used. They all taste pretty much the same, so give some others a try. It will add interest to your dish, especially when you serve the cooked egg whole or simply sliced.

- **FOR THE SAFEST RESULT,** use pasteurized eggs and store them at 45°F or lower.

- **TO TELL IF AN EGG IS FRESH,** put it in water. Really fresh eggs will sink to the bottom because their contents are dense. As they get older, they begin to incorporate air through the shell. As more and more air is incorporated, they start to float in water. First the large end of the egg will rise and eventually it will float. The more air in the egg, the more chance for bacteria. If your egg floats, throw it out.

- **CAN'T REMEMBER WHICH EGGS YOU HARD BOILED?** Spin each one. Hard boiled eggs will spin evenly because the cooked contents are solid. Uncooked eggs will wobble because the liquid contents slosh around.

- **EGGS CAN BE SUCCESSFULLY FROZEN.** You just have to take raw eggs out of the shell. (Shells can crack and allow bacteria to get to the egg and whole eggs also get tough.) Crack them into a freezer safe container. Stir very slightly so you don't add air to the eggs and you can freeze them for up to a year. Do mix because freezing affects the texture and they won't mix as well afterward. Be sure to mark how many eggs are in the container on the outside because chances are you won't remember. Either freeze them in batches or use sanitized ice cube trays so that each cube represents one egg. Once the eggs are frozen, you can transfer them to freezer bags. I find this especially helpful if we are going on vacation and I have eggs in the refrigerator that won't last until we get back. Separate some of the egg whites and yolks before freezing for use in recipes that call for one or the other. Thaw frozen eggs in the refrigerator for 24 hours, then use them immediately. (Cooked yolks can be frozen, but cooked whites don't freeze well.)

- **STORAGE:** Storing eggs at room temperature decreases the amount of time you can use them drastically. One day at room temperature is like a week in the refrigerator. If you store eggs at cooler temperatures, look for "sell by" date. You will find this date on the end of most egg cartons as well as a code that indicates the plant that packed them and the date they were packed. If you check it when you buy the eggs, you can choose cartons that have the most recent pack date and therefore the longest shelf life when you take them home. Generally, you can use eggs up to three weeks after their "sell by" date.

- **POWDERED EGG WHITES** are dried pure albumen. They can be purchased in cake decorating stores are can be stored for up to 12 months. They are normally pasteurized and you use them by mixing them with warm water. They work out pretty well and can even be whipped into meringue. You just mix 2 teaspoons of powdered egg white with 2 tablespoons of warm water.

- **EGGS ARE NOTORIOUS FOR STICKING TO THE PAN.** Instead of adding a lot of grease to the dish, try using cooking spray. A two second spray adds only about 20 calories to the dish.

- **EGG EQUIVALENTS:**
  1 whole egg = 3 tablespoons
  6 whole eggs = 1 cup
  6 yolks or 5 whites = 1/2 cup
  1 yolk = 1 tablespoon
  1 egg white = 2 tablespoons
  1 dried egg = 2 tablespoons powder +
      2 tablespoons warm water

# Breakfast Soufflé     *Serves 8*

Over the years, I have gotten lots of requests for this recipe. You can use a wide variety of ingredients. Make it your own by including all of the things you like to eat with eggs.

12 slices soft bread (wheat or white)

Whole butter for greasing baking pan

¼ cup olive oil

1 large yellow onion, small dice

1 cup red pepper, small dice

1 clove garlic, minced

3 cups cooked ham, smoked sausage removed from casings or loose sausage

4 cups Cheddar cheese, shredded

2 tablespoons all purpose flour

1½ cups half and half

12 eggs

1 teaspoon Tabasco® sauce (optional)

2 tablespoons prepared mustard

Salt and pepper, to taste

Garnish: Fresh parsley

1. Butter a 9 X 11-inch pan.

2. Cut the crusts from the bread and cut the bread into ½ inch squares. Fill the pan with a single layer of the bread.

3. In a frying pan, sauté the onion and pepper in the olive oil until soft. Add the garlic and sauté for another minute.

4. Mix in the ham or sausage and cook until no longer pink (if it is not already cooked). Then pour it evenly over the bread.

5. Top with the shredded cheese.

6. In a small bowl, whisk the flour with several tablespoons of half and half until smooth. Add the rest of the half and half, eggs, Tabasco® sauce, mustard, salt and pepper. Whisk it all together and pour it evenly over the casserole. Sprinkle the top with salt and pepper.

7. Refrigerate at least 4 hours or overnight.

8. At serving time, preheat your oven to 350°F and bake for about 45 minutes, until golden brown and puffed. Garnish with fresh parsley.

### Chef Lynn's Secrets:

- This casserole makes a perfect breakfast main course when you have guests or a hurried morning. Make it the night before; then just preheat your oven and pop it in. You have 45 minutes to set your table and prepare some biscuits or toast. No need to get up early to put a beautiful breakfast on the table!

- You can make this into a great appetizer by baking the mixture for approximately 20 minutes in greased mini muffin cups or pastry shells.

- I love it made with loose Jimmy Dean® hot breakfast sausage.

# Shirred Eggs   *Serves 8*

These are simply baked eggs. Make your own variations by using different toppings and serve with toast points (page 49).

8 eggs

4 tablespoons butter

2 cups coarsely grated Parmesan cheese

1 cup sun-dried tomatoes, sliced into thin strips

Salt and freshly ground pepper

4 tablespoons freshly chopped chives

1. Preheat your oven to 375°F.

2. Place four individual large ramekins or small casserole dishes on a cookie sheet with sides (jelly roll pan).

3. Butter the baking dishes and then carefully break 2 eggs into each dish. The dishes should just hold 2 eggs. (Don't break the yolks.) Sprinkle the tops with salt and pepper.

4. Bake the eggs for 10–12 minutes. Remove them from the oven, quickly sprinkle the cheese and tomatoes on top, and return them to the oven for 2-5 more minutes, just long enough to melt the cheese and finish cooking the egg whites. The whites of the eggs should be firm but not brown. The yolks should be soft and runny.

Optional: Sprinkle with fresh, chopped chives and serve immediately.

## Chef Lynn's Secrets:

- The beauty of baked eggs is meal timing. You can set your table, have any other dishes you want to serve ready — pop them in the oven, make the toast while they are baking, and voila, everything is hot and ready at the same time.

- **Here are some variations:** Top with other types of cheese, for example, Cheddar or Manchego. Substitute chopped ham, diced shallot, onion or sweet peppers for the sun-dried tomatoes. Or come up with your own version. Anything that tastes good with eggs will be perfect. You could also sprinkle on homemade toasted breadcrumbs... or in season... truffles!

# Chicken Noodle Casserole   *Serves 4*

This is a very user friendly recipe! If you have extra ingredients, definitely add them. Put this together the day before, refrigerate it, and then just heat to serve.

1½ lb. boneless chicken breasts

¼ cup olive oil

Salt and pepper

4 cups uncooked extra-wide egg noodles

3 cups fresh green beans, ends trimmed and cut into bite-sized pieces

4 tablespoons olive oil

1 shallot, minced finely

1 cup green or red pepper, diced small

1 cup mixed fresh mushrooms, diced small

½ cup slivered almonds

3 cups béchamel sauce (cheese variation – page 219)

1 cup yogurt

2 ⅓ cups Pepperidge Farm® Herb Flavored Stuffing

½ cup butter, melted

Salt and pepper, to taste

### Chef Lynn's Secrets:

- You can make this casserole as much as a day ahead. Cover and refrigerate as soon as possible. Bake just before serving.

- Any leftovers will keep up to 7 days. Simply reheat again at the same temperature and for about the same amount of time and serve.

- Leftovers can be kept for up to a week. The general rule is "Seven days and out!"

1. Preheat your oven to 350°F.

2. Brush the chicken pieces lightly with olive oil and sprinkle it with salt and pepper. Bake until it's just cooked through (20–25 minutes). Set aside to cool.

3. In a 3-quart saucepan, heat 2 quarts of water mixed with 1 teaspoon salt until boiling. Cook the noodles just until tender, about 7 minutes. Drain and cool.

4. Fill the pan again with water and 1 teaspoon salt, and cook the green beans just until done, about 3 minutes. Drain and cool quickly under running cold water.

5. Heat 4 tablespoons olive oil in a small frying pan and sauté the shallot and peppers until soft, about 2 minutes. Add the mushrooms and sauté another 2 minutes. Cool.

6. Dice the cooked chicken.

7. Butter a 9 X 11-inch casserole pan and sprinkle ⅓ cup stuffing across the bottom. Then layer the chicken, pasta, shallot mixture, almonds and green beans in the pan. Mix the béchamel cheese sauce with the yogurt. Using a spatula, spread the sauce on top.

8. Mix the rest of the stuffing (2 cups) with the ½ cup of melted butter and sprinkle it on the top of the casserole.

9. Bake just until heated through, about 25 minutes.

# WAYS TO LIGHTEN UP RECIPES

**MAKE LEAN MEAT TASTIER:** Lean meat does not have fat to keep it juicy so it will dry out faster. This means that you have to be especially careful not to overcook it. Poaching and braising are gentle cooking methods that work well to retain moisture. They also add flavor because some of the cooking liquid is absorbed. You can even sauté with a little stock instead of butter to reduce calories. Marinades also add moisture to meat and you can always add extra spice to increase flavor in dishes that don't have a lot of components. Spicy dishes can make you feel fuller and their tastes linger longer.

Just as the fat in your body helps to keep you warm, the absence of fat in lean meats causes them to cool down quicker. You can increase the density of the food by adding a low fat sauce. If you don't want to add the calories of a sauce, come up with a presentation where the food is close together on the plate or stacked. Then all of the elements will stay warmer.

**REDUCE FAT IN INGREDIENTS:** Read labels and choose ingredients with lower fat content. Dairy products are easy ones in this category. You can buy reduced calorie versions of most of them. You can replace milk and cream with evaporated skim milk. Mayonnaise and sour cream can be replaced by yogurt, etc. Check out the Substitutions Appendix (page 246) for more ideas.

Many of the recipes in this book call for cooking spray instead of butter for greasing pans. Spraying for 2 seconds adds only about 1 gram of fat or 9 kilocalories. You don't have to cook with a lot of butter in your dishes either. Adding just a little at the end can bring that great buttery taste forward.

**REVIEW YOUR COOKING METHODS:** Roast, steam, simmer, poach, grill and blanch instead of frying in fat.

**MAKE YOUR OWN STOCK** or buy fat free stocks. The fat in stock separates when cooled so you can easily scrape it off the top.

**USE REDUCTION AS A METHOD OF THICKENING:** Reducing the liquid in soups and sauces by simmering to evaporate some of the liquid takes longer but ensures that you don't have to add flour or other thickening products. For those who need gluten free products, this can be especially important. Soups and sauces can also be thickened by incorporating starchy vegetables like potatoes and beans. In addition to thickening, they add nutrition.

**PORTION CONTROL:** Eating less is unfortunately the best way to lighten up a meal. Part of this, however, is psychological because your plate doesn't look full. To combat this, add things to fill up the plate that don't add a lot of calories, like low fat sauces or salsa. Sliced vegetables like tomatoes also take up a lot of space but add very few more calories.

# Eggs Benedict  *Serves 4*

I love this dish for breakfast, lunch or dinner! To serve it hot, call everyone to the table when you slide the eggs into the poaching liquid and you're set.

8 eggs

1 tablespoon butter

8 circular slices Canadian bacon

4 English muffins

Salt and freshly ground pepper

Hollandaise sauce

1. First make the hollandaise sauce (page 225). Set aside and keep warm.

2. In a medium sized frying pan, melt the butter and fry the Canadian bacon until it is slightly browned. Set aside and keep warm.

3. Toast the muffins and set two on each serving plate. Top each with a slice of the cooked Canadian bacon.

4. Heat a saucepan of water to 180°F; then turn off your burner. Carefully crack the eggs and break each one slowly into the water. Let cook until the whites are just firm, about 3 minutes. Remove with a slotted spoon and place directly on top of the bacon. Note: If you have several batches of eggs to cook, try to keep your water temperature constant by turning the burner underneath on and off.

5. Spoon warm Hollandaise Sauce over the egg. Sprinkle with salt and pepper and serve immediately.

### Chef Lynn's Secrets:

- No one seems to agree on the origin of this lovely egg dish called Benedict. It is, however, my absolute favorite breakfast dish. I don't order it in restaurants much because it's difficult to serve hot. Making it at home easily solves that problem. Call everyone to the table when you slide the eggs into the poaching liquid and you're set!

- For poaching, an induction burner and pot come in very handy. You can set the temperature and it will hold it steady.

- Pictured right: Eggs Benedict with a twist: Fried fresh sausage is substituted for the Canadian bacon.

## Chef Lynn's Poaching and Flipping Secrets

If you find poaching eggs difficult, try the shirred eggs on page 113. They are a cross between poached and sunny side up eggs — lending themselves more toward one or the other depending on how long you cook them. The presentation is beautiful and fail proof.

**If you want to get poaching down though, here are some tricks:**

1. Use only a few inches of water — just enough to cover the egg. Carefully crack the egg in half and hold it just above the water as you pull the shell apart. Slide the egg into the water and leave it alone until the whites are cooked to your liking. Then carefully lift them out with a slotted spoon. I find it helpful to spray the pan with cooking spray before putting the water in it or to use a nonstick pan.

2. If you have 3-inch cake or egg rings, you can place these in the water and break the eggs into the rings. This will make them perfectly round. when the eggs are cooked, pull the rings out first and then remove the eggs with a slotted spoon. Again, it's helpful to spray the rings with cooking spray before you put them in the water.

Speaking of eggs, ever wonder why you can't flip them without using a spatula? You may be using the wrong pan. A sautoir is a pan with straight sides and if you are using one you don't have a chance at flipping. A sauteuse is a pan with curved sides. You need the curved sides to execute the flip. Lift the handle to slide your food down into the curve to make sure it's not sticking and to get it in the correct position for a good flip. Give the front of the pan a quick flip upward and then move it slightly forward to catch it. Flip and catch — just 2 steps. Try it!

Begin with a small, omelet sized frying pan and dry toast. Just concentrate on turning the toast over. It doesn't need to fly three feet in the air. When you can flip the toast well, try an egg and then move on to larger things.

# Grown Up Mac and Cheese     *Serves 8*

This grown-up version of mac and cheese is heaven on earth! Serve it with a crisp salad and you've got a really satisfying lunch.

1 pound mezze or regular penne pasta

1 whole black truffle, sliced paper thin (1 oz.)

Optional: 1 cup ham, cut into tiny cubes

Butter for greasing the pan

6 tablespoons butter

1 shallot, minced finely

6 tablespoons cake flour

4 cups whole milk (or half and half)

1 cup chicken broth

2 tablespoons truffle oil

1 teaspoon garlic salt

1 teaspoon freshly ground white pepper

2 cups white cheddar cheese, grated

**Topping:**

¼ cup Italian breadcrumbs

¾ cup Parmesan or Cheddar cheese, grated

2 tablespoons butter

1. Preheat your oven to 350°F.

2. Cook the pasta in boiling water with 1 tablespoon salt until just cooked through, about 7 minutes. Drain and cool.

3. Mix the pasta with the truffle slices (and the ham if you choose to use it). Place in a buttered 9 X 11-inch baking dish.

4. Make the sauce: In a 3-quart saucepan, melt 6 tablespoons butter. Add the shallot and cook for one minute. Whisk in the flour and cook for several minutes. (This mixture should be the consistency of peanut butter. If it isn't, add a little more flour.)

5. Whisk in the milk (or half and half) and chicken broth. Cook slowly over low heat for 20 minutes. Whisk often and keep the sides of the pan scraped down so a skin doesn't form.

6. Whisk in the truffle oil, grated white cheddar cheese, garlic salt and white pepper. Pour over the pasta.

7. Mix the breadcrumbs with 2 tablespoons melted butter and sprinkle them on top of the pasta mixture. Top with grated Parmesan or Cheddar cheese.

8. Bake until hot and the crumbs are slightly browned, about 25 minutes.

**Chef Lynn's Secrets:**

- This can be made the day before or hours ahead. If you let it stand after baking, it will cut into cleaner pieces. Cut first and then reheat in a 350°F oven for about 20 minutes.

- Truffles are a type of mushroom and can be found in many markets, usually near the meat counter. Black (winter) truffles are easier to find than the more fragrant white ones that are harvested in early autumn. If you don't have fresh truffle you can make this anyway. Truffle oil will give it plenty of taste.

# Pasta Salad    *Makes 2 Quarts*

This recipe spices up some standard picnic fare with lots of crunch!

½ pound mini penne pasta

⅓ cup garden onion (about 3), sliced very thin

½ cup red pepper, diced very small

½ cup green pepper, diced very small

¾ cup water chestnuts, drained and diced very small

½ cup Parmesan Reggiano cheese, coarsely grated

1 cup mayonnaise

3 tablespoons Dijon mustard

1 teaspoon each salt and pepper

1 teaspoon champagne vinegar or white wine vinegar

**Optional:** 3 hard boiled eggs, diced small

**Garnish:** Red paprika and fresh chives, chopped tiny

1. In a large saucepan, bring 2 quarts of water mixed with 1 tablespoon salt to a boil. Add the penne pasta and cook for about 7 minutes, just until cooked through but still firm. Drain and run under cold water to cool. Transfer to a large bowl.

2. Add the rest of the ingredients and mix well.

3. Taste and adjust the seasonings if necessary.

4. Chill before serving, at least 2 hours.

## Chef Lynn's Secrets:

- The secret to pasta salad is the ratios. The right flavor mix and the right ratio of soft pasta to crunch is what will make it stand apart. Contrasting colors also add to its appeal.

- If you add the eggs, you may need to add a little more mayonnaise and a little more salt. Taste and adjust.

- To boil the eggs, bring 2 quarts water to a boil. Lower the whole eggs into the water using a spoon. I use a gravy ladle because it keeps them very stable. Cook for 10 minutes. Drain and cool. This will keep that pesky green ring from forming around the yolk.

# Homemade Pasta  *Easy and from Scratch*

Making pasta can be simple if you understand three things:

1. For extruded pasta shapes (in other words, dough that is forced through a machine), you can use much harder dough because the machine can apply so much more pressure than you can by hand. The more semolina you have in the dough, the harder or tougher it will be.

2. If you want to make pasta by hand, you can save yourself some headaches by using softer dough that can more easily be rolled thin... especially when making ravioli, which needs to form itself around the filling. You can make softer dough by changing some or all of the semolina to all purpose or bread flour and/or adding some olive oil.

3. Let your pasta rest at least 30 minutes before cooking to relax the glutens in the flour. This makes it more tender. It will also be easier to roll and won't "pull back" as you try and roll it out. Keep it covered when you are not working with it so that it doesn't form a skin.

So let's go! Here are doughs that work for the three purposes: extruded pasta, hand rolled pasta and ravioli.

## Traditional Extruded Pasta:

(To use with a pasta machine)

2 pounds Semolina flour

1 cup whole eggs or water or a combination of both (Add a bit at a time until a stiff dough forms. You may not need all of the liquid. Many machines mix the dough for you. Just put the ingredients in and let it do the work.)

1. Mix in the machine and extrude (let the machine push the dough through the die that makes the shape). Let rest 30 minutes before cooking or dry for later use.

2. Mix 1 quart chicken stock with 1 quart water and 1 tablespoon salt. Bring to a boil. Cook about 7 minutes. Remove with a slotted spoon and served spoon and serve.

## Hand-rolled Pasta and Ravioli:

5 cups bread flour

1 tablespoon olive oil

4–5 whole eggs or 1 cup water

1. Mix all ingredients and knead for 5 minutes.

2. Let rest covered with plastic for at least 20 minutes.

3. Roll out with a rolling pin. If necessary, add flour until it rolls without sticking.

4. Cut into shapes and let them rest for 30 minutes or let them dry overnight.

5. Mix 1 quart chicken broth with 1 quart water and 1 tablespoon salt. Bring to a boil. Cook the pasta about 4 minutes or until tender. Remove with a slotted spoon and serve.

# Variations (Flavored Doughs):

Mix the following with the basic mix above (first with the flour and then add any liquid):

**Garlic Flavored Pasta:** Add 4 roasted and chopped garlic cloves.

**Onion Flavored:** Add 1 small onion, minced.

**Basil and herb flavored:** Add 1 cup chopped fresh basil leaves. Chives, tarragon, thyme and oregano all work well. For rosemary flavored, just use ½ cup and be sure to chop it very tiny.

**Carrot Flavored:** Add 3 carrots, peeled, steamed and chopped tiny. Work the dough until it's orange.

**Green or Black Olive Flavored:** Mince a dozen olives. Mix them with the flour and then add the egg.

**Spinach Flavored:** Add 8 oz. fresh spinach, steamed and chopped. Mix it first with the flour and then add the liquid.

**Spinach, Tomato, Beet, etc.:** Mix 4 tablespoons powdered vegetable (available online). This adds a lot of beautiful color but doesn't change the original pasta taste too much. (Turmeric makes a beautiful yellow colored pasta that looks rich and eggy, although it isn't.)

**Pepper Flavored:** Add 2 tablespoons coarse grind black pepper.

**Squash Flavored:** Add 1 cup cooked and minced squash.

**Turmeric Colored:** Add 4 tablespoons turmeric.

You get the idea... Now invent your own!

Above: Left to right: Pasta dough flavored with turmeric, tomato and spinach powders.

## Chef Lynn's Secrets:

- Keep the dough covered at all times so that it won't dry out!

- If you want to roll your pasta out using a hand cranked roller, work with small pieces. The knob on the left of the machine is numbered from 1 to 7. Start rolling the dough through on seven (the widest setting). Fold the edges in to keep them even and roll again. Turn the number on the knob to 6 and repeat. Keep working the setting down to at least 2 and 1 if you can. It must be thin. If necessary, add flour until it rolls without sticking.

- Do not overcrowd the pan when cooking. It's better to cook the finished shapes in batches to ensure they are cooked evenly.

- To add taste, use a mix of half chicken broth and half water for cooking.

- When drying pasta, make sure there is sufficient air around it or it can mold. Hang it or place it on wire mesh in a way that air can circulate around it.

# Quick Pasta Sauces: Red and White

Sauces purchased in stores are extremely expensive compared to these simple alternatives.

# Roux Based Sauce: *Makes 3 cups*

Roux is a traditional thickener, made with equal parts of clarified butter and cake flour. Whisk in milk and a few spices and you have just made a standard French béchamel.

The reason to use roux in a sauce is because it makes a very stable sauce that will easily keep in the refrigerator for a week and reheat well. The only trick is to be sure to cook it for at least 20 minutes to stabilize the starch and to get rid of the flour taste. Here is an example with some variations. Just multiply it if you want more.

3 tablespoons clarified butter (page 23)

3 tablespoons cake flour

Approximately 3 cups milk

Salt

White pepper

Lemon juice

**Optional flavorings:**

⅓ cup grated cheese

¼ cup fresh chives or any other herb that
   complements your dish, chopped

1. In a medium sized frying pan over low heat, whisk together the butter and flour. Cook for 3 minutes.

2. Whisk in milk, a little at a time. It should incorporate about 3 cups.

3. Then flavor it as you like, but always add salt, white pepper and a little fresh lemon juice to spike up the flavor.

**Chef Lynn's Secrets:**
- Another simple but tasteful pasta sauce is pesto made with fresh basil (page 243).
- Save any leftovers to use as a quick vegetable or meat topping.

# Tomato Based Sauce   *Makes 3 cups*

A basic tomato sauce can be used for so many things that it's hard to know where to begin. Use as a topping, a base for gazpacho soup or a layer in a lasagna casserole all rank high on the list.

2 cups very ripe tomatoes – any type

4 tablespoons olive oil

¼ cup yellow or white onions, diced small

¼ cup peeled celery, diced small

½ cup red pepper, diced

Salt and pepper, to taste

2 teaspoons hot sauce (Tabasco® etc.)

¼ cup chives

4 tablespoons tomato paste

2 tablespoons fresh lemon juice

1. Heat the olive oil in a 2-quart saucepan.

2. Add the onions and celery and sauté until soft and golden.

3. Add the red pepper and cook several minutes more.

4. Add the rest of the ingredients and cook several minutes more.

5. Purée in a food processor or using an immersion blender to the consistency that you like. It can be slightly chunky or very smooth — as you like.

6. Taste the sauce and add more seasonings or tomato paste if necessary.

# Ravioli   *Makes one pound of pasta*

Ravioli is the quintessential homemade pasta specialty. With the right dough, it can be easy.

4 cups bread flour (or a mix of flour and semolina)

1 teaspoon salt

1 tablespoons olive oil

4–5 eggs, lightly beaten

Large bunch of fresh basil leaves

Filling recipe: See next page

Water for brushing around the filling

1. Whisk the flour and salt together.

2. Make a well in the middle and add the olive oil and the eggs a few at a time. Add just enough egg to form a stiff dough.

3. Let the dough rest for 20 minutes.

4. Using a hand crank pasta machine, press a small piece of dough through the widest setting. Keep passing the same piece of dough through, narrowing the rollers each time. Fold it over and re-roll any time it gets out of shape. When you are finished, you should have a long, thin strip. Set this strip on your counter and cover it with clean, fresh basil leaves.

5. Make another strip exactly like the first and lay it on top of the basil leaves. Carefully lift up the strips and run them through the thinnest setting one more time.

6. Cut the strip in half so that you have two pieces.

7. Place 1 tablespoon filling 2-inches apart all along one strip. Brush around the filling lightly with water. Top with the other strip and press around the filling mounds with your fingers. Using a pastry cutter, cut out squares being careful not to get too close to the mounds.

Ravioli rolled with basil leaves (uncooked).

# Fillings

Choose one or make a combination: You can mix these fillings up with any of your favorite cheeses. If you choose a hard cheese, grate it. Soft cheeses that will mix well can be left as is.

### Ricotta and Chevre (Goat) Cheese:

Mix 1 cup Ricotta with ½ cup goat cheese. Add a pinch of salt and pepper. Then add any or all of the following: ¼ cup toasted pine nuts, ½ cup chopped tomatoes and ¼ cup basil or chives.

### Three Cheese:

Mix 1 cup Gorgonzola cheese with ½ cup Asiago or Parmesan cheese (coarsely grated), ½ cup Mozzarella and a pinch of salt and pepper. Mix in ½ cup fresh breadcrumbs.

### Spinach and Cheese:

Chop 6 cups fresh spinach and steam it until soft. Drain and cool. Mix with ½ cup minced shallots, 1 cup grated Manchego cheese, 1 cup ricotta cheese, a pinch of salt and a pinch of pepper.

### Chevre and Sun-Dried Tomatoes:

Mix 1 cup chevre cheese with ¾ cup sun-dried tomatoes cut into small slivers. Mix in ½ cup chopped fresh basil and if desired, ½ cup toasted pine nuts.

### Sausage Stuffing:

Mix 1 pound Jimmy Dean® hot sausage (fried until no longer pink), ¼ cup minced shallots, ½ cup each of Ricotta, grated Mozzarella and grated Asiago cheeses. Also add a pinch of salt and pepper.

### Mushroom Stuffing:

Sauté ⅓ cup minced shallot in butter or olive oil just until soft. Add 2 cups chopped morel mushrooms and continue to sauté until they are soft, 3 or 4 more minutes. Cool and mix with 1 cup fresh breadcrumbs and one lightly beaten egg, salt and pepper to taste.

### Chef Lynn's Secrets:

- If your dough sticks in the machine, just add a little more flour. Fold and re-roll if your piece gets out of shape. If it gets too long, just trim it.

- If you roll the final piece with the basil inside more than once, the leaves will start to break up. The more you roll it, the more it will mix and actually end up coloring the dough. Stop at any stage. It's all pretty.

- You can make your ravioli any size. I like to make them large and stuff them with lots of delicious filling.

- I like to cook the ravioli in a large frying pan with tall sides. I mix ½ quart water with ½ quart chicken broth and add 1 tablespoon salt. Then I carefully slide in the raviolis, being careful not to overcrowd the pan. They take about 7 minutes to cook through. They are delicious with just a little melted butter on top, sprinkled with chives or another herb. No need to make a fancy sauce!

# Spinach Lasagna  *Serves 8*

Make this lasagna with or without meat. If you don't include the meat, you won't miss it.

10 oz. spinach (or 15 oz. if not using sausage)

1 cup chicken or vegetable broth

¼ cup pine nuts, toasted

Optional: 1 pound regular pork sausage

4 tablespoons olive oil

1½ tablespoons clarified butter

1½ tablespoons cake flour

2 cups whole milk

12 lasagna noodles

3 cups tomato sauce (homemade or purchased), divided

1 cup fresh tomatoes, diced very small

Salt and pepper, to taste

¾ cup ricotta cheese

2½ cups shredded Cheddar or mozzarella or a mix of both

3 tablespoons Minute Tapioca®

¼ cup Parmesan cheese

**Chef Lynn's Secrets:**

- The key to this yummy and not so runny lasagna is the Minute Tapioca®. By thickening the sauce, it works along with the cheese to give support and hold the squares together when you cut them.

- It can be made with or without meat. It's great family food, either way.

1. Preheat your oven to 350°F.

2. Remove any thick stems from the spinach and chop it. In a large frying pan, cook it in the broth until it wilts, about 3 minutes. (It will absorb all or most of the broth.)

3. Toast the pine nuts on a cookie sheet. Place them in a 400° F oven for about 7 minutes.

4. If using sausage, in a medium frying pan, cook it in the olive oil until it is no longer pink. Mix with 2 cups of the tomato sauce and purée it in a food processor. Mix in tomato.

5. Make the white sauce: In a small frying pan, mix 1½ tablespoons clarified butter with 1½ tablespoons cake flour. Heat for several minutes. Gradually whisk in 2 cups whole milk and cook for 15 minutes.

6. Cook the lasagna noodles about 7 minutes. In boiling water seasoned with 1 tablespoon salt. Drain.

7. Spread about 4 tablespoons plain tomato sauce in the bottom of a square baking pan or a small oblong casserole pan. Then layer in the ingredients as follows:

   - Noodles — tomato sauce — fresh tomatoes — ½ of the spinach — ricotta — tomatoes

   - ½ cup grated cheese — pine nuts

   - 1½ tablespoons Minute Tapioca® — salt and pepper

   - Noodles — white sauce — 1½ tablespoons Minute Tapioca® — salt and pepper — ½ of spinach — ½ cup grated cheese

   - Noodles — tomato sauce — fresh tomatoes —1½ cups grated cheese — ¼ cup coarsely grated Parmesan cheese

8. Bake for 30 minutes, until lasagna is warmed and cheese is melted. Serve hot.

# Spaetzle  *Serves 4*

These fantastic noodles are native to Switzerland and Germany.

2¼ cups all purpose flour

1 teaspoon salt

1 egg, well beaten

¼ to ¾ cup water

2 quarts water mixed with 1 tablespoon salt for cooking

**Other flavor options:**

¼ cup grated Parmesan cheese

¼ cup very finely minced shallot

**Optional Toppings: (Also see Secrets)**

1½ cups breadcrumbs or 1½ cups Parmesan cheese

Make Ahead Gravy (page 221)

**Chef Lynn's Secrets:**

- Spaetzle are little noodles, common in both Germany and Switzerland. You will see them in soups or as a side dish prepared in different ways. Sometimes hot melted butter is simply poured over them. Sometimes breadcrumbs or Parmesan cheese are sprinkled over them.

- Most commonly, the spaetzle noodles are cooked in boiling water as in this recipe and then later fried in butter until they are golden and beginning to crisp. The most elaborate way is to add breadcrumbs or Parmesan cheese to the fried version and then pour your favorite gravy over the top. I love to make them when I make veal scallopini because the rich gravy is a perfect fit.

1. Over medium high heat, begin heating 2 quarts of water mixed with 1 tablespoon salt.

2. Whisk the flour and salt together. (If you are using Parmesan or shallot or both, also mix it in.)

3. Mix in the egg and then the water gradually. Use just enough to make a smooth dough. Press the dough into a strip on a small cutting board.

4. By now, your water should be boiling. Using a sharp knife, scrape off little bits of dough directly into the boiling water. Use about ⅓ of the dough at a time so you don't overload the saucepan. Cook 5 to 8 minutes, until done.

5. Remove them with a slotted spoon and place them on a platter in one layer. Repeat the process until you have used up the dough.

**NOTE:** If you are not accustomed to scraping the noodles, it will be an arduous process to scrape them directly into the water. I find it easier to scrape them onto a lightly floured piece of parchment paper — away from the heat! Then it's easy to dump them into the boiling water all together so they cook evenly.

# Sun-Dried Tomato & Vegetable Quiche *Serves 6 to 8*

Quiche can be a stand alone entrée or a delicious accompaniment to other main courses.

**For the crust:**

1 cup flour

1 teaspoon salt

⅓ cup white Cheddar cheese

½ cup butter

⅛ cup very cold water

**For the filling:**

½ cup sun-dried tomatoes (about 2 oz.)

2 tablespoons olive oil (flavored with basil is nice if you have some, see page 227)

1 shallot, minced

½ cup red pepper, chopped small (1/2 pepper)

1 cup grated white Cheddar cheese

½ cup fresh mozzarella cheese, chopped very small

½ cup chopped basil

5 eggs + 3 egg yolks

1¾ cups half and half

2 tablespoons prepared mustard

½ teaspoon each, salt and pepper

Cooking spray

1. Preheat your oven to 425°F.

2. **Make the crust:** In a small mixing bowl, whisk the flour and salt together. Mix the cheese through. Cut the butter into small pieces and mix with your hands, pressing the butter into the flour until it looks like peas. Make a well in the middle and pour in the cold water. Mix until it forms a ball.

3. **Prepare the crust:** Spray a 10-inch fluted quiche pan with cooking spray. (If you don't have one, use a pie pan.)

4. On a floured counter, roll the crust out until it is slightly bigger than your quiche pan. Fold it in half and lift it into the pan. Lightly press it down so that it completely fills the pan. Trim the edge by pressing down along the edge with your thumb.

5. **Make the filling:** Slice the sun-dried tomatoes in half lengthwise. Then cut tiny strips crosswise. Set aside in a bowl.

6. Heat 2 tablespoons olive oil in a small frying pan. Over medium heat, sauté the shallot just until it's soft. Add the red pepper and continue to heat for 2 minutes. Cool and add to the sun-dried tomatoes. Also add the cheeses and basil and mix thoroughly. Season with salt and pepper, to taste. Line the crust evenly with the mix.

7. In a separate bowl, whisk the eggs with the half and half, mustard, salt and pepper. Carefully pour it into the crust.

8. Bake on the bottom rack of your oven until lightly browned on top, 40–50 minutes. Serve hot.

Above: Sun-dried Tomato & Vegetable Quiche, garnished with fried basil (page 239) and a fried quail egg.

## Chef Lynn's Secrets:

- Never mix hot ingredients into raw eggs. It will cause them to immediately cook and ruin the consistency of your finished product.

- You can easily use this quiche as a main course. In season, a simple side of sliced tomatoes drizzled with a flavored olive oil and sprinkled with salt and pepper make an outstanding accompaniment.

- Baking on the bottom rack of the oven helps the crust to cook through because it is then closer to the heat source.

- When the quiche first comes out of the oven, it will look "puffed". Let it sit 5 to 10 minutes before cutting so it has a chance to settle down.

# Chapter Seven
# *Breads*

# Lesson Seven

## *What's important to know about making breads?*

- **IN BAKING, EVERYTHING HAS ITS PURPOSE.**

  As Robert L. Wolke says in his wonderful book, What Einstein told his cook, "Never gamble with a cookie!"

  Robert was talking about salt, but actually ALL of the elements of baked goods have important functions, so be careful when reducing or omitting ingredients. In addition to nutritional value, for example:

  **MILK** makes the texture of bread softer, adds flavor and causes a deep crust color to develop.

  **FLOUR** gives structure, so if you reduce it or add too much, your result will be too soft or too tough.

  **SUGAR** tenderizes, adds sweetness and crust color, attracts moisture, helps the butter to cream together with the other ingredients and is food for the yeast so it helps the dough to rise.

  **SALT** adds flavor and helps to control the yeast because it eventually kills it.

  **EGGS** also help with structure as the proteins within coagulate. They also help with rising and add moisture and flavor as well as a deep crust color.

  **FATS** add moisture, help to tenderize, help the finished product to last longer and add flavor.

- **RATIOS ARE IMPORTANT.** Measure very carefully. A little bit of this or a little bit too much of that can throw the whole thing off and cause everything from falling to complete failure.

  A scale is worth its weight in gold because it gives you the most precision. Dipping a measuring cup into flour or pouring flour into a measuring cup, for example, can result in different amounts each time you do it. The proper way is to spoon the flour into the cup. Then level it off with the spoon handle or a knife.

- **WATCH YOUR SALT RATIOS.** Do not use pre-salted products. For example, always use unsalted butter in all types of cooking. That will give you complete control over how much is added to flavor your dish at the end.

- **PREPARE YOUR PANS FOR A GOOD RELEASE.** Greasing pans is important to keep your baked goods from sticking. Use a fat that can withstand high heat and won't burn – like Crisco® or clarified butter or a cooking spray. For extra protection, you can lightly flour the pan after you rub on the fat.

- **STORAGE:** This will surprise some people, but when you have a beautiful finished bread, don't store it in plastic or the refrigerator. Plastic and refrigeration both will soften the crust and speed up staling. For best results, store at room temperature in a paper or cloth bag.

- **ALWAYS PREHEAT YOUR OVEN.** Baked products need to be placed in an oven that is already hot and stays consistent. This is extremely important when baking products that need to rise. Don't open the oven door during the baking process.

  You can simulate a professional oven by leaving a baking stone on the bottom rack of your oven. It will help to hold the heat and keep it even. Pies and bread can be baked directly on it.

- **ROOM TEMPERATURE INGREDIENTS:** If your recipe calls for room temperature ingredients but yours are cold, you can rush the process. Butter can be microwaved for 20 seconds to soften it without melting. Eggs can be warmed in a bowl of warm water and other ingredients can be placed in a metal bowl that is placed in another bowl of hot water.

- **IF YOU FORGET TO EGG WASH**, using a pastry brush, you can give your bread or rolls a sheen by painting a small amount of butter on the top. Very small though, or you will compromise its crustiness. If the butter is whole, you will need to pat it with a paper towel after painting because the milk solids will separate from the fat.

# Potato Bread    *Makes 2 loaves*

With or without the potatoes, this bread is good for making sandwiches or simply slathered with butter and jam.

1 medium potato

Warm water

5 teaspoons dry yeast (2 packages)

2 tablespoons sugar

1 cup whole milk

2 tablespoons butter

3½ cups bread flour

3½ cups all purpose flour

1 tablespoon salt

## Chef Lynn's Secrets:

- I've been making this easy bread for over 30 years. It never ceases to please.

- If you don't have a mixer, you can mix it by hand. Just knead it for about 10 minutes.

- Cut it thick for wonderful French toast. Slice it up, wrap it tight and freeze it to pull out on a whim for toast. Chop it up for wonderful breadcrumbs. In every variation, the comment is always "YUM!"

- P.S. If tightly wrapped, it freezes well for up to 3 months.

1. Peel and dice the potato. Place in a small saucepan. Cover it with water and simmer until it's cooked through and very soft, about 15 minutes.

2. Drain the water off the potato, but keep it. Add more water to make a cup if necessary. When the water cools to lukewarm, mix it with the yeast and sugar in your mixer bowl.

3. Mash the potato with a fork and add it to the yeast mixture.

4. Heat the milk and butter to lukewarm and add it to the yeast mixture.

5. Using the dough hook, mix in the flours and last, the salt. After the flours are thoroughly mixed in, turn the machine to high and beat it for 2 minutes.

6. Place the dough ball in a greased bowl. Then turn it over so the whole thing is greased. Cover it with a thin kitchen towel and set it in a warm place until it doubles, about 45 minutes.

7. Punch the dough down with your fist. Re-cover it and let it rise about 30 minutes more.

8. Form into loaves: Roll dough into a large rectangle. Fold it over twice. Then fold the ends under and place in greased loaf pans. Pat down to release any air. Let rise again for about an hour. The dough should rise above the pan.

9. Preheat your oven to 375°F and bake until browned on top, 40-45 minutes.

10. Remove from the pans and cool on wire racks. Wait at least an hour before eating if you can! The bread will continue to relax and finish baking.

# Calzone    *Serves 4*

This is pizza in a pocket! Eat them hot or cold.

1 recipe Pizza Dough (page 144)

1 medium yellow onion, minced

2 tablespoons olive oil

1 cup sausage (or cooked ham, diced)

1 tablespoon Dijon mustard

1 cup ricotta cheese

1 cup mozzarella cheese

1 egg

1 cup spinach (fresh or frozen)

½ teaspoon each salt and pepper

1 tablespoon hot sauce, like Tabasco®

Small amount of water in a small dish

Egg wash: 1 egg whisked with 2 yolks and
    1 tablespoon cream

Cooking spray if baking on a cookie sheet

1.  Make the pizza dough and divide it into 8
    equal portions. Let them rest while you
    prepare the filling.

2.  Preheat your oven to 425°F.

3.  Sauté the onion in the olive oil. Add the
    sausage and continue to sauté until the
    sausage is cooked through and no longer
    pink. Add the spinach and if fresh, cook
    until it's wilted. (If frozen, just mix drained
    and thawed spinach through.) Let this
    mixture cool and then mix it with the
    ricotta, mozzarella, egg, mustard, salt,
    pepper and hot sauce.

4.  Roll each piece of dough into a circle.
    Top one half with the filling, keeping it
    2 inches from the edge. Using a pastry
    brush, lightly brush the edge around the
    filling with water.

5.  Lift the other half over the filling and press
    the edges together. Flute with your fingers
    or press with a fork to seal. Lightly brush
    with egg wash.

6.  Bake on a hot pizza stone or sprayed
    cookie sheet until lightly browned, about
    20 minutes.

7.  Serve hot.

**Chef Lynn's Secrets:**

• Be careful to brush on the egg wash lightly and
  completely cover the calzone. Areas without egg
  wash will brown differently than those with it.

• Always, always, always taste what you have
  cooked before presenting it to others. In this
  case, taste the filling and adjust the seasonings if
  necessary before baking the calzone.

# Cheese Bread Sticks    *Makes 24 cheese bread sticks*

Cheese Bread Sticks can be made in many shapes and sizes to suit your occasion.

2¼ teaspoon active dried yeast

1 cup lukewarm water

1 teaspoon sugar

3½ cups all purpose flour

2 tablespoons Coleman's® dry mustard
    powder

1 teaspoon salt

1¾ cups white Cheddar cheese, coarsely
    grated

1 shallot, minced

2 tablespoons butter for greasing the bowl

½ cup Parmesan cheese for topping, finely
    grated

Cooking spray

Egg wash: 1 egg + 1 yolk whisked with
    1 tablespoon cream

## Chef Lynn's Secrets:

You can also form these into dinner rolls or
loaves or shorter, fatter sticks. Just don't egg
wash them until you are ready to bake or the
crust can become soggy. Here are some ways to
change it up: Add:

- ½ cup chopped fresh herbs (basil, chive
  or tarragon)

- 1 cup cooked ham or cooked sausage, diced
  very small

- 2 garden onions, washed and cut crosswise
  into very thin slices

- Swiss, Manchego or pepper jack cheese
  instead of the Cheddar

At best, serve immediately or the same day.
Or you can store them in a loosely covered
container at room temperature for about 3 days
or freeze in freezer bags for up to 3 months.

1. Mix the yeast, water and sugar. Set aside until
   it bubbles.

2. Mix the flour with the mustard powder and
   salt. Mix in the coarsely grated cheese, the
   shallot and any other flavorings you choose.
   (See Chef Lynn's tips).

3. Add the yeast liquid to the dry ingredients
   and mix to a stiff dough. Knead by hand for
   3-5 minutes.

4. Rub the inside of a large bowl with butter.
   Place the dough in it and then turn it over.
   (This greases the top and bottom both.)
   Cover the bowl with a thin damp cloth and let
   it rest until the dough doubles, 30 minutes to
   an hour.

5. Divide the dough into 24 equal pieces. Form
   into bread sticks by rolling into "snakes".
   Start rolling with one hand. Then place both
   hands together in the middle and roll out
   to the ends. Brush with egg wash and roll
   through Parmesan as the last step. Place on
   baking sheets sprayed with cooking spray.

   *Note: When you work the dough, the proteins
   will seize up and pull back, making the sticks
   a little shorter than you initially roll out. As
   they rest, they will tenderize again and become
   more pliable.*

6. Let the bread sticks rise until double in size,
   about 30 minutes.

7. While waiting, preheat your oven to 375°F.

8. Bake 15 to 20 minutes. Cool.

# Cinnamon Bread (& Rolls)    *Makes 2 loaves*

5½ to 6 cups bread flour, divided

½ cup sugar

2 teaspoons salt

4½ teaspoons active dry yeast

⅓ cup whole butter

1 cup cold milk

¾ cup cold water

3 eggs

3 tablespoons  butter for greasing the
   bowl and pans.

**Topping:** ¼ cup melted butter

½ cup sugar

1½ tablespoons cinnamon

**Variation:** Add 1 teaspoon rum extract
   to the filling

**Chef Lynn's Secret:**

- Make sure your yeast is well within its
  "use by" date on the package.

- You can add a crumb topping to this
  bread by mixing ⅓ cup flour, ⅓
  cup packed light brown sugar and 2
  teaspoons cinnamon with 3 tablespoons
  whole butter. Just rub it through your
  fingers until it's crumbly. When the
  loaves are ready to bake, brush them
  with egg wash and sprinkle on the
  topping.

1. In your mixer bowl, whisk together 2 cups
   of flour, ½ cup sugar, 2 teaspoon salt and
   4½ teaspoon yeast.

2. In a small saucepan, melt ⅓ cup whole
   butter. Remove from heat and pour in
   1 cup cold milk and ¾ cup cold water.
   Immediately pour into the mixer bowl with
   the dry ingredients and mix for about 3
   minutes at medium speed. Scrape down the
   sides of the bowl.

3. Add 3 eggs and 1 more cup of flour and
   mix again for about 3 minutes. If you have
   a dough hook, switch to it now. If not,
   proceed by hand.

4. Mix in about 3 more cups of flour and mix
   until completely blended. Beat with the
   dough hook for 3 more minutes or knead
   by hand for about 10 minutes. The dough
   should pull away from the sides of the bowl
   while mixing and feel stiff.

5. Rub whole butter all over the inside of
   the bowl. Place the dough in the bowl and
   then turn it over so that the top is greased.
   (This will help to keep it from drying out.)
   Place in a warm place for about 40 minutes
   to rise. The size of the dough ball should
   double.

6. While the dough is rising, melt ¼ cup butter
   and set aside to cool. In a small bowl, mix
   ½ cup sugar and 1½ tablespoons cinnamon.

7. When the dough has doubled, punch it
   down with your fist and divide it in half.
   Using a rolling pin, roll each out into a
   rectangle. Roll the length first to about
   14 inches. Then roll the width to about
   12 inches. Paint each heavily with melted
   butter and sprinkle half of the sugar-
   cinnamon mixture on each.

8. Roll up lengthwise. Fold the ends of the roll underneath and press down on the top so they stay underneath. Place this in a well buttered loaf pan and press down again to release any air pockets. Place the loaf pans in a warm place and cover them with a thin kitchen towel. Let them rise again until they fill up the pan and rise over the top to look like a loaf, about 45 minutes.

9. Bake in a preheated oven at 375°F for about 45 minutes or until well browned. Cool and wait at least an hour to slice so that it will finish with its carryover baking.

## Cinnamon Rolls

This recipe can easily be made into cinnamon rolls. After rolling the dough up, just cut it into 1 inch slices and lay them cut side down in a well buttered baking dish. Bake until lightly browned. Glaze with confectioner's sugar mixed with just enough water to make it the consistency of drizzled frosting. Mix in a little at a time until it's just right.

Both versions freeze well. Cool and wrap tightly and freeze up to 3 months. Thaw at room temperature before serving or gently reheating.

# Crackers    *Serves 6*

Makes approximately 24 large crackers.

**Basic Cracker Mix:**

1 cup all purpose or wheat flour

5 tablespoons cold, unsalted butter, cut into small pieces

*Liquid: 2½ tablespoons

*Spices, to taste

*Cheese: Up to 2 cups, if desired

*Other Flavoring: Up to 2 cups

Cooking spray

**Chef Lynn's Secrets:**

- The most important thing about crackers is that they should be very thin. Roll them carefully with your rolling pin on a very lightly floured surface. Work with very small pieces of dough and re-roll scraps only once. I like to cut the edges with a fluted pastry cutter so they look both pretty and professional.

- You can store these crackers in an airtight container for several weeks.

- For a crispier cracker, leave the butter out, but note that you may need a little more water. Milk also makes a softer, browner crust than water.

- To easily pick up the cracker shapes you have rolled out, slide a sharp French knife underneath and lift them on to the baking sheet.

1. Preheat your oven to 400°F.

2. Mix the flour well with any spices and flavorings.

3. Drop in the butter and press between your thumb and fingers until the mix is the consistency of streusel.

4. Add enough liquid to make stiff dough.

5. Roll very thin. Cut out shapes and place them on a baking sheet sprayed with cooking spray.

6. Bake until lightly browned and firm, about 12 minutes. Cool on the cookie sheet.

**\*Variations:**

**Sun-Dried Tomato and Cheese Crackers:**

Liquid: Water (2½ tablespoons)

Spices: ½ teaspoon salt, 1 teaspoon white pepper, ¼ teaspoon cayenne pepper, ⅛ teaspoon garlic powder

Cheese: 1½ cups white Cheddar cheese

Other flavoring: ⅔ cup sun-dried tomatoes, sliced very tiny. If packed in oil, dry them off with a paper towel.

**Peppered Swiss Crackers:**

Liquid: Milk (about 2½ tablespoons)

Spices: 1 teaspoon salt, 1 tablespoon coarse grind black pepper

Cheese: 2 cups Swiss cheese

Other flavoring: None

# Dinner Rolls  *Makes 24 Rolls*

The smell of home made dinner rolls baking is as good as the taste!

3 tablespoons sugar

½ cup warm water

2 packages active dry yeast

1 cup whole milk

¼ cup butter

1 cup whole wheat flour

3 cups all purpose flour

1 teaspoon salt

Optional: 1 cup olives, chopped

## Chef Lynn's Secrets:

- If you are using a bread stamp, push it ¾ of the way through each ball of dough.

- When your rolls come out of the oven, transfer them to a rack to cool and lightly brush them with melted clarified butter to enhance their appearance and give just the hint of the taste of butter.

- Let your rolls sit at least an hour before eating. They will continue to cook as they cool and need the resting time for the gluten to relax and tenderize.

- Variations: Add 1 cup of chopped olives or sun-dried tomatoes and/or ½ cup chopped fresh herbs such as basil.

1. Mix the warm water, sugar and yeast together. Set aside to make sure it starts to bubble and you know that the yeast is active.

2. Heat the milk and butter until it is very warm but not hot, or it will kill the yeast. You should be able to hold your finger under the running water without burning it.

3. Place the flours and salt in a large mixing bowl. Add the liquid and olives (if you are using them). Using a dough hook, mix on low speed until a dough forms. (You can also do this by hand.) Change speed to high and mix for 2 minutes.

4. Turn out onto a lightly floured surface and knead by hand for 5 to 10 minutes. You may need to add a little more flour.

5. Place in a greased bowl. Then turn the dough ball over so there is some grease on the top. This will keep it from drying out. Cover the bowl with a kitchen towel. Put it in a warm place and let it rise for about 20 minutes.

6. Grease the cavities in a muffin pan. Form rolls by placing 3 one inch balls into each cavity or making one large ball and pressing a bread stamp into it.

7. Cover and place in a warm place to rise to double in size (about 30 minutes).

8. Preheat your oven to 425°F. Bake about 12 minutes or until golden brown.

9. Remove from pan and cool on racks.

# Crusty Sour Dough Bread   *Makes two loaves*

Don't assume you can't make bread because it takes too long. You only need to be around to do small things here and there. Work the rising time around your errands and you can pull it off.

1½ cups lukewarm water

2½ teaspoons active dry yeast

2 teaspoons sugar

1⅔ cups starter*

4¾ cups unbleached white bread flour (or use half white bread flour and half whole wheat flour)

3½ teaspoons salt

Cornmeal or flour for sprinkling the pizza paddle

**Special Equipment:** Pizza paddle and pizza stone

Spray bottle filled with water

1. Mix the water, yeast and sugar together and let it stand 10 minutes. It should start forming little bubbles. If not, get some new yeast and start over because it isn't "alive".

2. Add the rest of the ingredients and mix in your mixer for 8 minutes on medium speed. If you don't have a mixer, mix and knead the dough for about ten minutes.

3. Cover with a thin, damp kitchen towel and let the dough rest for an hour and a half. If your oven has a setting called "proof", set it on that and put the bowl in your oven during this time. If you do not have this setting, set your oven to 90°F.

4. Remove from the oven and preheat it to 425°F.

5. Sprinkle a pizza paddle liberally with cornmeal. Handling the dough as little as possible, form it into a round and set it on the cornmeal. Let is rise until doubled in size, about an hour.

6. Slide the loaf onto the hot pizza stone and shoot 2 sprays from the water bottle on the sides of the oven. Quickly close the door. Bake until well browned, about 30 minutes.

### Chef Lynn's Secrets:

- This bread is the one I make most often. It's basically the same recipe used to make the famous Poilâne bread in Paris. I don't have a wood burning oven, but baked on a hot pizza stone sprinkled with cornmeal in a very hot oven, it's certainly very similar. I love it!

- *You can buy sour dough starter powder on line from a number of different sources. Then grow it by feeding it flour and water (enough to keep the consistency like thick cake batter). If you keep it at room temperature, you have to "feed" it every day. If you keep it refrigerated, you only need to feed it once a week. If your starter turns pink, it has gone bad, so throw it away. If you grow too much, just discard what you don't want or give it to a friend.

# Rich Baking Powder Biscuits   *Makes ten 3-inch biscuits*

These homey biscuits are delicious plain or with flavored butter. Add a fried egg and bacon for a great breakfast sandwich.

1¼ cups milk

2¼ cups all purpose flour

1 teaspoon kosher salt

2½ teaspoons baking powder

3 tablespoons sugar

5 tablespoons whole unsalted butter, cut into small pieces

1 egg

2 egg yolks

1 tablespoon cream

Cooking spray

**Make them plain or choose one of the following variations:**

**Option No. 1:** 1 cup sun-dried tomatoes, chopped very small and 8 large basil leaves, chopped very small

**Option No. 2:** 1 cup grated hard cheese (like Cheddar or Parmesan)

You can always add ½ cup fresh, chopped herbs

**Chef Lynn's Secrets:**

- You will have the best luck if you keep the butter and milk cold until use.

- Be careful not to over mix. It can cause "tunneling" (air pockets) in the biscuits.

- Place them very close together on the baking sheet and use tin foil to create a wall on the outside. (See photo) This will help them to rise up instead of out. Wrapped or in an airtight container, baked biscuits freeze well for up to 3 months.

1. Preheat your oven to 425°F. If making sun-dried tomato biscuits, first place the tomatoes in a small bowl. Stir in the milk and let them sit for five minutes to re-hydrate. Chop the basil and set aside. If not, proceed to step 2.

2. In a large mixing bowl, whisk the flour, salt, baking powder and sugar together. Add the butter pieces and mix together by pressing the mixture through your fingers until it resembles cornmeal. (If using basil and/or cheese, mix it in now.)

3. Make a well in the center and pour in the milk or milk/tomato mixture. Mix with your hands until it just becomes a dough.

4. On a floured surface, pat the dough into a square. It should be even and ¾ inches thick. Cut into circles or squares and place on a cookie sheet sprayed with cooking spray.

5. Egg wash the biscuit tops. (Whisk together 1 egg + 2 yolks + 1 tablespoon cream and paint it on using a pastry brush.) Cover the entire surface for even browning.

6. Bake on the middle oven rack for approximately 20 minutes, until nicely browned.

# Grandma Ogden's Banana Bread

*Makes 1 loaf (12 pieces)*

This makes a very dense and dark loaf.

½ cup whole butter (room temperature)

1 cup white sugar

3 ripened bananas, mashed

2 teaspoons real vanilla extract or black walnut flavoring

2 eggs

2 cups all purpose flour

1 teaspoon baking soda

½ teaspoon baking powder

1 teaspoon salt

1 cup black walnuts or hickory nuts, chopped

1. Preheat your oven to 350°F.

2. Grease one large or two small loaf pans.

3. Cream butter and sugar together. Mix in bananas and extract.

4. Mix in eggs, one at a time.

5. In a separate bowl, whisk flour, baking soda, baking powder and salt together. Mix in nuts. Then mix the dry ingredients into the wet mixture all at once.

6. Bake up to 1½ hours, until loaf is very brown and a toothpick inserted in the center comes out clean.

**Chef Lynn's Secrets:**

- This recipe is as old as the hills... My grandma called it "Mother's Banana Bread" so it must be circa 1885. I still love it!

- Instead of chopping the nuts, break them up with your fingers so they are very coarse. This gives it an artisan look and provides a crunchier taste. Mixing them into the flour first helps them to better distribute through the batter.

- For a rich, nutty taste, toast the walnuts in a 400° oven until very slightly browned, about 10 minutes. Cool and add to the recipe.

- For an intense banana taste, let your bananas ripen at room temperature until the skins are black.

- Make it a day or two ahead to maximize flavor. You can also freeze it for up to 3 months.

# Orange or Lemon-Ginger Scones   *Makes 6 to 8 scones*

Scones are traditional British breakfast fare. In England and Scotland, you will find versions that are less sweet than typical American scones like this one.

1 cup bread flour

1 cup cake flour

¾ cup sugar

2 teaspoons baking powder

½ teaspoon salt

2 teaspoons ground ginger

2 teaspoons cinnamon

Zest from 2 lemons or 1 orange

½ cup cold butter, cut into small pieces

2 eggs

Juice from 2 lemons or 1 orange

½ cup pineapple juice (or plain orange juice)

Extra flour to sprinkle your counter

Egg wash: 1 egg yolk and 1 teaspoon cream

Sugar for sprinkling tops

Cooking spray

1. Make sure you have a rack in the middle of your oven and preheat it to 425°F.

2. Whisk together the flours, sugar, baking powder, salt, ginger, cinnamon and zest.

3. Drop in the butter pieces and press them into the flour with your fingers until the clumps are the size of peas.

4. Add the eggs and juice and mix with your hands to form dough. Sprinkle some flour on your clean counter and set the dough on top of it.

5. Shape the dough into a flat circle. Cut into 6 or 8 pie shaped wedges, depending on the size you want your scones to be. (If you want to make mini scones, make two circles.) Place them on a cookie sheet sprayed lightly with cooking spray.

6. Brush lightly with egg wash and sprinkle them with sugar.

7. Bake until firm to the touch and lightly browned, about 20 minutes. Cool.

## Chef Lynn's Tips:

- Zest is grated peel, usually lemon or orange. Simply rub a micro planer or small grater against the outer skin to grind it off. Rub lightly and try to avoid the white pithy skin directly underneath, which can be very bitter. One lemon or one small orange will give you about 2 tablespoons of zest.

- Scones are best the day they are made, but can be successfully frozen in an airtight container for up to 3 months. Freeze before frosting.

- If you want to add a light glaze or frosting drizzle to the tops, just mix 1 cup of confectioner's sugar with enough water to make it slightly runny. Add 1 tablespoon at a time because it's easy to add too much liquid. Then just paint it across the tops or drizzle it off the end of a spoon.

- For extra pizzazz, serve with cinnamon flavored butter. Just blend 1 teaspoon cinnamon and 1 teaspoon sugar with ¼ cup soft butter.

- By the way, don't bother to invest in a scone pan unless you want small, perfectly shaped scones. Using the method described here, you can make rustic cut scones that to me are more attractive.

# Pizza – The Basics    *Makes 3 large, thin crust pizzas*

Pizza is definitely the ultimate crowd pleaser. This one sports chicken, artichokes, fresh corn and cheeses. The variation at the end comes from southern Germany and is called "Dinette."

1½ cups warm water (approximately 110° F)

2 tablespoons sugar

2¼ teaspoon active dry yeast (one package)

About 4 cups all purpose flour + ½ cup or more flour to place on counter

1 tablespoon kosher salt

3 tablespoons olive oil

3 cups of your favorite tomato sauce

Toppings of your choice, such as: Ham, pepperoni, cooked chicken, fresh corn, artichoke slices, ham, sausage, chopped fresh pepper, caramelized onions, shallot and olives...the list is endless! Note that if any of these ingredients are packed in oil, you can use that flavored oil in place of regular olive oil in the recipe.

3 cups mozzarella cheese, coarsely grated

3 cups sharp Cheddar cheese, coarsely grated

¼ cup Parmesan cheese, coarsely grated

Salt, pepper and cayenne pepper to taste

1. Preheat oven with pizza stone inside to 425°F.

2. Combine water, sugar and yeast, and let it sit until you see little bubbles.

3. If using olives or artichokes, drain them and reserve the oil. (Make sure to carefully pit the olives if necessary.)

4. Mix flour and salt in mixer bowl.

5. Add 3 tablespoons olive oil.

6. Knead on low speed or by hand for ten minutes. (Dough will be slightly sticky.)

7. Place dough in an oiled bowl; then turn it upside down so the dough is coated.

8. Punch dough down with your fist.

9. Cover bowl with plastic wrap and let rise until doubled (about 1 hour).

10. Divide into 3 pieces. Cover and let it rest for 15 minutes.

11. Form pizzas by pushing out from the center of the dough circle. Leave a fatter ring at the edges for a crust. Place one pizza at a time on a pizza paddle sprinkled with cornmeal or flour.

12. Brush the crust lightly with olive oil. Spread 1 cup of tomato sauce in the middle of each pizza.

13. Place toppings on the pizza, spice with the salt and peppers to taste and sprinkle with cheeses. Transfer to the hot stone. Bake until the crust is golden brown, about 25 minutes.

Above: Basic pizza topped with fresh corn cut off the cob, artichoke, chicken, tomato sauce, salt and pepper.

## Chef Lynn's Secrets:

- Bread flavor takes time to develop. A long, slow rise is ideal. You can make this dough the day before and store it in the fridge overnight (Step 7) to slow it down. Take it out and leave it at room temperature for several hours before making your pizza.

- Form into pizza shapes by pushing out from the middle of the ball of dough. Avoid the edges if you would like to have a thicker rim to hold the sauce.

- If you feel like the dough is fighting you, let it rest for 15 minutes and try again. When the proteins are relaxed the dough will cooperate!

- You can grill your pizza by throwing it on a hot grill. It will rise, so make it a little thinner than you want it to end up. Then add toppings and finish in the oven just long enough to melt the cheese and heat the toppings.

- Don't overload your pizza! Heavy pizzas are difficult to handle and won't properly cook through before the crust is burned.

- Add color by sprinkling your finished pizza with chopped basil or chives.

- A pizza stone needs time to heat up. Preheat your oven for at least 30 to 45 minutes before you bake. If you don't have one, just use a cookie sheet or pizza pan. It will be a little less crispy, but still delicious.

- Take care if you use cornmeal. It makes a delightfully crispy crust but will burn in the oven. If you are making lots of pizza, you will have to brush it out in between.

## Variation:

1. Fry two yellow onions cut into very thin rings and 1 cup chopped bacon.

2. Mix with ½ cup flour, 1½ cups sour cream, 3 eggs, 1 teaspoon salt, and ½ teaspoon pepper, 1 teaspoon garlic powder and 2 tablespoons caraway seed.

3. Prepare pizza, using the mixture above as a topping.

# Pretzels *Makes 14*

Best fresh, try and make these within hours of serving time.

1½ cups warm water

4½ teaspoons active dry yeast (2 packages) or best, 1 fresh yeast cake

1 teaspoon sugar

4½ cups all purpose flour

2 tablespoons butter for greasing bowl

2 egg yolks whisked with 1 tablespoon water

Coarse salt for sprinkling pretzels

Cooking spray

**Chef Lynn's Secrets:**

This recipe was given to me when I was living in Mainz, Germany in 1972. It's as close as I have ever seen to the real thing. However, commercial pretzels and pretzel rolls do have a tangier taste that is difficult to replicate at home. It comes from the fact that they are dipped in a 10:1 solution of water to lye. In this weakness, it is probably not harmful to eat (given all the pretzels that have been consumed), but it is poison and the mixture is dangerous to work with as it can greatly damage your eyes and skin if splashed. I don't know about you, but I prefer to take a pass on that and enjoy my pretzels as is.

Serve with your favorite pub mustard, of course!

1. In a large bowl, combine the warm water, yeast and sugar. Let stand for 30 minutes. (Be careful that the water is not too hot or it will kill the yeast. You should be able to hold your finger in it. This step tells you whether your yeast is alive. The bubbling is the yeast feeding on the sugar and you should see it almost immediately.)

2. Mix in the flour to form a dough and knead by hand for 7–8 minutes. (In a mixer with a dough hook, let it process for 2–3 minutes on high.)

3. Rub the bowl you mixed the dough in generously with butter and place the dough ball in it. Turn it over, so you now also have butter on the top. (This helps to keep it from forming a skin.)

4. Cover the bowl with a thin, damp cloth and let it rise about one hour or until it doubles in size.

5. Now make the pretzel shapes. Take a small piece of dough and roll it on the table, back and forth with your hand to form a long, snake shape. Leave the middle section a little fatter than the ends. Twist or knot into pretzel shapes. (If the dough cracks while being handled, very lightly oil the surface.)

   Place directly on greased baking sheets that have been lightly sprayed with cooking spray.

6. Using a pastry brush, and working on one pretzel at a time, lightly brush with the egg and water mixture. (Water in the egg wash instead of milk gives the pretzels a crispier crust.) Sprinkle liberally with coarse salt before the egg wash dries.

To make the pretzel shapes, try grabbing the left end of the rolled dough with your right hand and the right end with your left hand. Cross your hands back to make the middle twist. Then you just have to lay the ends down and over the fatter section of the pretzel. If your ends are too long, just cut them off. Practice makes perfect! This is soft, pliable and forgiving dough. You can re-roll and try again if you have a disaster.

7.  Let rise in a warm place, about 20 minutes.

8.  Preheat your oven to 425°F and bake on the bottom rack until golden brown, about 12–15 minutes. Cool on wire racks.

9.  When COMPLETELY cool, place in an airtight container for storage. (You can also freeze them in an airtight container, but they will never again be quite as good as the day they are baked.)

**NOTE:** If you have a pizza stone, keeping it in your oven more closely approximates a professional baker's oven. It will help to keep the heat more even and if you bake directly on it or even place your cookie sheets on it, it will cause your baked goods to be crispier. Crusts with fillings will also cook through better and will tend not to get soggy.

# Chapter Eight
## *Desserts*

# Lesson Eight

## *What's important to know about desserts?*

- **WHIPPED CREAM** that is homemade adds a professional touch. For the best whipped cream, keep a mixing bowl and mixer whip in the freezer. The cream will whip better if all ingredients and equipment are very cold. Use cold whipping cream. Place one cup of whipping cream in the cold bowl and start whipping. When peaks just start to form, shake in 2 tablespoons granulated or confectioners sugar — either one works — and finish whipping.

- **EGG WHITES** have rules that are the opposite of cream. The whites and all equipment should be room temperature. If you are in a hurry and your eggs are cold, you can warm them in a bowl of hot water for about 15 minutes and then proceed.

- **EGG WASH** is used to make things look evenly brown. That means that you have to brush it on evenly with a pastry brush. Every spot you miss will look uneven. The best egg washes have more yolk than white in them.

- **BUTTER** with the highest fat content will make your desserts taste the best. "European style" butters tend to have the most fat because governments in European countries allow producers to include more fat than in the United States. (That's why those butters from Normandy taste so good. They are actually different than the ones we have here.) Plugra® is an example of a high fat butter.

  Always use unsalted butter in your recipes. Salt contents in butters vary. If you start with an unsalted version, you can exactly control the amount of salt because you know how much you add in yourself. This way you keep the salt ratio correct in relation to the other ingredients.

- **KEEP FRUIT CRISP AND FRESH LOOKING.** If you are using ingredients that turn brown when exposed to air (such as apples), drop them in acidulated water to stop the process. To make it, mix lemon or other juices 50/50 with water. This mixture will coat the surface and keep the product fresh.

- **MIXING STICKY THINGS LIKE CHOPPED, DRIED CHERRIES** works better if you mix them with the flour. If you are using a sticky ingredient like raisin, chopped caramel, or anything gummy, mixing it in with the flour will cause it to distribute through the dough better. The flour will coat the wet areas and keep them from clumping together in the final stage.

- **MIXING IN FLOUR** can cause a rain of dust to fly all over your kitchen. Start your mixer slowly and gradually increase the speed. You can also cover the whole mixer with a piece of plastic wrap to contain the dust and still see what you are doing. Remember to always scrape your bowl down in between ingredient additions, so everything gets mixed in well.

- **OVENS VARY IN TEMPERATURE.** Even if you have a one-unit double oven, the two ovens within the unit can vary in the way they produce heat. A difference in the baking temperature can drastically affect cooking time as well as the end results. Keeping an oven thermometer inside every oven can help you to keep an eye on varying oven performance and allow you to set temperatures to compensate for any discrepancies.

- **SIMULATE A PROFESSIONAL OVEN** by always leaving your pizza stone on the lower rack. It will help to keep the oven heat even. For pies and other filled baked goods, bake right on it. This will help cook the bottom crust. Make a note, however, that pizza stones take awhile to come to their full heat. Preheat your oven 30 to 45 minutes in order to fully heat your stone.

- **BAKE PIES** with fillings on the lowest rack of the oven and best on a baking stone. This gives the bottom crust the opportunity to cook through and remain crispy despite the fact that the crust is covered by the filling.

# Oma's Apple Kuchen     *Serves 6 to 8 Makes one pie*

I know this is "Denglish" but that's what it's called! This pie is legendary in our family. It's a simple custard pie that is simply delicious and tastes to us like home.

**For the pie crust:**

2 cups all purpose flour

1 tablespoon granulated sugar

¾ cup cold butter

1 egg, lightly beaten

1 tablespoon milk

Cooking spray

**For the filling:**

2 Granny Smith apples

2 tablespoons all purpose or cake flour

1 cup sugar

1 teaspoon cinnamon, if desired

2 tablespoons whole butter, melted

4 to 5 egg yolks (Custard version) or
   3 whole eggs (denser version)

1 cup half and half or whole milk

**Chef Lynn's Secrets:**

- Another variation of this pie is to very thinly slice the apples and arrange them in a circular design on the bottom of the crust. (They will float up during cooking.)

- This pie needs to sit in order to condense before serving. Make it the morning of your dinner or even the night before. It only gets better!

- You can easily add a delicious citrus flavor to this pie. Just include the zest from an orange or lemon plus substitute ¼ cup orange or lemon juice for some of the milk.

1. Preheat your oven to 375°F.

2. First, make the crust: Whisk the flour and sugar together and then drop in the cold butter in small pieces. Mix with your hands, pressing the pieces of butter into the flour until you have a mixture resembling small peas.

3. Make a well in the center of the flour mixture and drop in the egg and milk. Mix with your hands to make dough.

4. Spray a 10-inch pie pan with cooking spray. Press the dough in the pan and up the sides.

5. Now make the filling: Melt the butter and transfer it to a mixing bowl. Add the flour and sugar and mix.

6. Add the egg yolks, a few at a time. Using a spatula, scrape down the bowl between additions. Add the half and half and mix again. Set aside.

7. Cut the apples into quarters. Peel and seed them. Cut them into medium sized dice. If desired, mix them with cinnamon. Place them evenly on the crust.

8. Pour in the custard (liquid mixture containing the eggs).

9. Bake for about 45 minutes, until the custard is set and the top is very lightly browned.

10. Cool completely and refrigerate until serving time.

11. Cut into wedges and serve.

# American Apple Pie     *Serves 6 to 8  Makes one pie*

Good old apple pie... Everybody makes it, so why not make yours extraordinary? This version is heavily spiced and adds the toasted goodness of baked walnuts. It's flaky, yet easy to handle — in fact, it's as easy as pie! Changing the nuts to candied or sugared ones raises the WOW factor even more.

**For the crust:**

2 cups All Purpose (AP) flour

1 teaspoon salt

¾ cup cold butter

½ cup cold water

**For the filling:**

5 large Granny Smith apples, peeled and
  sliced thinly (6 cups of slices)

2¼ cups sugar + 1 tablespoon for sprinkling

1½ tablespoons Minute Tapioca®

2 tablespoons fresh lemon juice

2 teaspoons nutmeg

4 teaspoons cinnamon

1 cup toasted walnuts

3 tablespoons butter (for dotting the filling)

1. **First prepare the crust:**

   Whisk the flour and salt together in a medium sized mixing bowl. Cut the cold butter into small pieces and drop them directly into the flour mixture. Press together with your fingers until the mix is well blended and looks like small peas. Make a well in the center and pour in half the water. Mix with your hands, adding water just until a dough forms. (You do not necessarily have to use all of the water.) Split the dough into 2 pieces, wrap each in plastic wrap and set aside in the refrigerator.

2. **Then make the filling:**

   Mix 2 cups sugar, Minute Tapioca®, lemon juice, walnuts and spices. Peel and slice the apples. As you finish each apple, toss it with the sugar mixture to keep it from browning.

**3. Now assemble the pie:**

  a. On a lightly floured surface, roll out the dough into a circle just larger than a 9 inch pie pan. Fold the dough back (in half) and lift it into the pie pan. Unfold the dough and gently press it into the pan. Sprinkle it with ¼ cup of sugar. Trim it to ½ inch overlap of the pan.

  b. Put the apple mixture on top of the dough and lightly press it down. Dot it with little pieces of butter, about 3 tablespoons.

  c. Roll out a second circle of dough, fold it, place it on top of the apples and unfold it. Once again, trim the dough to ½ inch overlap of the pan.

  d. Fold the top edge layer under the lower one so that it meets the edge of the pan. Crimp the edge with a fork or press into flutes using your thumb and pointer finger. Sprinkle the top with the remaining sugar.

  e. Using a sharp knife, cut slits in the top crust. Sprinkle the top with the remaining sugar.

  f. Bake at 375°F for 45-55 minutes, until the top crust is golden brown. Turn the oven off and leave it in there for another 20 minutes to continue gentle browning. Remove from the oven and cool.

Serve with purchased caramel sauce and/or ice cream. As an alternative, Cheddar cheese is a good accompaniment.

**Variation:**

For a praline version, substitute half of the sugar in the filling for packed light brown sugar and change the nuts to pecans. Dot with a little more butter before adding the top crust.

## Chef Lynn's Secrets:

- When you cut slits in the top of the pie (vents so that steam can escape and the pie won't buckle or crack) cut them where you expect to cut the pieces. That way your slices will be nice and even.

- If you have a rolling pin with a ball bearing mechanism, don't immerse it in water or you will rust out the inner parts. Wipe it off with a soapy dish rag and then a rinsed one.

- Bake your pie on a piece of parchment paper or tin foil to catch any drips. They can smoke and adversely flavor your pie. Besides, it makes for easy oven clean up .

- In an airtight container, this pie freezes well (baked or unbaked) for up to 3 months. If you freeze it unbaked, take the pie out and let it stand for an hour before baking. Baking time may be slightly longer.

# Applesauce Roll Cake  *Serves 10*

This cake looks tricky to make, but it's just a matter of having the right batter mix so it's spongy and easy to roll.

**For the cake:**

1 cup sugar

1 cup all purpose flour

1½ teaspoons baking powder

½ teaspoon salt

3 teaspoons cinnamon

½ teaspoon nutmeg

½ teaspoon cloves

1 tablespoon tapioca

2 large eggs, beaten

¾ cup thick applesauce

Approximately 3 tablespoons powdered sugar for sprinkling the towel

Butter for greasing the pan

**For the filling:**

8 oz. Philadelphia strawberry cream cheese, at room temperature

4 oz. regular cream cheese, at room temperature

1 cup powdered sugar

2 tablespoons butter, room temperature

1 teaspoon pure vanilla extract

2 cups walnuts or pecans, finely chopped

**Garnish:**

Fresh strawberries and/or ice cream

1. Preheat oven to 375°F.

2. Butter a jelly roll pan (17½ X 13-inch). Top with a sheet of waxed paper (or parchment paper) cut to fit the pan. Also butter the top of the paper.

3. **MAKE THE CAKE:** Whisk the sugar, flour, baking powder, cinnamon, salt, nutmeg, cloves and tapioca together.

4. Mix in the beaten eggs, followed by the applesauce.

5. Pour into the pan.

6. Bake until tester comes out clean in the middle of the cake (about 16 minutes).

7. While the cake is baking, lay two thin kitchen towels on your counter. Dust them with powdered sugar.

8. When the cake is done, remove it from the oven and run a table knife around the edges to be sure they are loose. Turn the cake onto one of the towels, paper side up. Remove the paper and top with the sugared side of the other towel. Roll the cake up and let it rest on the counter with the cut side down so that the cake is held together. Let it sit there and completely cool in the towels.

9. **MAKE THE FILLING:** Beat together the two cream cheeses and the cup of powdered sugar, 2 tablespoons butter and 1 teaspoon vanilla extract.

10. Unroll cooled cake. Spread the filling evenly over the cake. Sprinkle with nuts.

Above: Applesauce Roll Cake with strawberry cream cheese and chopped walnut filling. Chill thoroughly before slicing for the best success and clean your knife well after each cut.

11. Using the towel to help, roll the cake back up. Press as you roll and keep it tight. Trim the ends so they are even. Dust with powdered sugar.

12. Refrigerate until ready to serve. Cut into one inch slices at serving time and garnish as you like. Fresh strawberries and/or ice cream are nice!

## Chef Lynn's Secrets:

- A jelly roll pan is a baking pan (cookie sheet) with sides. Parchment paper is baking paper that helps to keep moist baked goods from sticking to the pan. It also provides support for cakes like this. Both sides are the same. There is no right or wrong side.

- If you over-bake this cake, it will tend to crack when you roll it. If that happens, you can save it by wrapping the cake in plastic wrap and twisting the ends so that the wrap is tight. Refrigerate until the cream cheese filling is firm and then it should hold together just fine.

# Banana-Coconut Cake   *Makes one 9 inch layer cake or 24 cupcakes*

Coconut lovers... Here's a piece of heaven!

**For the cake:**

½ cup butter, room temperature

1½ cups granulated sugar

2 eggs

1 teaspoon vanilla

¼ cup plain or vanilla yogurt
   (or sour cream)

1 cup mashed bananas (2 bananas)

2½ cups flour

1 teaspoon baking powder

1 teaspoon baking soda

1 teaspoon salt

7 oz. sweetened coconut flakes

**For the frosting:**

½ cup butter

4 cups confectioner's sugar

1 cup semi-sweet chocolate chips

3 tablespoons sour cream

1 teaspoon vanilla

1 fresh banana (sliced)

½ cup slivered almonds, walnuts or
   pecans, chopped

1 cup of the same nuts for garnish

7 oz. coconut for sprinkling the
   finished cake

**First make the cake:**

1.  Preheat your oven to 350°F.

2.  In a mixing bowl, cream the butter and sugar together.

3.  Mix in the eggs and vanilla; then the yogurt.

4.  Whisk the rest of the ingredients together and add them to the batter. Mix.

5.  Grease your cake pans with Crisco® or butter, top with a parchment paper circle (that you cut out) and grease and flour the top of the paper.

6.  Fill baking pans about ⅔ full.

7.  Bake for about 35 minutes, or until the cake is light brown on top and an inserted toothpick comes out clean. (Cupcakes will only take about 25 minutes.) Cool and frost.

**Then make the frosting:**

1.  In the top of a double boiler, melt the chocolate chips. (Alternatively, you can microwave the chips for 60 seconds and stir them.)

2.  Cream the butter and sugar together.

3.  Add the chocolate, sour cream, and vanilla.

4.  Put ⅓ of the frosting in a separate bowl and mix it with the sliced, fresh banana and ½ cup chopped nuts.

Above: Banana-Coconut Cake could easily become your family's new favorite dessert. Yogurt, bananas, coconut and chocolate... What's not to love?

## Assemble the cake:

1. Place a dab of plain frosting on a serving plate and set a cake layer on top of it. (This will stabilize the cake and keep it from slipping around when you carry it.)

2. Frost the top only with the frosting that contains the fresh banana.

3. Set the second cake layer on top of the filling.

4. Frost the outside of the cake with the plain frosting and sprinkle it all over with coconut. Garnish with the same kind of nuts you used in the filling.

5. Refrigerate for several hours before cutting.

## Chef Lynn's Secrets:

- If you're in a hurry and your butter isn't room temperature, zap it for 12 seconds in a microwave.

- This recipe also makes great cupcakes. Baking time will be reduced to about 20 minutes. Make half the frosting recipe as you will only be frosting the tops of the muffins. Or skip the frosting and just drizzle the cupcakes with powdered sugar mixed with water to a frosting consistency.

- **To cut the cake cleanly,** use a very sharp knife. Make a cut, wipe it off, then dip it in a container of very hot water and wipe it and clean again. Repeat between every cut.

# Berry Sherbet    *Makes 2 Quarts*

Sherbet is a frozen dessert that falls somewhere between sorbet and ice cream. It contains berries or juice like a sorbet, but also milk or cream like ice cream without the eggs.

4 cups frozen berries without juice

1 cup sugar

2 teaspoons fresh cold lemon juice

2 cups cold milk

1. Place completely frozen berries in the work bowl of a food processor. Use the knife blade.

2. Put the sugar and lemon juice on top of the berries. Then pour in the milk.

3. Process for about two minutes.

4. Churn in an ice cream machine for about 20 minutes and then freeze for at least 4 hours.

Alternatively, just pour the mixture into a 2-quart container. Seal it and place it in the freezer for at least 4 hours.

**Chef Lynn's Secrets:**

- I have always called this "cheater" sherbet because it turns out well even if you don't churn it in an expensive ice cream machine.

- If you have fresh berries, freeze them before using so the mix is very cold.

- The sherbet works equally well with raspberries, strawberries, blackberries or blueberries.

# Pears Poached in Pinot

*Serves 4*

This is so easy and so impressive! In my book, that's a perfect recipe.

4 pears, (Anjou, Bartlett or Bosc)

One bottle good quality Pinot Noir wine (about 3 cups or 750 ml) or one bottle Riesling (fruity white wine)

2 cups sugar (or 1 cup if using Riesling)

1 tablespoon whole cloves, crushed with the side of a knife

2 teaspoons ground cinnamon

**Cheese Accompaniment:**

Mix together and put a scoop in the center of each cavity:

1 cup Mascarpone Cheese

½ cup whipped cream

2 tablespoons vanilla sugar

**Garnish:** Mint leaves or chopped nuts

**Chef Lynn's Secrets:**

- To keep the pear from sliding around on the plate, slice a very thin flat spot across the bottom of the pear.

- Mascarpone is actually closer to cream than cheese. It's an Italian invention made from crème fraîche. You will find it in a tub in the dairy section of your local market.

- Instead of the Mascarpone cheese mixture, you can fill the pear cavity with ice cream or whipped cream or yogurt.

- Mix butter lettuce, goat cheese and pecans. Add a dressing of raspberry vinaigrette (page 228 - Basic vinaigrette + raspberries) just on the salad and lay sliced, marinated pears on top. You could also serve this salad at the end of the meal, as they do in some European countries. Yum!

1. Preheat your oven to 400°F.

2. Wash and peel the pears. Cut them in half. (If you like, you can leave the stem on both sides, but it won't always be possible.) Use a melon baller to cut out the seeds in a perfect circle. Use a sharp knife to cut out the tough part of the stem. Place the pears in an oven proof pan just big enough to hold all of the pieces.

3. Whisk the wine, sugar, cloves and cinnamon together until well blended. Pour over the pears.

4. Bake for 1 hour. Turn the oven off and leave them in there for another 45 minutes with the door closed.

5. Cool and refrigerate in the juice until serving time.

6. At serving time, plate each half pear. Fill the cavity with your choice of filling. Decorate with mint and/or chopped nuts.

NOTE: Leftovers will keep for up to 2 weeks. Continue to enjoy the pears and either boil the liquid down separately to make a sauce or serve it as a delicious pear infused after dinner drink.

# Blueberry Crème Brulée    *Serves 6 to 8*

Thick, creamy custard in a beautiful dish makes a lovely dessert.

4 cups heavy whipping cream

3 vanilla beans

Zest of 1 lemon

¾ cup granulated sugar

¼ cup Grand Marnier liqueur

12 egg yolks

8 tablespoons granulated sugar,

    for caramelizing tops

¼ cup Grand Marnier in a spray bottle,
    also for caramelizing tops

1 quart blueberries

1. Cut the vanilla beans in half, but not all the way through the ends. Place them in the cream. Add the zest (grated peel) of 1 lemon. Cover and refrigerate overnight to intensify the vanilla and lemon flavors.

2. Preheat your oven to 375°F.

3. Place 6 large or 8 small ramekins on a jelly roll pan (a baking sheet with sides).

4. Place the vanilla flavored cream in a four quart, heavy bottomed saucepan. Using your fingers, scrape the vanilla seeds out of the pods and discard the pods, leaving the seeds in the cream.

5. Beat the eggs with the sugar.

6. Heat the cream until it just starts to boil. Take it off the heat. Now you want to combine the eggs with the hot cream, but if you pour them together too fast, the eggs will cook. Instead, whisk the eggs and then add the hot cream slowly. Using a heat proof measuring cup with a pour spout works well. While whisking with one hand, stream in the hot cream a half cup at a time, until you have added it all. Then whisk in the salt and the Grand Marnier.

7. Carefully pour the cream mixture (custard) into the ramekins. Pour slowly so air bubbles do not form. Drop 4 blueberries into each ramekin and gently press into the custard with a spoon.

8. Fill a 2-quart container with hot water and have it ready. Place the ramekins in the oven and then pour the hot water into the pan around them to make an instant hot water bath. Do this quickly so you don't lose a lot of heat from the oven. Reset the oven to 350°F and bake for 25 to 35 minutes, until the

custard is set. When you jiggle it, it should seem firm. Cool and refrigerate.

9. Up to several hours before serving, sprinkle evenly with 1 tablespoon sugar. Immediately spray the sugar lightly with Grand Marnier and torch the sugar until it's golden brown and crispy.

**To carmelize the tops:**

Up to several hours before serving, sprinkle evenly with 1 tablespoon sugar. Immediately spray the sugar lightly with Grand Marnier. Torch the sugar until it's golden brown and crispy. (Be careful and torch on an angle away from your face.) Realize that the sugar will continue to cook after you move the torch away, so practice pulling the flame back just before you see the level of brown that you want.

**Chef Lynn's Secrets:**

- Most people don't realize that Crème Brulée can be made ahead of time. Make the cream base, refrigerate it and cook it as you need it for up to a week. Once it's cooked, you can hold it for several days. Just caramelize the sugar on the day you will serve it and add any berry toppings just before serving or the moisture in the berries will destroy the sugar. Your goal is fresh berry, crackly sugar and creamy custard in every spoonful!

- Add fresh fruit or berries just before serving. Don't do this earlier or the moisture in the berries will cause your custard to deteriorate.

- Cut the vanilla beans in half almost all the way to the end so that the bean makes a V shape. It will release its wonderful flavor but it will be easier to retrieve from the hot custard mix.

# Chambord Cheesecake     *Serves 16*

In this 25 year old "Bon Appetit" recipe, I have changed some of the ingredients and a lot of the method to make it more accessible for home cooks. You only need a small piece of this rich dessert.

**For the meringue circles:**

1 tablespoon flour for dusting circles

Butter for greasing pan

6 egg whites

7 oz. almonds, ground

1 cup sugar

1 tablespoon cornstarch

**For the cheesecake:**

18 oz. cream cheese

1 cup sugar

4 eggs

¼ cup Chambord liqueur

1 teaspoon vanilla extract

**For the Frosting:**

8 oz. cream cheese

1 cup unsalted butter

1 teaspoon raspberry extract (flavoring)

5 oz. semisweet chocolate chips, melted

8 oz. fresh raspberries

**Garnish**:

6 cups fresh raspberries or blackberries

— OR —

3 cups chopped pecans

1. Preheat your oven to 300°F.

2. **To make the meringue circles:** Set a 10-inch cake pan on a piece of parchment paper and draw around it to make a circle. Repeat twice so that you have three circular pieces. Cut one circle out with scissors, just inside the line you have drawn. Place the other two pieces on cookie sheets.

3. Butter the inside of the cake pan. Place the cut out circle in the pan and butter the top of it. Shake 1 tablespoon of flour around the pan to dust it.

4. Whip the egg whites to stiff peaks and then mix them with the almonds, sugar and cornstarch. Pour half the mixture in the center of the two circles drawn on parchment paper. Using a spatula spread the mixture out to within ¼-inch of the drawn circle. Pour half the mixture in the center of the two circles drawn on parchment paper. Using a spatula spread the mixture out to within ¼-inch of the drawn circle. Bake the circles for about 40 minutes, until set. Remove from oven and cool. You can make them a day ahead. Refrigerate until ready to use.

5. Preheat your oven to 350°F.

6. **Make the cheesecake:** Mix the room temperature cream cheese, sugar, vanilla, eggs and Chambord until well blended. Pour into the prepared pan and set the pan on a jelly roll pan (cookie sheet with sides). Fill the jelly roll pan with water until it comes halfway up the sides of the cake pan. (This is called a hot water bath). Bake at 350°F for about 40 minutes or until set. Remove from oven and cool. Refrigerate until ready to use.

7. When ready to assemble the cake, make the frosting. Mix together 8 oz. cream cheese, 1 cup butter, 1 teaspoon raspberry flavoring and the cooled chocolate. Divide the frosting into two bowls. In one bowl, mix in the 8 oz. of fresh raspberries.

8. Assemble the cake: Make a swipe of frosting on the plate to keep it from slipping. Put a piece of the almond meringue on the plate and spread it with the chocolate frosting- raspberry mixture. Then unmold the cheesecake by running a knife around the edge and inverting the pan over the cake plate. Top that with more of the raspberry frosting, then the other meringue layer. Frost the cake with the remaining plain frosting.

9. Let the cake sit at room temperature for 2 hours so that the frosting blends with the meringue. Then refrigerate until serving time.

**Chef Lynn's Secrets:**

- Egg whites whip best at room temperature and batter and frosting ingredients combine best at room temperature. So think ahead and set everything out well in advance of your preparation time.

- Sometimes mistakes can be the mother of invention. If your frosting is a little lumpy, choose to garnish the cake with chopped nuts to hide the imperfections. Sneaky, but delicious!

- Make it ahead! Make everything the day before you need the cake and just assemble it the day you need it.

- In season, top this cheesecake with luscious fresh berries and it's irresistible. You can spoon them on top of each piece, create a pattern on top of the cake or arrange them at the side of each piece on individual serving plates. Do this at the last minute because over time the moisture in the berries will make the frosting runny.

# Crêpes — Sweet and Savvy! *Makes 24 crêpes*

You don't need a special machine to make crêpes. Try them in an omelet nonstick frying pan for sure success.

1¾ cups all purpose flour

½ cup granulated sugar

Pinch of salt

1½ tablespoons vanilla sugar

6 eggs

3¼ cups whole milk

**Optional:**

1½ tablespoons brandy, Grand Marnier liqueur or rum

Olive oil for seasoning pan

Fillings: (See ideas – next column)

1. Mix the flour, sugars and salt together.

2. Lightly whisk the eggs and thoroughly mix them into the dry mixture, scraping down the sides.

3. Add the milk and liqueur (if using) and whisk until thoroughly blended.

4. Let the batter sit for 30 minutes before proceeding.

5. Heat a nonstick omelet pan. Brush it very lightly with olive oil. Pour one ounce of batter into the pan and quickly swirl it around to coat the bottom. Cook until you see tiny bubbles appearing all over the batter and the crêpe is relatively firm and lightly browned on the bottom. Loosen edges with a spatula and flip to brown the other side. Remove to cool. (Keep them separated and don't stack until cool.)

6. Choose your filling, roll up and drizzle with chocolate, caramel or fruit coulis.

**Chef Lynn's Secrets:**

- Dessert crêpes are make ahead, easy and fun for everyone. You can successfully freeze cooled crêpes between sheets of waxed paper for up to 3 months. Just take out what you need and leave the rest for later. Your kids will enjoy filling their own.

- As a party idea, set up a crêpe bar with various fillings for a kids' party and let them dream up their own concoctions. A scoop of ice cream at the end and you're a star!

- Leftover crêpes can be frozen between sheets of waxed or parchment paper for up to 3 months. Simply thaw, fill and serve.

**Here are some ideas:**

- Spread the crêpe with Nutella® chocolate spread. Cover with chopped pecans. Drizzle with caramel sauce.

- Fill with sliced strawberries and whipped cream. Drizzle with fruit coulis.

- Fill with cooked apples and drizzle with caramel sauce.

- Fill with grilled pineapple and sprinkle with hazelnuts. Drizzle with chocolate sauce.

- Spread with whipped cream or Greek yogurt and top with fresh berries. Drizzle with fruit coulis or chocolate.

- Using a melon baller, fill with small scoops of ice cream and drizzle with chocolate sauce.

- Fill with fresh, diced pears and figs. Sprinkle with ground cloves and top with whipped cream. Drizzle with chocolate.

- Mix gorgonzola cheese with just enough cream to make it spreadable. Top with fresh, cooked pear. Sprinkle with walnuts. Drizzle with fruit coulis.

- Spread lightly with maple syrup. Top with cooked peaches and whipped or sour cream. Sprinkle with cinnamon and chopped pecans. Drizzle with chocolate.

Need I say more? Just consult your taste buds!

## Raspberry Coulis:

2 cups fresh or frozen raspberries, puréed

½ cup sugar

1 teaspoon clear gel (page 213)

1 tablespoon lemon juice

1. In a small saucepan, mix the berries, sugar and clear gel. Bring to a rolling boil.

2. Cook until the coulis starts to thicken and has a nice sauce consistency.

3. Mix in lemon juice. Use or store in the refrigerator for up to two weeks.

# Individual Cheese Course  *Serves 4*

Offering a nicely presented fresh cheese course is a special and sophisticated dessert, not often found in a home setting.

**GUIDELINES:**

Include both soft and hard cheeses.

Arrange everything from mild to strong.

Incorporate something sweet like fig or quince jam.

Add something salty.

Add a little something spicy.

Add some eye appeal.

Choose a mild tasting bread or cracker that won't interfere with the taste of the cheese.

Choose the right wine accompaniment.

**Chef Lynn's Secrets:**

- Cheese is the perfect ending to any meal. Combine it with something sweet and something salty and not only will you enhance the taste, there's no need for anything to follow.

- Indulge your guests with an individualized presentation of your personal selections. Just arrange them from mild to strong so one won't overpower the other.

- Store cheeses in the refrigerator between 35° and 40°F. They will taste best, however, at room temperature, so take them out and let them warm up several hours before serving.

**CHOOSE:**

Something sweet:

- Grilled fruit: Peach or pineapple slices
- Fig or quince jam or fruit chutney
- Slice of dried fruit: pineapple, date or apple
- Fresh dates, apple or pear slices
- Fresh berries

Something salty:

- Walnuts
- Pecans
- Almonds

Something spicy:

- Flavored balsamic vinegar
- Spicy nuts
- Edible Nasturtium flower (peppery taste)

Something for eye appeal:

- Blue cheese balls: Mix equal parts blue cheese and butter. Wrap this around a small, green grape and roll it in ground pistachios.
- Mix equal parts blue cheese and cream cheese and wrap it around ½ fresh fig. Roll in ground almonds or walnuts.
- Include a slice of brie marinated in wine (page 240)
- Edible flowers or fresh herbs

Choose the right bread or cracker:

- Water crackers or French baguette are the best.

Choose the right wine if you wish to serve it:

- The wine should be sweeter than the sweetest item you are serving.

**Here are some pairings that I particularly like:**

- Amish blue, Gorgonzola and Roquefort cheeses + apples or grapes
- Brie or camembert + cherry jam
- Fontina + almonds or dried pears
- Gruyère + walnuts
- Parmesan + fresh dates, fig or quince jam

Example of an individual cheese tray

Bleu cheese balls

# Individual Cheese Course *(continued)*

Here are two delightful cheese ideas to add to your cheese plate or to use simply as snacks or garnish.

## Parmesan Wafers

12 tablespoons coarsely grated
Parmesan cheese

**Chef Lynn's Secrets:**

- The wafers will get crispy as they air dry. You can also refrigerate them to speed up the process.

- Circles are not the only shapes that work with this recipe. Use your imagination and try others like squares or triangles. Just be careful to keep the edges straight. Setting a simply shaped cookie cutter on the baking sheet and dropping the cheese inside is a good way to make other shapes.

1. Preheat your oven to 400°F.

2. Place a piece of parchment paper on a cookie sheet.

3. Using 2 tablespoons of the cheese, form six circles.

4. Bake until completely melted, bubbly, and slightly brown, about 5 minutes.

5. Cool completely and transfer to paper towels to dry.

## Bleu Cheese Balls

¼ cup crumbled Gorgonzola or other bleu cheese

¼ cup butter or cream cheese

Salt and pepper

Small green grapes

1 cup pistachio nuts, chopped

1. Mix the bleu cheese and your choice of cream cheese or butter together. You can do this by hand or in a food processor.

2. Season with salt and pepper.

3. Using your fingers, form the mixture around small green grape so that the grape is completely enclosed. (Mix will be sticky and it doesn't help much to refrigerate it before proceeding.

4. Roll in chopped nuts. Refrigerate until serving time.

5. Place one grape on each cheese tray or serve as an appetizer.

# Cynfull Cheese Straws

No, that's not a misspelling! These munchy, crunchy straws came from Cynthia and they are so good that if you start eating them before the meal you will be too full to make it to the main course! Definitely, they are yummy.

½ cup butter

1 pound extra sharp Cheddar cheese, grated

¼ teaspoon cayenne pepper

¼ teaspoon salt

2 cups all purpose flour, sifted

**Optional:** Add 1 tablespoon spice, for example: coarsely ground pepper, cayenne pepper, or garlic powder. Make them your own by choosing to add spices that you like.

1. Beat all ingredients except the flour together until it forms a thick paste.

2. Add the flour and mix until thoroughly blended. Let dough rest about 30 minutes.

3. Press out small strips through a star-shaped cookie press or fill a pastry bag and pipe strips through a large star shaped tube.

4. Bake at 350°F for 15 minutes until light brown. Cool and store in a tin or freeze in an airtight container for up to three months.

**Chef Lynn's Secrets:**

- Grate the cheese while cold. Then set it aside and bring it and the butter to room temperature before proceeding. Not only will the dough be easier to handle, it will be tastier.

- Don't skip the 30 minute rest period. This allows the gluten to relax and will make your dough more tender and easier to handle.

- Making the shapes: Using the cookie spritz press, you can pipe long strips and then cut to size if you prefer. Using small pieces of dough at a time, you can also skip the press and roll it out very thin using a rolling pin . Then cut strips or cracker shapes and bake as indicated. Last, you can roll bits of dough into shapes between your fingers.

- Cheese straws will keep about a week in the refrigerator.

# Lemon Mousse    *Serves 6*

5 egg yolks

1 cup of sugar

Zest and juice from 2 large lemons

1 envelope of gelatin

¼ cup water

2 cups heavy whipping cream

2 tablespoons sugar

1 quart water

**Optional Garnish:**
1 cup whipped cream + 1 tablespoon sugar
    and sliced strawberries

1. In the top of a double boiler, mix the yolks, sugar and lemon. (Use a small strainer to catch the seeds as you squeeze in the lemon juice. Discard the seeds, but add any pulp to the mixture.)

2. In a small bowl, bloom the gelatin by mixing it with ¼ cup water and setting it aside.

3. Whip the cream. When it is ¾ of the way whipped, sprinkle in 2 tablespoons granulated sugar to sweeten it. Finish whipping until you see the cream forming soft peaks.

4. Heat 1 quart of water to a boil in the lower pan and immediately turn down the heat so it is simmering. Place the top pan over the water and whisk vigorously, until it coats the back of a spoon (approximately 170° F).

5. Stir in the gelatin.

6. Fold in the whipped cream and place immediately in serving dishes or glasses before it sets up.

7. At serving time, make another cup of whipped cream to use as a topping or garnish with fruit.

## Chef Lynn's Secrets:

- Mousse, like Crème Brulée, has a custard base. This one is, however, solidified by using gelatin and then it's lightened up with the addition of whipped cream.

- So start with any of your favorite custard pies that contain gelatin – Key lime, lemon etc. Add whipped cream and maybe a few spices and voila! There's a delicious mousse patterned after one of your favorite tastes.

- If you chill your mixing bowl and whip attachment in the freezer before whipping the cream, it will whip quicker and lighter.

# Chocolate Coffee After Dinner Cake   *Serves 6*

Simply stated, nothing ends a meal in a more satisfying way than chocolate!

6 tablespoons unsalted butter + 1 tablespoon butter to grease the molds.

5 oz. chocolate, broken into small chunks

3 tablespoons Grand Marnier, cognac or rum

1 tablespoon coffee extract
*(Note: If you don't like the taste of coffee, just skip adding it.)*

3 large eggs, separated

¼ cup granulated sugar

1½ tablespoons flour + a sprinkling for the molds

Confectioner's sugar for dusting cake tops

Berries and mint leaves for garnish

1. Preheat your oven to 400°F.

2. Lightly coat six soufflé molds or ramekins with butter. Dust with flour. Set aside.

3. In the top of a double boiler, mix the chocolate, Grand Marnier, coffee extract and 6 tablespoons butter. Heat just until the chocolate is melted. Cool almost to room temperature.

4. Transfer the egg whites to the work bowl of a mixer and beat until they hold stiff peaks.

5. Reduce speed to low and add the sugar, yolks and 1½ tablespoons flour. Mix just until fully incorporated. Fold this into the chocolate mixture with a rubber spatula.

6. Fill each ramekin ¾ full.

7. Bake for 8–10 minutes or until cracks appear in the top of each cake.

8. Dust with confectioners' sugar and if you like, garnish with fresh berries and mint leaves.

## Chef Lynn's Secrets:

• To me, a simple and small ramekin (little ceramic dish) of chocolate fits the bill as a perfect ending to any meal. This cake is fudgy in the middle and almost like eating ganache. It will puff up in the oven and then collapse as it cools. This is normal. Serve it warm, turned out of the mold or simply (and more easily) in the ramekin it's baked in. A dab of caramel sauce in the middle of the top is always welcome!

• If you turn the cake out of the ramekin into a bowl, you could powder sugar the bottom (which would now be the top) and surround it with sliced strawberries. It also pairs nicely with a scoop of vanilla ice cream.

# Chapter Nine
## Cookies & Snacks

# Lesson Nine

## *What's important to know about making cookies?*

- **DROP COOKIES** come out best if baked in a hot oven, 375° to 425°F. Use a scoop to portion them so they look uniform. The more similar they are, the more professional they will look.

- **MEASURING:** Worth mentioning again is that ratios of components are very important in baking. Whenever possible, use a scale to measure the weight of ingredients so that they are exact. When measuring flour, don't scoop it out or you can pull out a different amount every time. Instead, spoon it into the cup and then level it off by scraping the spoon handle across the top of the cup. Measure powdered sugar the same way. Brown sugar, on the other hand, is very dense and needs to be packed into the cup. To measure spices, dip them out with a measuring spoon; then level them off.

  When measuring eggs, avoid unwanted bits of shell by first cracking them into a measuring cup or small bowl. When you are sure they are free of shells, mix them into your batter.

- **MIXING:** Your cookies will mix and blend together if all ingredients are at room temperature. If your butter is cold and you don't want to wait, you can put it in the microwave for 20 seconds to warm it up. If it still needs to be a little softer, give it another 5 seconds. Use small increments of time so that it doesn't melt.

  Mix flour in slowly so its dust doesn't fly all over your kitchen. You can drape a thin kitchen towel over the whole machine and bowl to contain it or better yet, drape a large piece of plastic wrap over the whole thing. Then you can see what you are doing.

- **BAKING SHEETS:** I like to use a brand of baking sheet called "Cushion-Aire®". They keep the cookies from browning too much on the bottoms before the tops are cooked through.

- **TECHNIQUE:** Make your cookies all as close to the same size as possible so that they will bake evenly and be done at the same time. Also, your overall batch will look more professional.

- **DO A DOUBLE CHECK:** When your dough is ready, take the time to bake off one cookie by itself. I know this seems extreme, but it will point out any problems and allow you to fix them without a lot of waste.

- **BAKING:** Always preheat your oven. I have not said that in every recipe in this book, but it goes without saying. Recipes are formulated to be baked at a steady temperature. If your oven is not preheated, you cannot depend on any cooking times in any recipe and your recipe may even totally fail. While we're on the subject, open the door only as necessary while you are baking. Try to keep the temperature as consistent as possible.

  Another trick is to preheat the oven ten degrees higher than the temperature indicated in the recipe. After you open it and insert your food, close the door and re-set to the temperature to the one indicated in the recipe. This will compensate for the loss of heat from opening the door, but is generally only necessary when making a soufflé that could fall if the temperature is not hot enough.

- **STORAGE:** If your cookies get hard during storage, a slice of apple placed in an airtight container with your cookies will soften them up.

# Common Cookie Problems and how to fix them:

The difference between a good cook and a great cook is experience gained from errors. Great cooks have learned about the interaction of ingredients and know what to do when things don't look right. Don't be afraid to make mistakes. Mistakes are valuable lessons. Here are some cookie secrets to get you started.

CRACKED COOKIES: Probably baked too quickly. Temperature is too high.

COOKIES ARE TOO HARD: Not enough liquid in the mix.

COOKIES ARE TOO SOFT: Not baked long enough. Could be that cookies are too large to cook through.

COOKIES SPREAD TOO MUCH: Baking temperature too low. Too much sugar in the mix. Can also be too much liquid in the mix.

ROLLED OUT COOKIES ARE TOUGH: Use as little flour as possible when rolling and don't re-roll leftover dough more than once. For sugar cookies, you can roll the dough out on sprinkled sugar instead of flour, but don't re-roll too much or they will get too crispy.

COOKIES ARE NOT CHEWY ENOUGH: Not enough eggs.

COOKIES ARE NOT CRISPY ENOUGH: If you add sugar to a recipe, it will make your cookies crispier.

COOKIES GET TOO BROWN: Baked goods will continue to brown slightly after you take them out of the oven, so take them out just before they are as brown as you would like them. Cookies have carryover cooking too! Let them sit on the hot cookie sheet for a few minutes before removing them to the counter or wire racks to cool. This will allow the cookies to "set" and better retain their shape.

# Almond Apple Delights

*Makes 60 cookies*

The delicious chunks of fresh apple in these cookies help to keep them fresh and caused them to be voted "favorite cookie" by the BHCC caddies.

2 Granny Smith apples

1 lemon

⅓ cup apple juice

3 cups slivered almonds

1 cup butter

½ cup granulated sugar

1½ cups powdered sugar

1½ cups light brown sugar

2 large eggs

2 teaspoon real vanilla extract

2 teaspoon cinnamon

1 teaspoon nutmeg

1 teaspoon baking soda

1½ teaspoons kosher salt

4½ cups unbleached flour

**What is lemon zest?** To make zest, rub a fine grater against the skin of a fresh lemon. Rub lightly to create tiny yellow shavings. Avoid scraping the more bitter white pith underneath.

**Chef Lynn's Secrets:**

- Be sure to toast the nuts and to let the apples get slightly browned. This intensifies their flavors.

- This dough is wet. Dip your fingers in granulated sugar and roll a small ball with the tips of your fingers. Drop it in sugar, swirl the bowl to coat it and then roll it again with your fingers.

1. Preheat your oven to 375°F.

2. Core, peel and dice the apples. In a small saucepan, cook over medium heat for about 5 minutes. Some but not all of the apples will be mushy. Stir in ⅓ cup apple juice and the juice and zest of one lemon. Cool.

3. Place the slivered almonds on an ungreased baking sheet and bake in a preheated 375°F oven for about 8 minutes. The nuts should be very slightly browned and you should detect a nutty smell.

4. Using a mixer, blend the butter and three sugars together. Scrape bowl to get any extra dry ingredients mixed in. Add the eggs and vanilla and mix just until blended. Remove from mixer.

5. By hand, blend in the apple mixture.

6. Mix the dry ingredients (cinnamon, nutmeg, baking soda, salt and flour) and nuts together.

7. Form into balls. Roll lightly in granulated sugar.

8. Bake on lightly sprayed baking sheets for about 15 minutes. Cookies should be lightly browned and firm to the touch.

9. Let rest on hot cookie sheets for 5 minutes before removing to counter to finish cooling.

# Chocolate-Walnut Fudge  *Makes 4 ½ pounds (Recipe can be cut in half)*

This is my take on a recipe that is as old as the hills! The basic recipe was originally found in the Battle Creek Enquirer (circa 1957).

2 lbs. 4 oz. high quality semi-sweet chocolate

2 cans sweetened condensed milk

Large pinch of salt

3 teaspoons walnut extract

3 cups walnut halves

**Variations:**

1. Substitute milk chocolate for the semi-sweet, vanilla or maple flavoring for the vanilla extract and pecans for the nuts.

2. Substitute white chocolate for the semi-sweet, vanilla for the extract and whole almonds for the nuts

3. Substitute almond extract for the vanilla and almonds for the nuts..

1. Break the walnut halves into irregular, coarse pieces with your fingers.

2. In a double boiler, begin melting the chocolate.

3. As the chocolate melts, place the milk, salt, extract and walnuts in a large, heat proof mixing bowl.

4. Place a large piece of waxed paper on a cookie sheet.

5. When the chocolate is melted, pour it into the mixing bowl and stir until everything is well mixed and smooth. Use a rubber spatula to get all of the fudge out of the bowl, to stir and to push the mass to shape the rectangle.

6. Mound into a rectangle (approximately 7 X 11-inch) on the waxed paper covered cookie sheet.

7. Cover and chill for at least 2 hours.

8. Cut into pieces and fill your candy dish!

**Chef Lynn's Secrets:**

- Homemade fudge makes a great hostess gift. Cut it into 1-inch slabs just like you see in candy stores in northern Michigan. Wrap it with patty paper (available at cake baking and decorating supply stores) and place it in decorative boxes or bags tied with a cloth ribbon.

- Stored in an airtight container in the refrigerator, this fudge will keep well for several weeks.

# Chocolatey-Chocolate Chip Cookies    *Makes 36 cookies*

The blending of favorite flavors as well as the contrasting textures make these cookies special favorites.

1 cup butter at room temperature

1 cup white sugar

1 cup light brown sugar

2 eggs

2 teaspoons pure vanilla

1 teaspoon baking soda

1 teaspoon salt

2¼ cups flour

18 oz. mini semi-sweet chocolate chips

1 cup toasted walnuts (See Secrets below)

2 cups coconut

Cooking spray

1. Preheat your oven to 400°F.

2. Mix butter and sugars together.

3. Add eggs and vanilla, scraping bowl after each addition.

4. In a separate bowl, whisk together baking soda, salt and flour. Then mix into wet mixture.

5. Dump the chocolate chips onto the top of the dough.

6. Toast nuts and toss hot nuts onto the chips. Mix through.

7. Mix in coconut.

8. Form into balls and place on cookie sheets lightly sprayed with cooking spray.

9. Bake until lightly browned and set, 10 to 12 minutes.

## Chef Lynn's Secrets:

- Toasting the nuts at 400°F just until lightly browned (about 7 minutes) will intensify their flavor.

- Tossing the hot nuts into the dough mixture melts some but not all of the chips and spreads the chocolate flavor through the dough.

- Provide more texture variety by chopping the nuts by hand so the shapes are irregular.

- Make ahead: Cool and freeze for up to 3 months in airtight bags. Defrost at room temperature as needed.

# Coconut-Macadamia Nut Cookies     *Makes 36 cookies*

This is my most sought after cookie recipe... a definite crowd pleaser!

¾ cup butter at room temperature

½ cup white sugar

¾ cup light brown sugar

2 teaspoons pure vanilla

2 large eggs

14 oz. moist coconut

2 cups roasted macadamia nut halves

½ teaspoon salt

½ teaspoon baking soda

2¼ cups flour

1. Preheat your oven to 375°F.

2. In a mixer bowl, cream butter and sugars together.

3. Mix in vanilla and eggs, scraping bowl down after each addition.

4. Mix in coconut and nuts.

5. In a separate bowl, whisk salt, soda and flour together. Then add to wet mixture, mixing thoroughly.

6. Form into small balls and place on ungreased baking sheet.

7. Bake 10 to 12 minutes.

**Optional:** With the coconut, mix in 2 cups of white chocolate chunks.

**Chef Lynn's Secrets:**

- Bake these cookies until they are just set and very lightly browned. Keeping your coconut moist is key. Be sure to store them in an airtight container.

- **Make ahead:** Cool and freeze in airtight bags for up to 3 months. Defrost at room temperature as needed with beautiful results.

# Milk Chocolate Dips    *Makes about 50 cookies*

These cookies smell heavenly and will entice your loved ones to follow their noses to the kitchen!

1 cup butter

1 cup granulated white sugar

¾ cup brown sugar, packed

1 tablespoon pure vanilla extract

2 large eggs

2½ cups whole wheat pastry flour

1 teaspoon baking soda

1 teaspoon salt

Two - 11.5 oz. packages Nestle ® Real Milk Chocolate Chips

24 oz. chocolate bark or other chocolate candy coating

2 cups ground pecans

1.  Preheat your oven to 375°F.

2.  Cream the butter and sugars together. Mix in the vanilla and eggs.

3.  Whisk together the whole wheat pastry flour, baking soda and salt. Then mix into the liquid ingredients.

4.  Mix in two 11.5 oz. packages of Nestle® Real Milk Chocolate Chips.

5.  Spray cookie sheets with nonstick cooking spray. Form the dough into 1 inch balls and place them about 2 inches apart on the cookie sheets.

6.  Bake for about 17 minutes, until lightly browned. When they are firm, remove them from the oven and let cool on cookie sheets.

7.  Melt the chocolate bark and dip the cookies in it. Additionally, dip half in the ground pecans.

8.  Store in an airtight container. Cookies will keep about 2 weeks or can be placed in an airtight container and frozen for up to 3 months.

**Chef Lynn's Secrets:**

- I love Cushion Aire® cookie sheets and they're not paying me to say this. They have two layers separated by air and really protect cookies from burning — especially cookies like these that are loaded with chocolate, which burn easily.

- Chocolate bark coating is available in cake decorating stores and often in regular grocery stores during the holidays.

# Lemon Biscotti    *Makes about 18, depending on how you cut them*

Traditionally, biscotti (pictured on page 173) are made with oil. This buttered version is rich and slightly crumbly. The lemon flavor of these delightfully crunchy cookies will give whatever you drink with it a brighter flavor.

½ cup butter

1 cup sugar

3 eggs

2 teaspoons vanilla

3 cups all purpose flour

1½ teaspoons baking powder

½ teaspoon salt

2 lemons, zest and juice

1 cup almonds, ground

Egg wash: 1 egg white whisked with
    1 tablespoon water

### Chef Lynn's Secrets:

- Much of the biscotti you buy in stores has been around awhile, which obviously affects the taste. There is a huge difference between those and fresh homemade versions. These crunchy and flavorful cookies are loved by themselves. You can dunk them in coffee or tea, but you don't have to in order to enjoy them.

- When you cut your biscotti, note that the bigger the angle, the longer the cookie. Nice, small pieces are perfect for everyone and bigger eaters can always take two!

- You can successfully freeze biscotti in an airtight container for up to three months. When you thaw it, it will still taste fresh.

- You can also successfully freeze leftover fresh lemon juice and lemon zest. Freeze the juice in ice cube trays and the zest in plastic freezer bags.

1. Preheat your oven to 350°F.

2. Cream the butter and sugar together.

3. Add the eggs, one at a time, scraping down the bowl in between and then add the vanilla.

4. Whisk together the flour, baking powder and salt and then mix this with the wet ingredients.

5. Add the lemon zest and juice and the almonds. Mix thoroughly.

6. Cover a cookie sheet with parchment paper.

7. Sprinkle a little of the flour on a clean counter and turn the batter out on top of it. Use just enough flour so that you can handle the dough. Split it in half and form two logs about 2 inches wide and 10 inches long. Lift the logs onto the cookie sheet, leaving about 4 inches of space between them. Lightly brush them with egg wash.

8. Bake until lightly brown, about 35 minutes. (The bars will spread quite a bit during baking.)

9. Remove from the oven and cool completely. Reduce the oven temperature to 325°F.

10. Using a serrated knife and cutting on an angle, carefully cut the bars into strips and turn each strip on its side. Bake again for about 15 minutes on each side, until lightly browned.

# Peanut Butter Cookies     *Makes about 40 cookies*

These are for kids of all ages. I call them disappearing cookies!

1 cup whole butter at room temperature

1 cup granulated sugar

1 cup light brown sugar

2 eggs

2 teaspoons pure vanilla

2 cups creamy peanut butter

1 teaspoon baking soda

1 teaspoon salt

2¾ cups all purpose flour

**Optional:** 2 cups salted Virginia peanuts, coarsely chopped

1. Preheat your oven to 375°F.

2. Cream together butter and sugars.

3. Add eggs and vanilla, scraping down bowl after each addition. Mix in the peanut butter and peanuts (if using).

4. Whisk baking soda, salt and flour together; then add to wet mixture.

5. Form into balls and place on ungreased cookie sheet about 5 inches apart.

6. Flatten lightly with fork dipped in water.

7. Bake just until set and very lightly browned, about 12-14 minutes.

**Chef Lynn's Secrets:**

- Use a large serving fork with wide prongs to flatten these cookies instead of a more traditional table fork. The wider ridges provide a more interesting mouth feel.

- Make them ahead! Cool and freeze in airtight bags for up to three months. Defrost at room temperature as needed.

# Molasses Cookies    *Makes about 50 cookies*

Soft and highly spiced, for molasses lovers, these cookies are a dream come true.

1 cup butter

1 cup sugar + sugar for sprinkling cookies

2 eggs

1½ cups dark molasses (12 oz. bottle)

½ cup whole milk

5 to 6 cups cake flour

2 teaspoons baking soda

3 teaspoons cinnamon

3 teaspoons ginger

1 teaspoon cloves

1 teaspoon salt

1. Preheat your oven to 425°F.

2. In a 5-quart mixer, cream the butter and sugar together.

3. Add the eggs and mix, scraping down the bowl to incorporate them.

4. Mix in the molasses and milk.

5. In a separate bowl, whisk together the flour, baking soda and spices. Then add them to the wet mixture and blend well. (The dough is very wet.)

6. Drop by teaspoons onto a greased cookie sheet. Sprinkle with a pinch of sugar.

7. Bake 10–12 minutes, just until set. (The cookies will spread while baking.)

8. Sprinkle with another pinch of sugar and let them sit on the hot cookie sheet for 5 minutes before transferring to the counter to finish cooling.

**Chef Lynn's Secrets:**

- In a well sealed container, between sheets of parchment or waxed paper, you can freeze these cookies for up to 3 months.

- Cake flour is the starchiest of all flours and the lowest in protein. Therefore, it easily absorbs fats and baked goods made with it are lighter and fluffier than those made with other flours. You will find it in most grocery stores, but look for it in a box, not a bag.

# Oatmeal-Maple Granola   *Makes 4 quarts*

Here's some granola that is reminiscent of oatmeal cookies. Bet you can't eat just a handful!

3 cups regular old fashioned rolled oats (oatmeal)

¾ cup wheat germ

1 cup dark raisins

1 cup whole almonds

2 cups whole pecans

2 cups whole cashews

1 cup flaked coconut

1 cup maple syrup

½ cup corn oil

½ cup light brown sugar

2 teaspoons ground cloves

5 teaspoons cinnamon

1 teaspoon salt

½ cup dried apples, cut into ¼ inch cubes (dice)

½ cup dried cherries

Cooking spray

1. Preheat your oven to 300°F.

2. Spray a jelly roll pan (cookie sheet with sides) with cooking spray.

3. In the biggest mixing bowl that you have, mix the oats, wheat germ, raisins, nuts, and coconut together. Set aside.

4. In a small saucepan, stir and heat the oil, maple syrup, sugar and spices until the sugar is dissolved and the mixture starts to boil. Pour the hot mixture over the oat mixture and using a spatula, stir it all together.

5. Bake for 20 minutes. Add the dried apples and cherries and bake for 20 minutes more, until the oats are lightly browned. Turn your oven off and leave the granola in the oven for 15 more minutes.

6. Remove from the oven and cool. Store in an airtight container for up to 2 weeks.

## Chef Lynn's Secrets:

- It's best to use regular old fashioned oats for granola as opposed to the quick cooking type. They hold together better and the taste is richer.

- To make the mixture cluster together, wet your hands and squeeze bits of the mix together with your fingertips before baking.

- You can use honey and/or molasses in this recipe, as replacements for the maple syrup, or any combination of the three ingredients, to fit your taste buds.

- Baking at a low temperature ensures that all ingredients are thoroughly heated through and baked.

- The reason for adding the dried fruit later in the baking process is so it retains enough of its moisture.

## Leftovers:

Use the granola as a crunchy topping on yogurt or a crisp salad. It also makes a nice trail mix on a hike or bike ride.

# Old Fashioned Peanut Brittle    *Makes 2 quarts*

Here's one straight out of the past. It reminds me of getting ready for Christmas at home with mom.

1½ cups raw peanuts

2 tablespoons butter

1 teaspoon baking soda

1 cup granulated white sugar

½ cup light corn syrup

¼ cup water

1 teaspoon salt

**You will also need to have ready:**

A clear glass of ice cold water

Candy thermometer (Optional)

1 large, buttered baking sheet

**Chef Lynn's Secrets:**

• Peanut brittle makes a great homemade gift at Christmas time. Look for beautiful, decorative tins or bags at the dollar store.

• Other nuts like macadamia and almonds can give this brittle a more sophisticated flair.

1. Measure the peanuts, butter and baking soda separately and set near by so they are ready to use.

2. In a heavy bottomed saucepan, mix the sugar, corn syrup, water and salt together.

3. If using a candy thermometer, clip it to the side of the pot, making sure that it is not touching the bottom.

4. Turn the burner on medium-high and heat until the sugar mixture is boiling.

5. Toss in the peanuts and continue to cook and stir over medium heat until the thermometer reads about 250°F, about 8 minutes. Whether using a thermometer or not, check it as follows: When it turns brown, drip a small amount of the hot mixture from a spoon into the cold glass of water. If it forms a hard thread, it's done. Immediately remove from the heat.

6. Add the butter and baking soda. Stir quickly until the butter is all melted. The mixture will foam up.

7. Using oven mitts, pour the hot mixture onto the buttered cookie sheet to form a rectangle. Don't stir. Let it settle down naturally.

8. Cool thoroughly. Break into irregular pieces.

# Twisted Oatmeal Cookies    *Makes 55–60 cookies*

These cookies have an irresistible, nutty taste, the texture of a flourless cake and the crunch of sweet coconut, plus the hometown goodness of oatmeal.

1 cup brown sugar

1 cup white sugar

1 cup butter

2 eggs

5 tablespoons sour cream

1 cup whole wheat flour

1 tablespoon baking soda

2 teaspoons cinnamon

1½ cups all purpose flour

3 cups oatmeal

2 cups ground pecans

1 cup raisins

1 cup coconut

Cooking spray

1. Preheat your oven to 375°F.

2. Cream the sugars and the butter together.

3. Add the eggs and sour cream, mixing well and scraping down the sides of the bowl to incorporate it all.

4. In a separate bowl, mix the flour, cinnamon and baking soda together. Then add in the oatmeal, nuts, raisins and coconut.

5. Mix the dry and wet ingredients together.

6. Using your fingers and a tablespoon of dough for each cookie, roll into a ball and then slightly flatten it with your fingers. Place each on a cookie sheet, lightly sprayed with cooking spray.

7. Bake about 15 minutes, until lightly browned.

8. Leave on hot baking sheets for 5 minutes before transferring to counter or racks to finish cooling.

# Popcorn + Variations   *Serves 6*

## POPCORN

8 ounces popcorn kernels

Peanut or corn oil

Salt

1. Coat the bottom of a 4-quart pot with peanut or corn oil.

2. Heat on medium high heat for 30 seconds. Next, toss in a single layer of popcorn kernels and place a cover on the pot.

3. When popcorn starts to pop, shake every 15 seconds. When popping slows, remove from heat and let sit until popping stops.

4. When removing from the pan, watch for uncooked kernels and discard them.

5. Sprinkle with regular salt, to taste.

## CARAMEL CORN

6 quarts popped popcorn

1½ cups light brown sugar

½ cup dark brown sugar

1 cup butter

½ cup light corn syrup

1 teaspoon salt

1 teaspoon baking soda

1 teaspoon butter flavoring

10 oz. mixed nuts, optional
   (Can be salted)

1. Pop 6 quarts of popcorn. Place in large roasting pan. If using nuts, place nuts on top of popcorn.

2. Preheat oven to 250°F.

3. In a pan with high sides and a thick bottom, mix sugars, butter, syrup and salt together.

4. Cook over medium high heat, stirring, until the mixture reaches a full, rolling boil. Turn heat to medium-low and boil for about 5 minutes. (Mixture should make a hard ball when dripped into a glass of cold water.)

5. Remove pan from heat. Add butter flavoring and stir, then add the baking soda by itself. Stir well. Mixture will foam up, so be sure the sides of your pan are tall enough. I use a 4-quart pot with 5-inch sides.

6. Pour mixture over the popcorn and nuts. Using a large spatula, carefully toss and fold the mixture through. Do this carefully. The mixture is very hot. As you mix, try not to break up the popcorn. When the caramel starts to harden, stop.

7. Place in preheated oven for 15 minutes to loosen the caramel. Remove from the oven and stir.

8. Cool. Store at room temperature in an airtight container if you have any left!

# KETTLE CORN

Regular popcorn, salted to taste

Caramel Corn

Mix the two kinds of popcorn 3 to 2 (3 parts regular popcorn and 2 parts caramel corn).

**Chef Lynn's Secrets:**

- A full, rolling boil is a boil you cannot stir down.
- Soak any dishes with caramel residue in them in hot, soapy water. Then they will easily clean.
- Don't know how much a quart is? 1 quart equals 4 cups.
- This is lovely to make at a party and to serve warm.

Caramel Sauce after soda is added

Caramel Corn

# Chapter Ten
## *Sandwiches & Chili*

# Lesson Ten

## *What's important to know about sandwiches?*

- **SPICE IT UP.** Spicing up your sandwiches is all about using your imagination. Think about your leftovers first. Think about what tastes best together, make it the right consistency — chop things in a way that they won't fall out when the sandwich is picked up — and then pile your favorite things between two slices of bread. By the right consistency, I mean thick enough so that it won't drip out when you eat the sandwich and so it won't make the sandwich soggy. Then all you have to do is spice it up with specialty mayonnaises and sauces or butters or even nothing if it isn't necessary. A sandwich should be easy to neatly eat.

- **NO SOGGY BREAD!** Dense and crusty breads are best for sandwiches because they don't fall as easily as soft breads. They also don't destroy the integrity of your sandwich by soaking up too much of the mayonnaise or other condiments. Think about focaccia, ciabatta, pita, sour dough, French baguette sliced on a long angle, pumpernickel and whole grain breads. They don't have to be plain though! Consider cinnamon, raisin or fruit breads. The list is almost endless.

  Speaking of soggy... sometimes it's helpful to create a vapor barrier. In other words, if your sandwich ingredients are a bit wet or if you need to make them ahead, you can protect the bread by covering it with a thin coating of butter or cream cheese. The bread retains its integrity because the ingredients can't leach through to make it soggy.

- **TIMING:** To limit the time that other ingredients have in contact with the bread, you can measure and set out your sandwich ingredients first. Then assemble your sandwiches all at once — as if in an assembly line — and serve them immediately and all at once. If your sandwiches must sit awhile, create a vapor barrier by lightly spreading each slice of bread with one of the flavored butters on pages 198 and 199.

- **ADD FLAVOR.** Don't underestimate the importance of flavored mayonnaise, pesto etc. These will give your sandwich uniqueness. Many products are on the market so you can buy them or even invent your own.

- **FRESH HERBS** add interest, color and texture to sandwiches. The possibilities are endless, but check pages 15 and 41 for some ideas.

- **THINK ABOUT YOUR LEFTOVERS.** What's in the refrigerator that could add something to the sandwich you are about to make? Leftover meats, meat loaf, both cooked and raw vegetables and lettuces would all be great additions. If you're wondering what might taste good together, check out the book, "Culinary Artistry" by Andrew Dornenburg and Karen Paige. You can look up almost any food or herb and see what complements it best.

- **STORAGE:** Also refer to the Section in this book called "What's Important to Know about Bread" on page 132. Tightly wrapping bread or storing it in the refrigerator isn't good for it and can actually encourage it to go stale.

- **FREEZING** whole sandwiches can work out OK if you don't put condiments on them beforehand. If you are packing lunch boxes or travel take along food that will not be immediately consumed, taking a frozen sandwich helps to lengthen the time they can sit at room temperature.

  I actually make sure I always have plain bread in the freezer for emergencies. Although it compromises the flavor and texture, it works out great if you just toast it. You can use it for breakfast toast, toast points or toasted sandwiches.

# Dense breads make great sandwiches!

Ciabatta means "carpet slipper" in Italian and is a dense, crusty flat bread.

Foccacia is a high gluten flat bread that can be found in many flavors and a variety of toppings.

French baguette is a sour dough bread, made simply from flour, water, yeast and salt.

Pumpernickel is dark, heavy German bread made with rye.

Raisin bread (pictured with whole wheat bread), usually combined with cinnamon, adds a lovely sweet touch to a sandwich.

Mixed breads add interest and varied nutrition to sandwiches.

# Chicken Chili  *Serves 4*

The ultimate sandwich accompaniment... Chili with traditional toppings. I was trying to create a chicken chili that tasted like traditional beef chili and here it is.

3 boneless chicken breasts

¼ cup olive oil

2 cloves garlic

1 cup yellow onion

3 scallions

3 large beefsteak tomatoes

One 15½ oz. can kidney beans

½ teaspoon salt

½ teaspoon freshly ground pepper

1 tablespoon hot sauce
   (Tabasco® or Red Devil®)

1 teaspoon chili powder
   (I used Penzey's® Chili 3000)

1 teaspoon Spanish paprika
   (I used smoked paprika)

½ to 1 teaspoon ground cloves (to taste)

1 tablespoon lemon juice; 4 oz.
   tomato paste

4 tablespoons sugar

**Toppings:** Chopped onions, sour cream
   or yogurt and grated Cheddar cheese

**Chef Lynn's Secrets:**

- The easiest way to cut chicken into bite-sized pieces is to partially freeze the chicken. Then, using a very sharp knife, slice into any size you desire.

- To easily peel tomatoes, cut a small X on the bottoms with a very sharp knife. Drop them in boiling water for about 20 seconds. Remove with tongs and cool. The skins should slide off easily when you peel it with your fingers.

1. Cut the chicken into bite sized pieces. Heat half the oil in a pan until it's very hot. Sauté the chicken pieces until just cooked through. Remove from the pan and place in a 4-quart saucepan.

2. Finely mince the garlic and dice the yellow onion. Finely slice the scallions, including the green stems. Add the rest of the olive oil to the same pan and sauté the garlic and onions until they are soft. Scrape them into the saucepan with the chicken.

3. Peel and dice the beefsteak tomatoes. Add them to the saucepan.

4. Drain the kidney beans well and add them also. Add the hot sauce, all of the spices as well as the lemon juice, tomato paste and sugar.

5. Cook over low heat for about 45 minutes, until well blended.

6. Serve with toppings on the side.

NOTE: If you want to change this to beef chili, use 1 lb. hamburger or chopped filet instead of the chicken.

# Chicken-Chutney Sandwich    *Serves 4*

½ cup pineapple juice or orange juice

½ cup water

1 large Granny Smith apple

24 oz. thin sliced cooked chicken

4 oz. very thinly sliced
   (or shaved) Swiss cheese

8 slices whole wheat bread

½ cup mayonnaise

2 teaspoons curry powder

Pinch of salt

Pinch of ground pepper

⅓ cup slivered almonds

4 tablespoons mango chutney

1. Mix the citrus juice with the water.

2. Wash the apple and cut it into 4 pieces. Using a very sharp knife, remove the core. Slice the apple as thin as you can and quickly place the slices in the juice/water mixture.

3. Divide the chicken and cheese into 4 equal portions. Set aside.

4. Mix the mayonnaise with the curry powder, salt and pepper. After it is thoroughly mixed, add the almonds and mix again.

5. Have the chutney and a measuring spoon ready. Drain the apple slices.

6. Assemble the sandwiches:

   a. Lay 4 slices of bread side-by-side with the other 4 slices of bread.

   b. Spread each with the mayonnaise/nut mixture.

   c. Top each slice of bread with 3 oz. chicken.

   d. Next, add equal portions of the apple slices.

   e. Spread 1 tablespoon chutney on the chicken. Top with cheese.

   f. Press down on the sandwich with a flat surface (a plate, for example). Slice in half and serve.

### Chef Lynn's Secret:

The juice/water mixture is called "acidulated water" because you have added citric acid to the water. The purpose of this is to keep the apple slices from turning brown. Now you can more leisurely prepare your sandwiches and they will not arrive at the table with brown spots.

# Chicken Burgers   *Serves 4*

1 lb. cooked ground chicken (or turkey)

½ cup slivered almonds, crushed in
your hand

¼ teaspoon each salt and freshly ground
pepper

¼ teaspoon cayenne pepper

4 tablespoons plum jam (or puréed chutney)

⅓ cup radish sprouts, chopped small

1 large shallot, minced

½ cup Italian breadcrumbs

8 tablespoons mayonnaise

8 tablespoons Dijon mustard

4 tablespoons olive oil

4 pieces Boston lettuce

4 slices beefsteak tomato or more if they
are small

1 cup shaved cheese (Parmesan, Cheddar
or Swiss)

4 Kaiser burger buns, wheat or white

### Chef Lynn's Secret:

If the burger starts getting too brown, you
can finish it in a 350°F oven. Bake it until a
thermometer reads 160°F. Take it out and it
will cook to 165°F — the safest temperature
for chicken — within a couple of minutes.
Serve immediately.

1. Mix the chicken, almonds, spices, jam,
   sprouts, shallot and breadcrumbs
   together well. Make sure the shallot is well
   distributed throughout the meat.

2. Form into four patties.

3. Heat the olive oil and sear the patties. Turn
   the heat down and cook until the meat is
   cooked through and not pink. Top with the
   cheese and cover the pan to slightly melt it.

4. Split the buns if necessary and spread the
   bottoms with mayonnaise and the tops
   with Dijon mustard. Top the bottoms with
   a piece of lettuce and then tomato. Place the
   burger next and then the top of the bun.

**Serving suggestion:** Sweet pickles and
matchstick potatoes or coleslaw are perfect
accompaniments.

# Vegetable-Spinach Burgers     *Serves one*

Ingredients are for one burger. Just multiply by however many you would like to make!

2 cups fresh spinach, chopped

1 cup vegetable stock

Pinch each of salt and freshly ground pepper

1 tablespoon shallot, minced

2 tablespoons fresh red pepper, minced

1 teaspoon fresh lemon juice

¼ cup Ricotta cheese

2 tablespoons Italian breadcrumbs

2 tablespoons Parmesan cheese, coarsely grated

3 tablespoons fresh corn, cooked and cut off the cob

2 tablespoons olive oil, preferably lemon

1. Heat the vegetable stock in a large saucepan. When it starts to boil, add the spinach and simmer for 2 minutes, until it is wilted. Drain through a fine sieve. Using a rubber spatula, press the spinach against the sieve to get as much moisture out as you can. Place the spinach in a mixing bowl.

2. Add the salt and pepper, shallot, fresh red pepper, lemon juice, ricotta cheese, breadcrumbs, Parmesan cheese and corn to the bowl and mix well.

3. Form into a patty.

4. Heat the lemon oil over low heat and fry the burger until crispy brown on the outside and heated through, several minutes on each side.

**Chef Lynn's Secret:**

When you fry this burger, keep the heat low so the cheese doesn't burn. There are just enough breadcrumbs to hold it together, so the burger is very soft. Turn it carefully and if necessary, reshape by patting the sides with the spatula.

# Flavored (Compound) Butters: A Primer

Nut Butters are easy. You just put them in your food processor and grind them up! However, different species of nuts have different fat contents and act a little differently. Just watch them carefully as you grind them up and you will immediately see the difference. Some nuts make a very thin butter. If you see this, refrigerate it to thicken it. After processing, add a pinch of salt. Taste and adjust.

| All times are approximate, but following is a basic guide to processing times and flavor matches: | |
| --- | --- |
| 1 minute: | pecans, walnuts (regular and black) |
| 2 minutes: | cashews, macadamia nuts, peanuts |
| 2½ minutes: | hazelnuts, slivered almonds |
| 3½ minutes | whole almonds, pistachios |

## Cheese Butters:

Cheeses like Parmesan, Asiago, Manchego and Cheddar make tasty butter. I also like Gorgonzola or other blue cheeses and Gruyère.

1. Bring ½ cup high quality unsalted butter to room temperature.

2. Grate hard cheeses and crumble soft cheeses. (You will want about ¼ cup of cheese.) Then process for 30 seconds in a food processor or mix with the butter by hand.

3. Add a pinch of salt. Taste and adjust.

## Truffle Butter:

Mix 1 tablespoon truffle oil with ½ cup room temperature salted butter.

## Herb Butter:

Mix ¼ cup chopped fresh herbs with ½ cup room temperature butter and a pinch of salt. Try chives, parsley, tarragon or oregano, but all herbs work well for this.

## Onion Butter:

Mix or process (in a food processor with the blade attachment) ⅛ cup finely minced shallots or any type of onion with ½ cup room temperature butter and a pinch of salt. Optional: ½ teaspoon garlic.

## Berry Butter:

Use fresh raspberries, blackberries, blueberries or strawberries. Mix or process ⅓ cup fresh berries with ½ cup room temperature butter and a pinch of salt.

## Lemon or Lime Butter:

Mix or process 2 tablespoons fresh lemon or lime juice with ½ cup room temperature butter and a pinch of salt.

## Maple Butter:

Mix 2 tablespoons maple syrup with ½ cup room temperature butter and a pinch of salt.

## Cinnamon Butter:

Mix 2 tablespoons cinnamon with ½ cup room temperature butter and a pinch of salt.

## Roasted Pepper Butter:

Process in a food processor until smooth, about 1 minute: 1 roasted pepper (any color) with 1 cup unsalted, room temperature butter, a splash of lemon juice and a pinch of salt.

## Avocado (or other cooked vegetable) Butter:

Process ¼ cup avocado or cooked vegetable (like carrots or asparagus) with ½ cup room temperature butter and a pinch of salt and 1 or 2 teaspoons lemon juice.

## Garlic Butter:

Process 3 roasted garlic cloves with ¼ shallot and ½ cup unsalted butter and a pinch of salt.

**Other suggested flavor matches for butters:**

- Parmesan or nut butter with a dinner roll

- Hazelnut butter on a chocolate croissant

- Almond butter for an apple muffin

- Blue cheese or onion butter on top of a grilled steak

- Lemon or lime butter on a blueberry muffin

- Raspberry or cinnamon butter on pancakes or scones

- Truffle butter on fresh, cooked pasta

- Dill or roasted pepper butter on top of fish

- Garlic butter on a grilled lamb chop

- Baked vegetable butter on vegetables

- All butters go well on sandwiches

**Chef Lynn's Secrets:**

- Grinding your own nuts for butters is a big advantage because you can make them the consistency you like. The more you grind, the smoother the butter.

- To mold butters, press them into a flexible mold using a spatula and put them in the freezer for 20–30 minutes. Unmold and transfer them to a covered freezer container. Place on parchment or waxed paper in the container and separate layers with a piece of the same. You can keep the molds frozen for up to 3 months. Place on bread plates a half an hour before serving time or top hot meats at the last minute so they will still be visible when you serve the dish.

- If you put flavored butter on something hot (for example a steak) do it at the last minute so it will still have some shape when served.

# Gourmet Beef Burgers    *Makes 2*

One 1 lb. sirloin strip steak

1 tablespoon lemon olive oil

Salt and pepper, to taste

4 thin slices (rings) of a large, raw onion
   (white or yellow)

2 slices ripe beefsteak tomato

4 tablespoons mayonnaise and/or mustard

2 large, fresh buns (with or without
   sesame seeds)

1.  Rub the steak on both sides with the olive
    oil. Sprinkle both sides with salt and pepper.

2.  Heat your grill until it is very hot. Sear the
    steak on both sides and cook to your taste.

3.  Transfer the steak to a cutting board and
    with a very sharp knife, slice the meat very
    thin, on an angle.

4.  Spread both sides of the bun with
    mayonnaise (and/or mustard). Top with
    the beef.

5.  Serve with an onion slice and a tomato slice.

### Chef Lynn's Secrets:

- Two things really kick up flavor and
  they are lemon and salt. Pairing the
  lemon with the olive oil is a perfect
  example of how flavored oil can add
  a sophisticated touch. The lemon sits
  in the taste background and is almost
  indistinguishable.

- Try using flavored lemon oil when you fry
  eggs for another delicious combination.

# Grilled Vegetable Pita   *Serves 4*

1 red pepper

1 green pepper

1 large yellow onion

1 small purple eggplant

1 very small zucchini

1 very small yellow summer squash

4 tablespoons olive oil

¼ cup pine nuts

8 oz. goat cheese (also called chèvre)

4 pieces mustard greens or
butter lettuce

**For the Vinaigrette:**

½ cup olive oil

¼ cup balsamic vinegar

1 clove finely minced garlic

1 tablespoon Dijon mustard

⅛ teaspoon each salt and pepper, or
more, to taste

**Chef Lynn's Secrets:**

- When removing the pepper skins, do not rinse them or you will rinse away a lot of the wonderful smoky flavor. You can rinse your fingers while you work, but not the flesh of the peppers.

- These sandwiches definitely have a make ahead component. Mix the filling completely the day before and let it marinate in the refrigerator overnight. The flavors will blend and it will be even better.

1.  Grill the peppers: Remove the stems on the peppers and grill them until they are blackened all over (20–30 minutes, turning with tongs as the sides blacken). Place in a plastic or paper bag to cool for 20 minutes. Peel off the black skin, remove the stems, seeds and cut the soft flesh into ⅛-inch strips. Place in a bowl and set aside.

2.  Grill the eggplant and zucchini: While the peppers are roasting, cut the onion, eggplant, zucchini and summer squash into quarter inch strips. Brush them with olive oil and grill until they are soft. Make lots of caramelized hatch marks on the vegetables.

3.  Cool and cut each piece crosswise into ¼ inch strips. Add to the peppers.

4.  Whisk together the ½ cup olive oil, vinegar, garlic, mustard, salt and pepper.

5.  Mix the pine nuts with the cheese.

6.  Open each pita half and fill with ¼ of the mixture, a piece of the mustard greens (or one piece of lettuce) and 2 oz. goat cheese.

# Hot Italian Wraps   *Serves 4*

8 hot Italian sausages, smoked or regular

1 yellow onion, cut into strips

3 cups chicken broth

2 Granny Smith apples, diced into
    ½-inch pieces

½ head of green cabbage, sliced into
    thin strips

¼ cup Mucky Duck® or Ingelhoffer®
    honey mustard

Salt and pepper, to taste

4 pieces flatbread

2 tablespoons olive oil

1. If your sausages are not cooked, add enough
   water to a saucepan to cover them and
   bring it to a boil. Add the sausages and boil
   them until they are cooked through, about
   5 minutes. Drain the sausages and slice
   them into pieces, on an angle. Then sauté
   them in 3 tablespoons of olive oil until they
   are crispy and browned. Place them in a
   heat proof bowl.

2. In the same frying pan, caramelize the
   onion strips (page 235).  Remove from the
   pan and add them to the sausages.

3. Peel the apples and chop them into ½-inch
   pieces. In the same frying pan, heat the
   chicken broth over medium heat. Add the
   apple pieces and simmer until they are soft
   but not mushy, about 5 minutes.

4. Add the cabbage to the apples and cook
   long enough to soften and wilt it, another
   4 minutes. Drain the mixture in a colander
   and press it with the side of a rubber
   spatula to get the moisture out. Add this
   mixture to the sausage.

5. Add the mustard to the sausage and mix well.

6. Spread ¼ of the sausage mixture in the
   middle of each piece of flatbread. Fold it
   over and place it cut side down on a serving
   plate.

**Chef Lynn's Secrets:**

• This sandwich tastes the best when the
  cabbage has a little crunch, so cook it just
  until it's wilted.

• The heat in this sausage is totally controlled
  by how spicy your sausage is, so choose
  accordingly.

**Heirloom Tomatoes** come from traditional vines that proliferate naturally, or are open pollinated. Seeds are saved and cultivated without any intervention and they are usually grown in organic soil. These tomatoes are not genetically modified, so some are prone to disease and some have issues with cracking. There are hundreds of delicious varieties, offering many different shapes, colors and flavors.

Vine ripened tomatoes are simply the best, no questions asked. If yours are not yet ready to eat, store them in a cool, dry place, away from the sunlight. Do not store them in the refrigerator until they are completely ripe. You can keep them a little longer then at colder temperatures. To speed up ripening, put them in a paper bag at room temperature. Tomatoes give off ethylene gas, which stimulates ripening and holding them in the bag will concentrate it. If any of your tomatoes are moldy, separate them from the group because fungus can spread rapidly.

The tomatoes shown on this page were grown by my friend, Louie Halatsis in Livonia, Michigan in soil that has been organic for over 40 years. Unfortunately, he is not a commercial grower and at least as of this writing, doesn't sell them. His vines grow seven feet tall, which reminds me to tell you to be sure to stake your tomatoes or use wire baskets because tomatoes that sit on the ground will quickly rot.

Pictured below: Left: Big Rainbow, with its awesome sweetness and variable colors.
Right: Kellogg Breakfast, a yellow, low acid variety with few seeds and Brandywine, the "poster tomato" of the Heirloom group.

# Lettuce Wraps  *Serves 6*

1 head iceberg lettuce

**For the filling:**

2 cups ramen noodles

3 cups chicken broth

3 cups water

4 tablespoons olive oil

3 entire green onions, washed and sliced

3 boneless chicken breasts cut into ½-inch pieces

1 cup water chestnuts drained and chopped (8 oz.)

½ cup straw mushrooms, drained and chopped (4 oz. can)

**For the sauce:**

⅓ cup soy sauce

⅓ cup dark brown sugar

1 tablespoon rice vinegar

1 tablespoon sesame oil

2 tablespoons hoisin sauce

½ teaspoon freshly ground pepper

½ teaspoon cayenne pepper

Salt and pepper, to taste

1. In a 2-quart saucepan, heat the chicken broth and water to a full rolling boil. Drop in the ramen noodles and cook them for 3 minutes. Drain the noodles and set them aside. When they are cool enough, transfer them to a cutting board and chop them into smaller pieces.

2. In a large frying pan, heat the olive oil and sauté the onion until soft. Add the chicken and sauté it on high heat until it is golden brown on the outside and white all the way through. Be careful not to overcook it. The chicken should be tender.

3. Add the noodles, water chestnuts and mushrooms and mix through.

4. In a separate bowl, mix the sauce ingredients together and add it to the pan. Stir to heat.

5. Separate the lettuce leaves from its stalk. Wash and cut a small "V" in each leaf to remove the tough part of the stem. Place on a platter.

6. Serve hot in a community bowl with the lettuce leaves on the side so each person can take what they want and fill their own.

Above: Lettuce wraps can be served as a first course or as a main course. Just set out the lettuce pieces and the filling and let each person build their own.

## Chef Lynn's Secrets:

- Cutting the "V" in the lettuce leaves not only removes the bitter part of the stem, but also causes the leaf to form a natural cup when you hold it in your hand and pull each side of the "V" across each other. Fold the sides around the filling and you have a nice, easy to eat pocket.

- This make ahead meal is even better if you can put the filling together the day before so that the flavors can steep together.

- Always taste your food before you spice it and again before you serve it. Soy sauce, for example, is already salty, so if it's in your recipe, you may not need to add any more salt.

- Change these to beef wraps by using sliced beef flank steak instead.

# Manchego Panini    *Serves 4*

3 slices bacon

3 thin slices (rings) of yellow onion

½ cup Manchego cheese

½ ripe yellow tomato

2 pieces sandwich bread

1. First, sauté the bacon until it's slightly crispy. Drain on absorbent paper towels. Snip into small bits with scissors.

2. Peel an onion and cut a small slice on the side so you have a flat edge to lay it on. Slice down the edge of the onion to make 3 very thin onion rings. Toss the onions in the same pan you used to sauté the bacon and cook until they are browned (caramelized). Set aside to cool.

3. Grate the cheese.

4. Thinly slice the tomato.

5. Now build the sandwich in the following order: Bread, grated cheese, bacon, onions, cheese, and then bread.

6. Heat the panini grill. Brush both sides of the grill lightly with olive oil. Place the sandwich inside and grill just until the grill marks are nicely browned and the cheese is melted, about 3 minutes. Cool slightly before cutting. Use a serrated knife and saw back and forth to make a clean cut.

7. Serve with coleslaw or chips.

### Chef Lynn's Secrets

- Spain's Manchego cheese meets Italy's panini. Now there's a match made in heaven. The secret with this sandwich is the cheese ratio. Too much and you have a mess and it's hard to eat. Too little and it tastes dry. This one has just the right amount.

- Placing the cheese on both sides of the bread holds the sandwich together and makes it easier to eat. Shaving or grating it allows it to melt evenly during the short time it's in the panini grill.

- I love making panini with crusty sour dough white or wheat bread. The chewy texture holds up well to the gooey cheese.

# Mayonnaise + Flavorings  *Makes about 2 cups*

2 egg yolks

3 teaspoons water

4 teaspoons white wine or champagne vinegar

1½ cups vegetable oil or olive oil

3 teaspoons lemon juice

Salt and white pepper, to taste

1. Place the yolks, water and vinegar in a mixing bowl and whisk using the whisk attachment.

2. Using a measuring cup with a pour spout, slowly drizzle the oil into the mixture, making sure that it fully mixes. Watch carefully so that the oil doesn't pool up. Really drizzle it in so that the whisk can keep up.

3. Add the lemon juice, salt and pepper a little at a time, tasting after each addition, until you find a taste you like. Do the same with the flavors below – a tablespoon at a time and taste after each addition. Always keep mayonnaise refrigerated.

**Flavoring Ideas:**

- For those of you who like Miracle Whip®, add 2 teaspoons sugar

- Horseradish or wasabi paste

- Anchovy paste

- 1 teaspoon mustard powder

- Dijon mustard

**Chef Lynn's Secrets:**

- The safest way to make mayonnaise is with pasteurized egg yolks.

- If you move your whisk in a circle, you are stirring. Whisking is a back and forth motion that forces the mixture through the tines of the whisk.

# Toasted Tuna Sandwich   *Serves 2*

½ pound raw sushi grade tuna steak, cut into a block

Salt and freshly ground pepper, to taste

4 slices Pepperidge Farm® sandwich bread (white or 100% whole wheat)

2 tablespoons lemon or regular olive oil

2 to 4 tablespoons wasabi mayonnaise or Dijon mustard

1 scallion, cleaned and sliced crossways into very thin slices

4 small pieces Boston lettuce or 1 cup baby spring lettuce

½ cup radish sprouts

½ fresh avocado, sliced and drizzled with fresh lemon juice

1. Preheat your oven to 400°F.

2. Sprinkle the tuna with salt and pepper.

3. Heat the olive oil in a small pan and quickly sear the tuna on both sides. It should be brown on the outside and rare on the inside. Cool and using a very sharp knife, slice the tuna crosswise into very thin slices.

4. Using a pastry brush, lightly brush both sides of the bread with clarified butter. Place on a cookie sheet and bake until golden brown, about 7 minutes. Flip the bread over and bake a few minutes more, until both sides match.

5. **To Assemble:** For each sandwich, spread two pieces of bread with wasabi mayonnaise (or Dijon mustard). Press the radish sprouts into the mayonnaise (or mustard) on one piece of bread. Then cover that piece with lettuce. Lay half of the tuna strips across the two pieces of bread, overlapping the strips. Sprinkle the tuna with scallions. Top one piece with slices of avocado; then fold the other piece carefully over it to make a sandwich.

**Suggestion:** Serve with vegetable, potato or onion crisps or potato salad.

Above: Toasted tuna sandwich served with fresh tomato slices. If you like your tuna cooked more thoroughly, you may want to add more mayonnaise for moisture.

## Chef Lynn's Secrets:

- Clarified butter has its milk solids removed. Just melt whole butter and skim off the white foam that rises to the top. Then the butter can withstand higher temperatures. If you paint your bread with it evenly, you will get perfect, even browning. The bread will not brown properly in areas that have no butter.

- Make your own wasabi mayonnaise by blending ½ cup mayonnaise with 2 or 3 tablespoons wasabi cream or 1 teaspoon wasabi powder.

- Watch the sides of the tuna as you sear it. You will clearly be able to see how much you are cooking the tuna through because it will quickly turn brown.

# Chapter Eleven

# *Stocks, Sauces &*
# *Salad Dressings*

# Lesson Eleven

## *What's important to know about stocks, sauces and dressings?*

Sauces are one of the most important parts of any cook's repertoire. They add color, moisture, and most of all a range of flavors that can make or break your dish. In the famous Chef Escoffier's time, there were five so called "Mother Sauces". These are called brown sauce (thickened beef stock + spices), velouté (chicken stock thickened with roux + flavoring), béchamel (milk thickened with roux + flavoring), Tomato and hollandaise (egg yolks emulsified with butter + flavoring). All other major sauces come from these basic sauces. You will find the recipes for them in this section and if you know these techniques, you can make a great sauce for any meat, poultry or fish by flavoring them differently to match your dish.

Today, however, people need less time consuming ways to make sauces. Good stocks and quick thickeners are readily available in all grocery stores. You can make some wonderful sauces without starting from scratch. This chapter will show you how. For example, if you buy stock in a store, simply simmer it for awhile until it reduces by a third. The process of reducing (extracting some of the moisture) increases the flavor. Then build your sauce from there. You will already have cut out hours of work. Look at the Variations listed after the main sauces and you will find ways like this to cut your effort and still add lots of flavor to your dish.

Quick, modern sauces can also be made by simply combining ingredients. For example, melt crème Fraîche over low heat. Whisk in ½ teaspoon cornstarch to thicken it and then flavor it with chives, tarragon or other herbs that compliment your dish.

Types of Thickeners for sauces:

Your sauce will not always be the "perfect" consistency that you would like. Here are some things you can use for quick fixes. Mix a very small amount at a time. Give it a few minutes to work and repeat until you get the thickness you desire. If your sauce is too thick, you can thin it with any liquid ingredient listed on the recipe.

- **Flour** (especially cake flour because it is the starchiest flour and makes the creamiest and quickest sauces) is derived from the grain of wheat. Make a slurry by mixing it in equal parts with liquid to a consistency a little thinner than paste. Add it to a hot product for thickening. You can make a slurry with water, but the best ones are made with wine or broth.

- **Cornstarch** is made from the starch found in corn. Use it exactly like flour, but does not require as much cooking time.

- **Arrowroot** is a starch made from a certain vegetable root. It has three times the thickening power of flour and thickens almost instantly. It can be used close to serving time with good results.

- **Roux** is a mixture of equal parts of cake flour and clarified butter. 3 oz. flour can thicken about 1 quart of milk (or half and half or cream). Roux requires 20 minutes of cooking time to completely gelatinize the flour, in other words, to get rid of the raw flour taste. The longer you cook it, the more impurities will cook out. This makes a very stable sauce that you can keep in the refrigerator for up to a week.

Roux can be white, blonde or brown, depending on how long you cook it before adding the liquid. Each is progressively more flavorful. Which you use depends on the color you want in the finished sauce. The lightest is the most powerful. You can make it ahead and store it in the refrigerator or make it as the beginning of the process for making your sauce.

- **Beurre manié** is similar to roux, but is whole butter instead of clarified butter. It's mixed together at room temperature with your hands.

- **Tapioca** is a starch that has no flavor, no odor and no protein. It is therefore a good thickener to use for gluten free diets. It also works great for thickening fruit desserts, for reducing the moisture in lasagna so that it cuts better and for thickening soups.

- **Clear Gel** is a liquid or powdered clear starch used for fruit based recipes, like fruit coulis, fruit berry sauces, jams, jellies and pies. It has no taste and literally disappears as it thickens the fruit juices.

- **Gelatin** is a tasteless thickener made from the collagen of animal's skin and bones. It is used to thicken meat, fruit and vegetable juices to give terrines and other forms their structure.

To check the sauce's consistency, put a tablespoon of sauce on a plate and swirl it to see how it acts. You can always thicken the finished sauce by adding a sprinkling of arrowroot and cooking it a little more or you can thin it by whisking in a little chicken broth or cream.

If you want to make your own stocks:

Stocks give the basic flavor to sauces, so it's important to pay attention to making them well. Almost unconditionally, stock recipes call for mirepoix. This is a mixture of chopped flavoring vegetables. The basic recipe for this is 50% onion, 25% carrot and 25% celery. While I'm chopping the vegetables, I usually pile them in sections in a pie plate or simply in a circle on the counter. Then I can clearly see the ratio. The ratio can, however, be changed to include other types of onions and leek as well as other types of white vegetables. The more variety, the more sophisticated the taste. The longer the cooking time, the larger you should chop these vegetables so the flavor can steep out slowly.

Body parts with joints are more gelatinous than others and therefore are better for making stock. Use a mix of bones, but these would include shank, neck bones, wings and feet. Younger animals are also better, so for example, veal would be better than beef.

Always start with cold water. Simmer – don't boil – and don't touch except to carefully skim often. These are the rules of the road for stocks and broths. Stocks are made from bones and broths contain meat. You can cool them quickly and then freeze them for up to 3 months.

Homemade stocks will acquire a consistency like jello when they cool. You can cut them into cubes and freeze them individually to make your own bouillon cubes.

Making your own Salad Dressings:

- If you are using a food processor you don't have to chop ingredients by hand. You can drop any solid ingredients (like shallots or figs) directly onto the running blade. Then add your liquid ingredients with a hand whisk. Processing olive oil can give it a metallic taste.

- This is a place where you should use your high quality olive oil because its ratio in the recipe is really high and its taste will come through. If you use one that has a peppery flavor, taste the final mix before you add any more pepper.

- These vinaigrettes are normally made with balsamic vinegar, but you can also use cider, white wine, red wine, or champagne vinegars. Try and match your choice with your flavoring choices.

# Balsamic Reduction Sauce *Makes about 3 cups*

Leonardo, an Italian chef I met in Düsseldorf, Germany taught me how to make this sauce. It's fantastic with beef.

2 tablespoons granulated sugar

2 cups high quality balsamic vinegar

1½ cups demi-glace (page 215)

Salt and black pepper

Fresh rosemary or sage

1. In a 2-quart saucepan, heat the sugar over medium heat until it turns light brown. Pull the pan off the heat and add the vinegar. Be careful because it can pop and splatter hot liquid. Whisk until blended. Return to the heat and cook for 2 minutes.

2. Add the demi-glace and a teaspoon of a few fresh spices, like rosemary or sage.

3. Simmer to a sauce consistency — about 5 minutes more. If necessary, strain through a fine sieve.

DON'T FORGET THE FIRST COMMANDMENT OF COOKING!

Be sure to TASTE your sauce and adjust the seasonings before serving.

**Chef Lynn's Secrets:**

- If you need to thicken this sauce, mix 1 teaspoon of cake flour or arrowroot with just enough water to make a runny paste. (This is called a slurry.) Add it sparingly; then cook and stir until the sauce is the right consistency. It it's too thick, whisk in a little more demi-glace.

- You can check your sauce for consistency, by spooning some on a plate and tipping it back and forth. It should be thick enough to hold its shape.

- If you don't want to make demi-glace, reduce 3 cups of purchased beef stock mixed with 1 tablespoon tomato paste by half. It's a decent substitute.

# Beef Stock + Variations: Sauce Español & Demi-Glace

*Makes 5 quarts*

8 pounds beef bones, with some meat on them

5 quarts water

2 large yellow onions, diced into large pieces

3 stalks celery, chopped into large pieces

3 carrots, peeled and chopped into large pieces

4 bay leaves

1 tablespoon black peppercorns, crushed with the flat side of a knife

3 fresh parsley stems (leaves removed), also crushed with the flat side of a knife.

## Chef Lynn's Secrets:

- Making your own stock will greatly improve the flavor of your homemade gravies and sauces. I also use it for cooking risotto and for simmering vegetables. It takes time and effort, so I like to dedicate a day every so often to making it. Freeze it in different sized containers so that it's always handy. Just hold the container under hot running water until it loosens and then heat it in a saucepan. It will be ready in no time.

- Need a quick substitute? Boil down "store bought" sauce by 1/3 to intensify the flavor. Thicken it and add spices and you will have a good sauce or gravy. See the Variation shown with chicken stock. Just substitute the reduced beef stock and proceed in exactly the same way to create beef sauce or gravy.

- For quick Español, sauté one large yellow onion, diced very small. Add 4 tablespoons tomato paste and heat. Mix it with 2 quarts of purchased beef stock and reduce it by half.

1. Preheat your oven to 400° F. Place the bones in a large casserole pan so that you only have one layer. Brown them in the oven for 30 minutes. Add the onions, carrots and celery and bake another 30 minutes or until it all browns. Remove from the oven and transfer the meat and vegetables to a large stock pot. Be sure to scrape out all of the drippings in the pan. You can add water to the pan to loosen up bits that are left. This is all flavor!

2. Add water to 2 inches above the meat and vegetables and simmer for 5 or up to 18 hours. About halfway through, add the bay leaves, peppercorn and parsley stems. Skim the foam off the top as often as you can. These are impurities rising to the top and your stock will be of higher quality if you do this.

3. Place a large piece of cheesecloth in a large, fine sieve and strain the broth.

4. Chill in an ice bath (a larger bowl of water and ice) to reduce the temperature quickly.

5. Refrigerate for up to 7 days or freeze for up to 3 months.

## Sauce Español:

When you roast the bones, brush the meat and vegetables with tomato paste about 20 minutes before you take them out of the oven. You will use 4-6 oz. of tomato paste. (This is called pincé.) Otherwise, make exactly like the beef stock.

## Demi-Glace:

Combine equal parts of Sauce Español and beef stock. Simmer the mixture until it is reduced by half.

These techniques can also be used for lamb, veal and pork.

# Chicken Stock  *Makes 5 Quarts*

8 pounds raw chicken bones

5 quarts water

(Try and use 25% wings and/or feet because they contain the most gelatin and make good stock)

2 yellow onions, chopped into large dice

4 stalks celery, chopped into 1 inch pieces

4 carrots, peeled and chopped into 1 inch pieces

4 bay leaves

1 tablespoon peppercorns

4 parsley stems (leaves removed), crushed to release their flavor

1. Rinse the bones in cold water and place them in a large stock pot.

2. Add the onion, carrot and celery.

3. Cover with water to 2 inches above the bones.

4. Bring to a boil and then immediately reduce heat to simmer for 3 or no more than 8 hours. Using a small strainer or spoon, carefully skim often.

5. Add the bay leaves, peppercorns and parsley stems during the last hour.

6. Strain through a fine sieve lined with cheesecloth.

7. Cool in an ice water bath to bring the temperature down quickly.

8. Keeps up to one week refrigerated or up to 3 months frozen.

## Chef Lynn's Secrets:

- The difference between stock and broth is that broth is produced with pieces of meat as well as bones. When making stock, however, you should have some meat on the bones for flavor and richness.

- You can tie the spices in cheesecloth, but I don't always bother because straining the stock at the end will catch any little pieces that you don't want to transfer through to the stock.

- If you start with frozen bones, cover them with water and bring it to a boil. Then strain it off and start over with cold water to complete your stock. This will remove some of the impurities and is called blanching.

# Quick Variation: Chicken Gravy   *Makes 2 cups*

3 cups "store bought" chicken stock
　or broth

1 carrot

1 stalk celery

½ yellow onion

1 bay leaf

4 peppercorns

2 parsley stems (leaves removed), crushed
　with the flat side of a knife

Arrowroot or cornstarch

Salt, pepper and cayenne pepper

**Chef Lynn's Secrets:**

- You can make this quick gravy ahead and heat it on the stove at serving time. It will keep up to 7 days in the refrigerator.

- You can also just reduce the stock, thicken it and add the spices. It will still be good.

- Speaking of "store bought" stock, whenever I'm using that I put it on to simmer for as long as I have time for, up to a half an hour. This reduces the water content and intensifies the flavor.

1. Buy a good quality stock at your local grocery store.

2. Place 3 cups of stock in a large saucepan with 1 carrot, 1 stalk celery and ½ yellow onion, cut into large dice. Add 1 bay leaf, a few crushed peppercorns and a couple of crushed parsley stems if you have them. Simmer until the liquid is reduced by ⅓ to increase the flavor. Skim off any foam on the top.

3. Strain the stock to remove the vegetables and spices. Thicken it with arrowroot or cornstarch mixed with just enough water or white wine to make a paste. Start with one teaspoon of thickener. Whisk it in and cook it for 3 or 4 minutes. If it's still not thick enough, repeat until the sauce is the consistency you desire.

4. Add ½ teaspoon each salt and white pepper and a pinch of cayenne pepper. Now taste the sauce. If you like more salt or pepper, add some more.

# Vegetable & Fish Stock    *Makes variable amounts*

These stocks make nice bases for light colored sauces.

### Chef Lynn's Tips:

- **Technique:** A "chinois" is a cone shaped sieve with a handle. To trap as many impurities as possible, line the sieve with cheesecloth before pouring your stock through.

- **Flavor:** Before using your stock, simmer it for about 45 minutes to reduce the water content and intensify the flavor.

- **Fish Stock** can be made using the same technique. In your freezer, save shells from shrimp and other crustaceans or use fish bones. When you have enough, use a ratio of 5 lbs. to 2 quarts water. Add mirepoix and spices, and simmer for an hour and a half. Skim and drain. Use to cook lobster or to make sauces for fish.

You can save a lot of money in the kitchen just by being resourceful. Make delicious stock by saving clean scraps and peelings from any of the following vegetables:

Cabbage, carrot, celery, leek, onion (yellow, white or red), parsnip, potato, shallot, turnip

Store in a covered container for up to 5 days, adding scraps as they become available. You can make the stock at any time.

### Method:

1. Cover vegetable scraps (however many you have) with cold water to 2 inches above the vegetables.

2. Add 5-6 sprigs fresh thyme, 6 crushed black or white peppercorns and 3 crushed parsley stems.

3. Bring just to a boil. Then immediately turn heat down to simmer for 1½ to 2 hours.

4. Strain into a clean container using a chinois or fine sieve.

5. Cool quickly and refrigerate for up to 7 days or freeze for up to 6 months.

**Note:** How much of each vegetable to include? Think about your end use and/or your favorite tastes. If you love the taste of carrot, for example, and are planning to use your stock to make carrot risotto, the stock could contain lots of carrot peelings to enhance the carrot taste. For general purposes, it should be 50% from the onion family (yellow or white onions, leek or shallot). Root vegetables for the rest are always good. Just do not use strongly flavored vegetables like asparagus.

# Contemporary Sauces

Note: Always taste your sauces just before serving. If necessary, adjust the seasonings.
To hold your sauces, place them in a small pan, then place that pan in a larger pan of hot water.

## Béchamel Sauce with Contemporary Variations:

- **Basic:** (Makes 3 cups) A traditional sauce with modern variations: (Pasta) Melt 3 tablespoons butter; then whisk in 3 tablespoons flour. Whisk often and cook for 3 minutes. Gradually whisk in about 3 cups of milk. Simmer for at least 20 minutes to cook out the flour taste. Season with ½ teaspoon salt, ½ teaspoon white pepper and ½ teaspoon nutmeg. For the variations, prepare the béchamel and add the other components at the end. Omit the nutmeg when making the variations.

- **Caper:** (Seafood) Stir in ½ cup caper berries.

- **Citrus:** (Fish and chicken) Stir in the juice and zest from 1 lemon or 1 orange.

- **Cheese:** (Pasta) Make the béchamel with milk or heavy whipping cream. Whisk in 2 tablespoons butter and ⅓ to 1 cup grated cheese at the end. Parmesan, Asiago, Swiss, Gruyère, Cheddar or goat cheese are especially good choices.

- **Horseradish:** (Meat) Whisk in ¼ cup meat broth, 3 tablespoons prepared horseradish, 1 tablespoons balsamic vinegar and 3 tablespoons sugar.

- **Mustard flavored:** (Seafood, meat, pasta) Whisk in 3 tablespoons Dijon mustard at the end.

- **Olive:** (Meat, pasta) Stir in ⅔ cup chopped olives, black or green.

- **Parmesan-Tomato:** Mix in 3 tablespoons Parmesan and 1 chopped, fresh tomato.

- **Sun-dried Tomato:** (Meat, chicken, pasta) Stir in ⅔ cup slivered sun-dried tomatoes and ¼ cup cooked minced onion. Add 2 tablespoons oil from the jar.

## Beurre Blanc

Flavored butter sauce – A traditional sauce with contemporary variations that is great with fish or seafood.

- **Basic:** In a small frying pan, sauté 2 tablespoons minced shallots. Add 2 tablespoons champagne or white wine vinegar and 4 tablespoons fruity white wine. Simmer until all of the liquid has evaporated. Remove from heat and whisk in 1 cup of whole butter, a little at a time. Season with approximately ½ teaspoon salt and ½ teaspoon white pepper. Serve as is or add a flavoring below before seasoning with salt and pepper.

- **Caper:** Stir in 4 tablespoons capers.

- **Chive:** Stir in ½ cup minced fresh chives.

- **Curry:** Stir in ¼ cup coconut milk, 1 tablespoon curry powder, 1 tablespoon sugar, 3 tablespoons fresh cilantro, ½ teaspoon salt, ½ teaspoon white pepper and a pinch of cayenne pepper.

- **Lemon:** Whisk in 1 tablespoon fresh lemon juice and 1 tablespoon lemon zest.

- **Sun-dried tomato:** Stir in ¼ cup sun-dried tomato, cut into slivers.

- **Thyme:** Stir in 1 tablespoon minced fresh thyme and ½ teaspoon ground thyme.

# Contemporary Sauces *(continued)*

## Boursin® Sauce:

(Chicken and Crêpes) Heat and thin Boursin® cheese with just enough heavy cream to make a sauce.

## Burgundy-Mustard Sauce:

Sweat 2 minced shallots in 1 tablespoon butter. Add 1 cup strong red wine from Burgundy and 1½ cups beef stock. Simmer until thick, about ½ hour. (If necessary, you can thicken it with a little arrowroot mixed with just enough wine to make a paste). Stir in 3 tablespoons Dijon mustard, 2 tablespoons butter and ¼ cup sun-dried tomatoes cut into tiny slivers. Season to taste with salt, pepper and cayenne pepper.

## Cassis Gravy:

(Meat) Sauté 2 tablespoons shallots in 2 tablespoons olive oil. Deglaze with ¼ cup red wine. Add 1½ cups beef or veal stock. Simmer to reduce and thicken if necessary with 3 tablespoons cake flour mixed with just enough wine to make a paste. Add 2 tablespoons cassis liqueur and 2 tablespoons whole butter at the end.

## Chicken Cream Gravy:

Melt 3 tablespoons whole butter. Whisk in 3 tablespoons cake flour. Gradually whisk in 2½ cups chicken broth. Simmer for 20 minutes. Whisk in about ½ cup heavy cream or a little more if it needs to be thinner. Taste and season with about 1 tablespoon fresh lemon juice, ½ teaspoon salt, 1 teaspoon white pepper and a pinch of cayenne pepper.

## Cucumber Sauce:

(Seafood or vegetables) Using a food processor, combine ½ shallot and 1 chopped English cucumber (no seeds). Add 1 tablespoon lemon juice, ¼ teaspoon salt and ½ teaspoon white pepper. Mix with 1 cup sour cream.

## Curry-Coconut Sauce:

Sweat ¼ cup minced onion in 1 tablespoon butter. Whisk in 1 cup coconut milk, ½ teaspoon ground ginger, 1 cup chicken or vegetable stock and 1 tablespoon curry powder. Heat. Season with ¼ teaspoon salt, ½ teaspoon white pepper and a pinch of cayenne pepper or to taste.

## Dried Mushroom Sauce:

(Beef, chicken or pasta) Place 4 tablespoons dried mushrooms in 2 cups water and let it sit for 30 minutes or longer to plump the mushrooms up. Drain the liquid and reserve it. Chop the mushrooms very small or slice them very thin. Sweat 1 minced shallot in 3 tablespoons butter. Stir in 3 tablespoons cake flour. Gradually whisk in ¼ cup white wine and about 2½ cups beef, chicken or vegetable stock and ½ cup heavy whipping cream. Simmer for at least 20 minutes. Season with salt, pepper and cayenne pepper. If the sauce needs to be thinned, add more stock or cream. Optional: At serving time, mix in 4 tablespoons chopped, fresh thyme.

## Fresh Morel Mushroom Sauce:

(Beef, chicken or pasta) Make as dried mushroom sauce, above, except use 1 cup fresh, thinly sliced morel mushrooms. Omit the step where you put the mushrooms in water. Use beef stock and serve with beef.

## Goat Cheese Sauce:

(Meat, chicken or pasta) In a food processor, combine 4 oz. goat cheese with 2 tablespoons heavy whipping cream (or more if it's too thick). You can also use Boursin® or bleu cheese. A good garnish is chopped pistachios.

## Gorgonzola Sauce:

(Meat, pasta) In 2 tablespoons olive oil, sauté 2 tablespoons minced onion. Add ¼ cup white wine and 1 to 2 cups chicken or other stock and ¼ cup cream. If necessary, thicken with cake flour or arrowroot mixed with just enough wine to make a paste. Stir in ¼ cup gorgonzola, and ¼ cup sun-dried tomatoes cut into small slivers, salt, pepper and a pinch of cayenne pepper.

## Mustard Dill Sauce:

(Seafood) Using a food processor, combine 2 cups fresh dill (leaves only, no stems), ½ cup mayonnaise, ½ cup Dijon mustard, ¼ cup champagne vinegar or white balsamic vinegar, pinch of salt, pinch of white pepper, pinch of cayenne pepper and 1 tablespoon olive oil. Process until well blended. If you need to thin it, use a little more olive oil.

## Parsley Whipped Cream Foam:

(Fish or chicken) Process the leaves only from one bunch of parsley in your food processor. Add ½ shallot and process again. Add 1 cup chicken stock and process again. Season with salt and white pepper. Chill until serving time. At the last minute, add ½ cup heavy cream, whipped.

## Pepper Foam:

Sauté 2 tablespoons onion in 2 tablespoons olive oil. Mix in 1 red pepper, chopped small. Add ¼ liter chicken broth. Salt, pepper and cayenne pepper to taste. Purée.

## Red Pepper Coulis:

This is a colorful sauce that pairs well with crab cakes, fish, chicken or even steak. You can also make coulis with other vegetables and fruits.

Ingredients: 3 tablespoons olive oil, 1 shallot, diced large, 1 large red pepper, diced large, ¼ cup fruity white wine, 1 tablespoon cake flour, 1 cup chicken broth, ½ cup cream or milk. ½ teaspoon each salt and pepper, 1 teaspoon fresh lemon juice and 1 teaspoon hot sauce.

Method: Over medium heat, in a one quart saucepan, heat 3 tablespoons olive oil. Add the shallot and pepper and sauté until soft. Pour in ¼ cup fruity white wine. Cook until wine is absorbed, about 5 minutes.

Stir in 1 tablespoon cake flour and cook for 1 minute. Then stir in 1 cup chicken broth and ½ cup heavy cream or milk. Simmer for about 10 minutes, until thick. Using an immersion blender or food processor, purée the sauce. Season with ½ teaspoon salt and ½ teaspoon pepper, 1 teaspoon lemon juice and 1 teaspoon hot sauce. Turn heat to low and simmer for about 15 minutes or until thick.

## Ricotta Sauce:

(Meat, chicken or pasta) Using a food processor, combine 1 cup ricotta with ¼ cup tomato sauce, ½ teaspoon salt, ½ teaspoon white pepper, and 1 teaspoon hot sauce (such as Tabasco®).

## Saffron Sauce:

(Chicken or seafood) Sauté 2 tablespoons shallots in 2 tablespoons olive oil. Add a large pinch of saffron. Add ¼ cup white wine and simmer for 3 minutes or until the saffron colors the liquid. Add 2 cups chicken broth and 1¼ cups heavy whipping cream. Simmer to reduce or thicken if necessary. At the end, stir in 2 tablespoons whole butter and salt and white pepper to taste.

## Tomato Salsa:

(Sausage or fish) Chop 3 cloves garlic and 2 tomatoes. Mix with 1 tablespoon granulated sugar and simmer until the garlic is soft, about 3 minutes. Add 1 teaspoon cinnamon and ½ teaspoon nutmeg, ¼ teaspoon salt, 1 teaspoon pepper and a pinch of cayenne pepper. Simmer for 15 minutes. Serve hot or cold.

## Wasabi Sauce:

(Meat or fish) Thin ⅓ cup wasabi mayonnaise (available in Japanese markets) with 2 tablespoons lime juice. Garnish with garden onion cut on an angle.

# Make Ahead Gravy    *Makes 3 cups*

½ cup fruity red wine

1 tablespoon balsamic vinegar

3 cups beef or chicken stock

1 shallot; 3 tablespoons butter

3 tablespoons cake flour

3 tablespoons apple cider reduction (page 223) or apple jelly

¼ cup heavy cream or milk

1. Place ½ cup of a fruity red wine, 1 tablespoon balsamic vinegar and 3 cups beef stock in a small saucepan. Simmer over medium heat until the liquid is reduced to ⅔, about 25 minutes. Keep the sides of the pan scraped off so the residue doesn't burn and ruin the flavor of your gravy. You will still be able to see how far it is reducing by the marks on the sides of the pan.

2. In the meantime, finely mince a whole shallot and sauté it over medium heat in 3 tablespoons butter until the shallots are soft and golden. Whisk in 3 tablespoons cake flour and cook over low heat for 3 or 4 minutes.

3. Whisk in the stock/wine reduction, 3 tablespoons apple jelly or cider reduction and ¼ cup cream or milk. Cook over low heat for 20 more minutes. (If necessary, thin with more cream or thicken with a little more cake flour mixed with cream or stock.)

**Chef Lynn's Secrets:**

- This gravy is really a lifesaver! It can be made several days ahead and refrigerated. Then just heat it up at the last minute and add the drippings from your pan and thin or thicken as required.

- You do not have to add cream to this recipe if you don't want the fat. It's delicious without it.

- If you don't like the looks of your gravy or if it's lumpy, you can always purée it using an immersion blender or kitchen machine.

- To check to see if your gravy is a good consistency, spoon some onto a plate and tilt it to see how it behaves. If it makes a run for it, you need to thicken it. If it sits there like a blob, you need to thin it.

# Cider Reduction

*Makes one cup*

This is one of the most delicious things you will ever taste. It's simple, inexpensive and adds a ton of flavor.

1 gallon fresh apple cider

1. Pour a gallon of fresh cider into 4-quart saucepan.

2. Simmer it until the liquid reduces to one or two cups (about 2 hours).

3. Refrigerate it until you are ready to use it.

As it cools, the reduction will firm up and become like jelly. You can reheat it any time to use as syrup for pancakes or to glaze a pork roast or a chicken before and after baking. Serve more in a little pitcher on the side! You can use it as is on toast or bread instead of jelly.

Try it. You will love this natural product that needs no processed sugar at all.

**Chef Lynn's Secrets:**

- In order for the reduction to gel properly, you need fresh cider without preservatives.

- Once the cider is reduced, you can flavor it with puréed fruit or berries. Use about 4 tablespoons purée per cup of cider reduction. Great examples would be fig, pear or strawberry. Note that if you add purée the cider may not firm up into solid jelly as it does by itself.

# Fresh Tomato Sauce    *Makes 6 cups*

This quick and easy tomato sauce is best in the summer when vine ripened tomatoes are available. You can make it in 15 minutes.

6 cups tomatoes, peeled and chopped

2 stalks celery, minced finely

1 shallot, minced finely

1 clove garlic, minced (or 1 teaspoon powdered garlic)

2 tablespoons high quality lemon extra virgin olive oil

1 teaspoon salt and 1 teaspoon freshly ground black pepper

2 tablespoons fresh oregano, chopped or 1 teaspoon dried oregano

½ cup fresh basil, chopped

1. Place the tomatoes in a colander. Sprinkle with salt. Drain one hour.

2. Sauté the minced shallot and celery until just soft. Add the garlic and sauté one minute more.

3. Combine the shallot mixture with the olive oil, salt, pepper and oregano. Then mix this with the tomatoes.

4. Garnish with fresh, chopped basil leaves.

**Chef Lynn's Secrets:**

• This is the time to use your best olive oil. The taste will really come through. Add in 1 tablespoon fresh lemon juice which will give the sauce a nice taste lift.

• On the other hand, if you feel that the tomato sauce tastes too acidic, add 1 tablespoon sugar for every 4 servings. The sweetness will counteract the acid and smooth it out.

• Uses: Pasta sauce, bruschetta topping or a sauce for meat, fish or poultry.

# Hollandaise Sauce    *Makes about 3 cups*

Hollandaise is the sauce for Eggs Benedict and is also perfect for topping fresh asparagus.

1 shallot, minced very finely

⅛ cup white or champagne vinegar

½ cup white wine

8 white peppercorns, crushed

6 egg yolks

1 pound butter (whole or clarified —
   4 sticks)

1 tablespoon fresh lemon juice

Salt and white pepper, to taste

**Chef Lynn's Secrets:**

- Work quickly and bring the heat up slowly so your sauce doesn't curdle! Never start with a hot pan.

- If your sauce gets too thick, you can thin it with a tablespoon of hot water.

- Hollandaise only lasts about 2 hours, so make it as close to serving time as you can. If you hold it, keep it warm. A thermos with a spout works great for this purpose.

- I have successfully reheated refrigerated leftover hollandaise for immediate use by my family. You can try it by putting the sauce into a metal container and setting that in a bowl of very hot water for just a few minutes. Then whisk quickly and serve. This sauce will break quickly so that's why I say serve and eat immediately. It will still taste very good.

1. Place the shallots in a small frying pan with the vinegar, wine and peppercorns. Simmer until the shallots look dry and the liquid has evaporated.

2. Melt the butter and place it in a measuring cup with a spout. Keep it handy.

3. Place the egg yolks in the top pan of a double boiler and set it aside. Heat the water in the lower pan until it starts to boil and is steaming. Turn the heat to very low. Now place the top pan over the heat and start whisking. Whisk constantly until the yolks become a creamy yellow color and are thick. Keep the yolk off the hot sides of the pan where they could cook too fast and become scrambled eggs.

4. As soon as the yolks are thick, drizzle in the butter, whisking all the time. Your sauce should gradually acquire the consistency of mayonnaise.

5. Season with lemon juice, salt and pepper. Flavor it if desired (see below).

**Flavoring Ideas:**

Add ¼ cup of any of the following:

- Fresh chives, chopped

- Roasted garlic, minced

- Capers

- Tiny slivers of sun-dried tomatoes

- Chopped olives

- Chopped fresh dill (especially to serve with fish)

- Tarragon and other herbs

- Invent your own!

# Parmesan-Tomato Sauce    *Makes 2 cups*

This sauce is especially nice for mixing with pasta or as a topping for vegetables.

2 tablespoons butter

1 tablespoon cornstarch

Salt and pepper, to taste

About 2 cups heavy cream

3 tablespoons Parmesan cheese, grated

1 large, fresh tomato

1. In a small saucepan over medium heat, melt the butter. Whisk in the cornstarch.

2. Cook over low heat for 20 minutes, slowly whisking in the cream.

3. Whisk in the Parmesan.

4. Slice the fresh tomato and then cut the slices into thin strips. Mix into the sauce.

5. Add salt and pepper, to taste.

**Chef Lynn's Secret:**

This sauce is a modern version of béchamel sauce. Drizzle it over steamed vegetables or vegetable terrines to add color, moisture and flavor.

# Flavored Oils & Vinegars

Flavor your own oils to make their tastes stronger, to invent your own combinations and to save money if you use a particular type a lot. Attractive, different shaped bottles can differentiate them.

**Oils:** Canola, **vegetable** or **olive oil** can all be flavored the same way.

1. Mix 2 quarts of water with ¼ cup of salt and bring it to a boil.

2. Blanche 1 cup of herbs in the salted water as indicated below. (You can either place them in a sieve with a handle and hold them in the water or leave your chopped herbs on the cutting board and scrape them directly into the boiling water. Then pour the water through a fine sieve when they are done.) Drain them and squeeze them dry. Then chop them into pieces.

3. Put 1 cup of oil and the herbs in a food processor and process until blended – about 2 minutes. Pour into bottles and refrigerate until you need to use them.

**Basil, chives, fennel, mint** and **parsley** have thin leaves and only require 10–15 seconds of blanching time.

**Rosemary** and **thyme** are thicker and require about 30 seconds of blanching time.

**Chef Lynn's Secrets:**
- Oils should be stored in the refrigerator. They will get thick when chilled, so store in a container with a large opening so you can scoop out the oil you need with a ladle.
- Young olive oil is best. It should be used within one year of the press date on the bottle.
- Aged vinegars can be very expensive. Save money by reducing less flavorful or younger vinegars to intensify their flavor. Simmer on low heat until they are reduced by ¹/₃ to ½.

**Vinegars:** are easier.

Just put your choice of ingredients into the vinegar and store it in a cool, dark place for 3–4 weeks. The amount of spices, etc. that you put in is variable, so invent your own. Here are some suggestions for additions to 2 cups of vinegar: (I suggest you make it with balsamic, white or dark.)

- 2 tablespoons fresh lemon juice and 2 fresh figs, chopped

- 1 cup chopped basil leaves or other herbs

- 5 cloves chopped garlic

You get the idea!

# Understanding Vinaigrette (Salad Dressing)

Vinaigrette is a basic ratio of oil to vinegar with a few seasonings. It's a base for most other dressings. Use the following table to learn how to invent your own, suited perfectly to your tastes!

Choose ingredients as indicated and simply mix together using a whisk: (Using a food processor can give oil a metallic taste.)

| Basic Vinaigrette Recipe<br><br>Use all ingredients | Flavorings<br><br>Choose One | Herbs & Spices<br><br>Choose one in addition to or instead of Column 2 | Enhancements<br><br>(Optional)<br>Choose one | Make it creamy<br><br>(Optional)<br>Choose one |
|---|---|---|---|---|
| ⅔ cup high quality olive or canola oil | ¼ cup fresh berries, puréed | 2 T fresh ginger | ½ shallot, minced | ½ to 1 cup sour cream or crème fraîche |
| ⅓ cup vinegar* | 2 T mustard (Dijon, Spicy Brown®, Mucky Duck®, honey mustard — whatever you like!) | 1 T horseradish | ¼ cup white, yellow or green onion, minced | ½ to 1 cup mayonnaise (Make a vegetable dip by adding more until it's thick.) |
| 2 teaspoons fresh lemon juice | ¼ cup figs, minced | ¼ cup fresh fennel, minced | For sweetness, add 1 T honey or karo syrup** | ½ to 1 cup whipping cream or buttermilk |
| ¼ teaspoon salt | ½ cup crumbled blue or goat cheese | 3 cloves fresh or roasted garlic, minced | | |
| ½ teaspoon pepper | ½ cup Parmesan or other cheese, finely ground | ¼ cup fresh herbs, minced (chives, basil, parsley, mint, oregano, etc.) | | |
| Pinch of cayenne pepper | 1 T truffle oil | 2 teaspoons poppy seeds | | |
| | | 3 T caraway seeds | | |
| | | 1 teaspoon garlic powder | | |
| | | 1 teaspoon onion flakes | | |
| | | 1 T dry mustard (Coleman's®) | | |
| | | ETC. | | |

*Vinegar can be (from light to heavy) champagne, rice wine, white wine, sherry, apple cider, red wine or dark balsamic vinegar.

**Granulated sugar will not properly dissolve unless you heat it.                    T = tablespoon

# Classic Salad Dressing Variations

All dressings can also be used as vegetable dips. Vinaigrette style dressings can be used as meat, poultry, or fish marinades. For marinades, leave out the salt and add it at cooking time.

## Blue Cheese Dressing:
Mix together:
6 oz. cream cheese
¼ cup mayonnaise
¾ cup sour cream
2 teaspoons minced garlic
1 tablespoon lemon juice
3 tablespoons buttermilk
1½ oz. crumbled blue cheese
Stir in ½ cup blue cheese chunks.

## Caesar Salad Dressing:
Whisk together:
¼ cup mild olive oil
2 tablespoons each mayonnaise and fresh
    lemon juice
1/3 cup white wine vinegar
1 teaspoon Dijon mustard
½ teaspoon Worcestershire sauce
1 teaspoon garlic powder; 1 teaspoon
    anchovy paste
Pinch each of salt and black pepper
Stir in: ¼ cup shredded Parmesan cheese

## French Dressing:
Whisk together:
¾ cup olive oil; 1 tablespoon sugar
¼ cup champagne vinegar
2 tablespoons finely minced fresh parsley
1½ teaspoon Coleman's® dry mustard
1½ teaspoon each onion powder, salt and
    paprika
½ teaspoon pepper; ½ teaspoon garlic powder

## Fresh Herb Vinaigrette:
Whisk together:
2/3 cup mild olive or vegetable oil
1/3 cup champagne vinegar
¼ cup minced shallot
1 teaspoon garlic powder
2 tablespoons each fresh parsley, thyme and
    chives, minced

## Green Goddess Dressing:
Mix together:
½ cup mayonnaise
½ cup crème fraîche
¼ cup minced green onions
4 tablespoons fresh chives, chopped tiny
2 tablespoons Italian parsley, chopped tiny
1 tablespoons fresh lemon juice
Pinch each of salt and pepper

## Hot Bacon Dressing:
Chop 2/3 cup bacon into small pieces and fry
    them in a frying pan.
Sprinkle with salt and black pepper.
Stir in: ¼ cup apple cider vinegar
    2 tablespoons sugar.
Toss with salad while still hot.

## Lemon Poppyseed Dressing:
Whisk together.
2/3 cup mild olive oil
1/3 cup champagne vinegar
1/3 cup fresh lemon juice
2 teaspoons minced shallot
1 teaspoon Dijon mustard
1/3 cup sugar
1 tablespoon poppy seeds

## Raspberry Vinaigrette:
Whisk together:
2/3 cup mild olive or vegetable oil
1/3 cup raspberry wine vinegar
½ cup sugar
1 tablespoon Dijon mustard
Pinch each of salt and pepper

# Chapter Twelve
# *Garnish & Decorative Sides*

# Lesson Twelve

## *What's important to know about garnish and decorative sides?*

There is really only one rule for garnish and it's that everything on your plate must be edible. Beyond that, it's up to you and that's it.

You can make beautiful plates in a variety of ways. I personally am not big on non-edible plate garnishes that you end up moving around with your fork and wondering where the rest of the food is. I like to see things that add taste, a little nutrition, a use for leftovers and always eye appeal. I feel like you should be able to eat your garnish and fit it on a spoon. For example, a big piece of kale that looks pretty but I'm not going to eat doesn't fit the bill. A beautiful, peppery edible nasturtium flower on the other hand, is delightful.

Here are some ideas:

- **Sliced, whole, cooked eggs**

- **Quail eggs**

- **Sieved, cooked egg yolk**

- **Bits of leftovers**

- **Tiny chopped vegetables** in contrasting colors that add taste as well as color, like peppers, onions, radishes, tomatoes, cucumbers, cooked mushrooms, etc.

- **Fresh herbs:**

  Note: Chop fresh herbs the day you plan to use them. You can store them for awhile and even overnight in a container covered with plastic in the refrigerator.

  Parsley and most other green, leafy herbs can benefit from double washing. I know that it seems contrary, but if you wash these herbs, chop them and then wrap them in a towel and squeeze them in the towel under running cold water to wash them again, you wash away some of the chlorophyll which is

what is making them "gummy". The result is a beautiful sprinkling of herb that adds color, taste and interest to your dish.

To store whole fresh herbs, place them in a dish with sides and cover them with a wet paper towel. Replace the paper towel daily. They should easily keep for several weeks.

- **Colorful berries:**

  To store berries, place a piece of parchment paper on a cookie sheet with sides. Pour the berries on this in a single layer so that air can circulate around them. Do not wash the berries until you are ready to use them. Each morning, remove any berries that have deteriorated.

- On a personal note, we have wonderful fresh markets where I live, but for garnish ideas and specialty greens that are trimmed just right, I head to the local Japanese market. The produce is especially fresh and often perfectly ripened. Somehow they seem to sell things like quail eggs for one quarter of the price I've seen them in other places. The best thing, though, is that you can buy just a little bit of different things. This way, you can have a lot of variety without a lot of leftovers.

- That's something that's key about the professional chef's kitchen. Because of their volume, they can always choose a little of this and a little of that to enhance the look of a plate or to add some interest to the meal. It's hard for the home cook to have that kind of variety available unless they have the ability to buy in small quantities. This is another reason that learning to use your leftovers is key. Great garnish ideas can come from a leftover that you can chop or slice or use to create an addition to the next meal.

Flavor has many elements: taste, smell, texture and last but certainly not least, eye appeal.

# Apple Chutney

*Makes about 3 cups*

3 Granny Smith apples (2½ to 3 cups diced)

⅔ cup champagne vinegar

1 cup golden raisins

½ cup dark brown sugar

½ cup light brown sugar

1 cup granulated sugar

1 tablespoon dried ginger

1 tablespoon dried lemon or orange peel

½ teaspoon garlic powder

2 teaspoons hot sauce (Tabasco® or Red Devil®)

1.  Peel and core the apples. Dice them into 1-inch pieces.

2.  Put the apples in a 4-quart saucepan. Add all of the other ingredients and stir thoroughly.

3.  Bring to a boil. Reduce the heat to low and simmer for one hour. (The sauce will thicken up.) Stir occasionally as it cooks.

4.  Cool. Transfer to a covered container and chill for at least 2 hours before serving.

## Chef Lynn's Secrets:

- Apple Chutney is a good accompaniment for pork and chicken. Serve it as a sauce or a side.

- When you stir the hot mixture, keep the sides scraped down so sauce that splashes there won't burn. Heat resistant spatulas are great for stirring down hot pots or to sauté with. Rubbermaid® makes a good one. You can identify it because it has a red handle.

- Using light brown sugar in this recipe will produce a chutney that is more golden in color.

# Applesauce  *Makes 2 cups*

4 tart apples

3 tablespoons granulated or brown sugar

2 teaspoon cinnamon

1. Peel, core and dice the apples.

2. Cook over low heat until the apples become mushy.

3. Mash and stir in the sugar and cinnamon.

NOTE: If your apples are not juicy enough and begin to stick to the pan, add a little water.

**Chef Lynn's Secrets:**

- Applesauce makes a perfect side dish for pork. I often make it in the autumn when apples in Michigan are fresh and abundant.

- I like to leave some chunks in the applesauce to make the texture a little chewy and more interesting.

- Granny Smith apples work well in this recipe, but any tart apple will make great applesauce.

# Caramelized Onions  *Serves 6*

This is the quintessential topping for steak, chicken or pork.

3 large yellow onions

¼ cup clarified butter or olive oil

1 large pinch each of salt and pepper

**Optional:** 1 tablespoon granulated sugar and/or 2 tablespoons apple brandy or cognac

**Chef Lynn's Secrets:**

- Resist the urge to stir! Stirring cools the onions and causes them to sweat and delay the browning process. The initial high heat is important for even caramelization, which gives this dish its beautiful color and also its rich taste. Stir just enough to keep the onions from burning.

- When you do stir, it's a good idea to use a heat proof spatula to keep the brown bits on the bottom of the pan stirred into the onions as much as possible. They contain a lot of wonderful flavor. Heat proof spatulas have red handles and can be obtained at www.jbprince.com, a great place to also find just about any chef tool you can imagine.

- To learn how to clarify butter, see page 23.

- Use caution when adding alcohol to a hot pan because it can flame up.

1. Cut the onions in half. Lay the flat side down on your cutting board and slice thinly. The onions are now cut into strips. (These are called julienne strips.)

2. Heat the butter or oil in a large frying pan. It should get hot enough so that when you drop a piece of onion in, you hear a sizzling sound (sauté) but not hot enough to smoke. Place the onions carefully in the pan in a single layer and stir only when you see they are browning. Once they start to nicely brown, you can reduce your heat slightly to medium high.

3. When the onions are completely brown, some chefs add a little sugar to sweeten them. You do not have to do this, but it does make them irresistible. Sugar is intoxicating and makes people want more, so use your own conscience in adding it.

# Cooked Greens   *Serves 4 as a side dish*

## Collard Greens

These are tougher and require much longer cooking time. You will need:

1 bunch or bag of collard greens

8 oz. bacon, sliced into small pieces (or 1 turkey leg, whole)

½ cup minced onion

4 to 5 cups broth (Beef, chicken or vegetable)

Salt and pepper, to taste

1. Collard greens purchased in a bag are usually already roughly chopped. Just use them as is. If you get a bunch of whole leaves, cut off the tough stem ends. Then chiffonade them as described above.

2. In a 4-quart saucepan with tall sides, sauté the bacon until it just begins to crisp. (If you are using a turkey leg, brown it in hot olive oil. Then add it to the pot.) Add the onion and continue to sauté until the onion is soft.

3. Add the greens and almost cover with broth. (The greens will wilt down into the broth as they get hot.)

4. Simmer on low heat uncovered, approximately 2–3 hours, until tender. Lift out with a slotted spoon. (If you are using a turkey leg, remove it, take the meat off the bone, chop it and return the pieces to the greens. Season with salt and pepper, as needed. Serve or reheat at serving time.

## Spinach, Cabbage, Beet greens and Swiss chard

The tender greens above can all be "wilted" the same way:

1. Use one bunch of greens. In the case of beets, cut them away from the beets.

2. Cut away any thick stem ends and discard. Roll 4 or 5 leaves together. Make ⅛-inch slices all across the roll. (Chiffonade)

3. Heat 2 cups of broth in a medium sized frying pan.

4. Add the greens and cook for several minutes, just until they are wilted.

5. Season with salt and pepper.

**Chef Lynn's Secrets:**

• Greens provide an attractive and edible base presentation for almost any meat or fish. Just spoon the greens onto serving plates and place the meat or fish on top of them.

• To easily slice the bacon for the collard greens, cut a pound of bacon strips in half. Then make ⅛-inch slices across all the strips at once. This will give you the perfect size for the greens.

# Fried Green Tomatoes   *Serves 4*

2 green tomatoes, sliced

¼ cup olive oil

2 eggs, lightly beaten

2 tablespoons cream or half and half

1 cup Italian or fresh breadcrumbs

1 cup Parmesan cheese, grated

½ teaspoon each salt and freshly ground pepper

About ¼ cup lemon olive oil for frying

1.  Prepare two bowls. In one, whip the egg and cream together. In the other, mix the breadcrumbs and cheese.

2.  Dip the tomato slices in the egg and then in the bread crumb and cheese mixture. Use one hand to dip the tomato into the egg and the other to press the crumb mixture into the tomato. Place on a cookie sheet covered with parchment paper and let them rest for 20 minutes. Whenever you fry anything that is breaded, the breading is less likely to come off if you let it sit before frying.

3.  Heat the oil (on high heat) in a large frying pan and fry both sides of the tomatoes until they are light brown and crispy, about one minute per side. Turn with a spatula, not tongs because the tongs can rip the tomatoes apart.

4.  Place on absorbent paper towels to cool. Move to a serving dish. These can be eaten hot or cold.

5.  Add salt and pepper. Check the seasoning and add more if you think it needs it.

## Chef Lynn's Secrets:

• You can use breadcrumbs, flour, cornmeal or panko (Japanese breadcrumbs) depending on what you have on hand. Breadcrumbs will add some taste but Panko is flavorless. I find that flour is fine, but cornmeal is a little gritty for my taste. For that reason, I like to use breadcrumbs in this recipe.

• Be careful not to crowd the pan when frying or the tomatoes will not get crispy and there's nothing worse than soggy breading! I like to use a small pan and fry them one or two at a time, changing the oil as necessary.

# Incredible Edible Garnish    *Serves 4*

Garnish has its place in the home as well as in the restaurant. We first generate appeal with our eyes. It should be edible and add taste, color and texture.

Basil Chiffonade

Daikon Radish Sprouts

**To double wash parsley and other flat leaf herbs:** First wash and chop the leaves. Then place them in a clean dishcloth and roll the cloth up so the leaves are in the middle. Hold the dishcloth under running water and twist to wring out the water. Continue until you don't see much green juice (chlorophyll) seeping out. Unroll and the chopped leaves will sprinkle much better.

## Incredible Edible Garnish

Think about the flavors and colors in your dish. Choose something that is bite-sized or smaller and complements it — both in taste and color.

Chiffonade:

For this technique, place 3 or 4 leaves on top of each other and roll them up from the side. Make thin cuts from one end to the other. The closer your cuts, the finer your chiffonade will be. Fluff the pieces into a pile to separate them.

- Basil (fresh)
- Beet and Swiss chard greens (wilted in hot stock)
- Bok choy (wilted in hot stock)
- Cabbage (fresh or wilted in hot stock)
- Lettuce (fresh or wilted in hot stock)
- Mint (fresh)
- Spinach (fresh or wilted in hot stock)
- Swiss chard (wilted in hot stock)

Chopped or Sliced (Julienne):

- Artichoke (steamed)
- Avocado
- Celery stalks (peeled)
- Cheeses
- Cooked vegetables
- Cucumber (small)
- Egg white, hard boiled
- Fresh corn cut off the cob
- Jicama
- Leaf herbs like cilantro, parsley and tarragon (double washed, See note at left.)
- Hard boiled egg
- Herbs like chives, dill, oregano, sage
- Leek
- Nuts
- Olives

- Onions, all types
- Peppers, fresh (several colors), cut into tiny, thin (julienne) strips and placed in a small nest
- Peppers, roasted
- Radishes
- Snow peas
- Sun-dried tomatoes
- Tomatoes (peeled, seeded and chopped tomato is called concassée.)
- Turnip (cooked in boiling, salted water)

Diced (Chopped) or Julienne strips:

- Red, green and yellow sweet pepper
- Bread (fresh or toasted breadcrumbs or croutons)
- Cooked or raw vegetables
- Cucumber
- Onions, all types
- Peppers (roasted)
- Summer squash
- Zucchini

Fried:

- Fresh basil leaves

    Drop in very hot oil for about 4 seconds, but toss in from a distance because they really splatter. **BE CAREFUL!!** Remove with tongs and drain on absorbent paper towel.

    These will keep for several days uncovered and on paper towels, They are very fragile, so make extra.
- Potatoes (cooked and sliced into tiny strips)
- Quail eggs (boiled and sliced or fried)
- Okra, (sliced and fried in oil)

Grated:

- Carrot
- Cheese
- Cooked egg yolk (pushed through a sieve)
- Radish

Ground:

- Nut
- Spices

- Sliced on an angle:
- Carrots and other cooked vegetables
- Garden onions

- Spiral cut (looks like long noodles on the plate):
- Carrot
- Cucumber
- Apple
- Radish

Whole:

- Berries
- Edible flowers
- Spices

Edible flowers

# Marinated Cheese     *Serves 4*

1 small wheel of Brie or Camembert cheese

3 cups good quality Pinot Noir wine

1. Cut the brie into 8 equal wedges. Pierce each one all over and all the way through. The best thing for this is a metal cake tester, but if you don't have one, use a slim toothpick.

2. Place the cheese in a quart container, leaving space around each piece.

3. Completely cover the cheese with the wine and let it marinate for two or three days.

4. Serve alone, with a piece of apple pie or with a cheese course.

**Chef Lynn's Secret:**

Very soft cheeses like Camembert and Brie work best for this technique. It works as an appetizer or is a nice addition to any after dinner cheese tray.

# Ogden Nine Day Sweet Pickles  *Makes 1 gallon of pickles*

These crunchy pickles are perfect with sandwiches, chicken or meat salads.

1 gallon pickling cucumbers
  (about 14, 4 to 6 inches long)

Water

1½ cups kosher salt, divided

1 cup vinegar

1 teaspoon alum

4 pounds sugar

1 quart cider vinegar

3 tablespoons pickling spice

**Special Equipment:**
  5 gallon stone or ceramic crock

## Chef Lynn's Secrets:

- **ALUM** is a chemical compound that acts as a preservative and helps to make and keep the pickles crisp.

- **PICKLING SPICE** is a mix of spices used to flavor the pickles. It usually consists of allspice, bay leaves, cardamom, cinnamon, cloves, coriander, dill seed, ginger, juniper berries, mace, mustard seed and peppercorns.

- You can find both in the spice section of your local grocery store.

**DAY ONE:** Slice cucumbers into ½ inch pieces. Place in a crock and cover with water + 1 cup of salt. Place a plate on top of the pickles and weigh it down so they all stay under water.

**DAY TWO:** Add ¼ cup salt.

**DAY THREE:** Add ¼ cup salt.

**DAY FOUR:** Drain the pickles, rinse them and cover with fresh water.

**DAY FIVE:** Repeat Day Four.

**DAY SIX:** Repeat Day Four.

**DAY SEVEN:**
1. Place the pickles in a large saucepot. Add 1 cup vinegar, 4 cups water and 1 teaspoon alum. Bring to a boil. Then turn the heat down and keep hot over low heat for 5 hours. Drain and return them to the crock.

2. In the meantime, make a solution of 4 pounds sugar, 1 quart cider vinegar and 3 tablespoons pickling spices wrapped and tied in a small piece of cheesecloth. Heat this solution and pour it over the pickles.

**DAY EIGHT:** Drain the sweet solution off of the pickles and into a large saucepan. Heat it to boiling and pour the same solution over the pickles again.

**DAY NINE:** Repeat DAY EIGHT, but this time put the pickles in boiling hot, sterilized jars and seal the lids according to the jar manufacturer's directions.

# Vegetable Crisps   *Makes enough for 4 to 6 people*

Use one beet, turnip, parsnip, sweet or white potato

1 quart canola, corn or peanut oil

Salt

**Chef Lynn's Secrets:**

- French mandolins are great, but rather expensive. You can find a small plastic version of this in Japanese markets that works just fine. I have both and tend to use my plastic one more because it's a lot easier to pull out and also to clean.

- With ANY mandolin, CAUTION is in order! Make sure your vegetable is dry, and your mandolin is stable. Hold your hand out flat when sliding the vegetable back and forth. Stop well before your hand gets close to the blade. If you get too close, you can rip your hand in a very bad way. Don't ask me how I know that!

- For even browning, fry vegetable chips and battered onions at 325°F. If you want to slice them the night before, you can store them in the refrigerator in water. This reduces the starch, so then you can fry them a little hotter, up to 350°F. If you do this, make sure you use paper towels to dry the chips off before tossing them into the oil. Do this with caution because the water can cause popping and even more frying danger than normal.

1. In a heavy pan, heat the oil to 325°F. If you fry a lot of chips, keep it at that temperature by turning the burner off and on.

2. Using a French mandolin or food processor blade, slice the vegetables very thin. You can control how large your chips are by the angle you use when you slice. This may take some experimentation. (Thin slices and the frying temperature are the secrets! Too hot and they will burn around the edges before they are done. Too cool and they will be mushy.)

3. Fry until crisp and very slightly brown. Note that the chips will continue to brown after you remove them from the oil, so take them out just before they reach your desired browning.

4. Use a slotted spoon to move the chips to absorbent paper towels. Lightly salt immediately, while the oil is still hot or it won't stick.

5. Store at room temperature and do not cover. You can make these 8 hours ahead and still have very fresh tasting chips.

# Pesto    *Makes one cup*

½ clove elephant garlic

8–10 large stems of fresh basil leaves
(3 cups)

5 tablespoons extra virgin olive oil

1/3 cup Parmesan cheese, coarsely grated

¼ cup pine nuts

½ teaspoon kosher salt

¾ teaspoon Lawry's® seasoned pepper

1. Place the garlic clove on a baking dish and drizzle it with olive oil. Bake in a preheated 350°F oven about 45 minutes, until soft. Cool.

2. Fill a food processor with fresh basil leaves. Pulse slightly to chop. Add the garlic and pulse again.

3. Add the oil and process for about 15 seconds, until all ingredients are uniformly mixed.

4. Add Parmesan cheese and pine nuts. Pulse a couple of times to mix. Mix in the salt and pepper.

5. Make this ahead for the flavors to blend. It will keep for weeks in the refrigerator.

**Variation:** Sun-dried tomato pesto:

Add 1 cup sun-dried tomatoes, chopped into small slivers.

## Chef Lynn's Secrets:

• Elephant garlic is a form of garlic with very large cloves. The taste is much milder than its smaller cousins. Roasting it makes it milder still.

• Fresh pesto is so versatile! It's great as a pasta or pizza sauce, as a topping for fish or poultry or simply spread on fresh bread. Basil is easy to grow in pots on your patio or balcony so you can enjoy it all summer long.

• Store leftover pesto in the refrigerator for up to a week . Top it with a light coating of olive oil to keep it from turning brown. As an alternative, you can cover it with plastic wrap as long as you press the plastic directly against the pesto to keep the air out.

# Roasted Garlic  *Serves 4*

1 head of garlic (any type)

Approximately 4 tablespoons extra virgin olive oil, plain or flavored

Optional if serving with bread: Salt and pepper

1. Place the garlic head on your cutting board, tip side down. Press with the heel of your hand to loosen the cloves.

2. Cut the tips from each clove and peel away the papery skin.

3. Pile cloves in a ceramic garlic baker and drizzle the cloves with the oil. (If you are serving the garlic with bread, you can lightly salt and pepper it if you like, or not. Your choice.) Cover and place in a preheated 350°F oven for about 45 minutes. (You can cook all sizes of garlic together. Just pile the smaller ones together to equal the height of the larger ones.) Turn the oven off and leave the covered garlic inside for another 45 minutes. Refrigerate to keep cooked garlic for several days.

4. Use as called for in another recipe or serve with slices of fresh French bread. You can also use plain oil for baking and serve with flavored oil. I like to use lemon oil in both cases.

**Chef Lynn's Secrets:**

- Many recipes for roasting garlic say to slice the top off of the garlic head, leave the papery skin on and drizzle the oil into the cloves. This makes it easy to squeeze the soft garlic out of the cloves when you are finished.

  I like, however, to peel and separate the cloves for a couple of reasons. First, you can see any bad spots in the garlic and cut them away. If you are using a garlic baker like the one pictured, you already have a nice presentation when you pull it out of the oven. Third, you can easily spread it with a knife or use it in another recipe with no further fuss.

- If you don't have a ceramic garlic baker, just place the cloves on a piece of tin foil, drizzle with olive oil and closely wrap the foil around the pile of garlic. Bake on a cookie sheet or casserole pan.

# Scotch Quail Eggs   *Serves 6*

6 quail eggs

½ pound minced chicken

2 tablespoons fresh chives, chopped

1½ teaspoon Dijon mustard

¼ cup shallot, diced small

¼ teaspoon each salt and pepper

1 cup all purpose or cake flour

2 eggs, lightly beaten

1 cup Italian breadcrumbs

Peanut or corn oil for deep-frying
  (1½ quarts)

1. In a 2-quart saucepan, bring a quart of water to a boil. Lower the quail eggs into the water with a spoon and boil for 4 minutes. Drain and let them cool. When cool, carefully remove the shells.

2. Combine chicken, chives, mustard, shallot, salt and pepper in bowl. Divide mixture into 12 equal portions.

3. Set up your counter with a bowl of flour, a bowl of chicken mixture and bowl with beaten egg. Follow these steps for each egg:

   a. Lightly dredge eggs in flour.

   b. Shape chicken mixture around each egg.

   c. Roll in the flour.

   d. Dip into beaten egg.

   e. Roll in the breadcrumbs.

4. Just before serving, deep fry in peanut or corn oil at about 325°F until golden brown. Drain on paper towels.

5. Serve halved eggs with puréed chutney or plum jam.

## Chef Lynn's Secrets:

- Traditional Scotch eggs are made with a chicken egg, which is quite large by the time you wrap it with chicken. I find it more attractive to use the smaller quail egg. Then the finished size is that of a normal egg. You will also find that the coating on this one is tastier.

- Be careful about your oil temperature. If the oil is too hot, the outside will get too brown before the chicken is completely cooked.

- Quail eggs can be found in specialty and Japanese markets.

Appendix A:

# Common Substitutions

Remember that with cooking, substituting ingredients is not just about replacing a certain flavor. It's also important to achieve the same texture and consistency that was intended for the original ingredient. Whenever possible, use the ingredient called for in your recipe. This list is only for emergencies!

Allspice (1 teaspoon dried)
- ½ teaspoon ground cinnamon + ½ teaspoon ground cloves

Amaretto (2 tablespoons)
- ¼ to ½ teaspoon almond extract

Apple Pie Spice (1 teaspoon)
- ½ teaspoon ground cinnamon + ¼ teaspoon ground nutmeg + ⅛ teaspoon ground cardamom

Baking Powder (1 teaspoon)
- ¼ teaspoon baking soda + ½ teaspoon cream of tartar.

Brown Sugar (Light - 1 cup)
- 1 cup granulated sugar (white) + 2 tablespoons molasses

Brown Sugar (Dark - 1 cup)
- 1 cup granulated sugar (white) + 2 tablespoons molasses

Buttermilk (1 cup) Do not combine with raw fish and this doesn't work well with salad dressings:
- 1 cup milk + 1 tablespoon lemon juice or white vinegar (Let stand 5 minutes before using.)
- 1 cup milk + 1 teaspoon cream of tartar

Cake Flour (1 cup)
- ⅞ cup all purpose flour + 2 tablespoons cornstarch

Cheese
- Asiago: Equal parts of Parmesan
- Ricotta: Equal parts of cottage cheese or quark

Chilies, Thai
- Scotch bonnet peppers

Chocolate, semi-sweet (1 oz.)
- 1 oz. unsweetened chocolate + 1 tablespoon sugar

Chocolate, unsweetened (1 oz.)
- 3 tablespoons unsweetened cocoa + 1 tablespoon butter

Chocolate Chips, semi-sweet (½ cup)
- ½ cup semisweet chocolate

Cornstarch (1 tablespoon)
- 2 tablespoons all-purpose flour

Cream, light (1 cup)
- 2 tablespoons butter + 1 cup minus 2 tablespoons milk

Cream, heavy (1 cup)
- 1 cup evaporated milk
  NOTE: This is not appropriate for whipped cream and many baked goods

Cream, sour (1 cup)
- 1 cup plain yogurt or quark

Eggs (2 large)
- 3 small

Fish Sauce (¼ cup)
- ¼ cup Worcestershire sauce

Flour (1 tablespoon — to thicken liquids)

- 1½ teaspoons cornstarch or 1 teaspoon arrowroot

Flour, self rising (1 cup)
- 1 cup all purpose flour + 1½ teaspoon baking powder + ½ teaspoon salt

Garlic (1 clove)
- ¼ teaspoon garlic powder or minced dried garlic

Gelatin (1 sheet)

- ¼ oz. unflavored powdered gelatin granules

Ginger, fresh (1 tablespoon)

- 1 teaspoon ground ginger

Half and Half (1 cup)

- ½ cup whole milk + ½ cup heavy cream
- ⅔ cup skim milk + ⅓ cup heavy cream

Herbs (fresh)

- To substitute dried herbs, divide the fresh amount by 3.

Honey (1 cup)

- ¾ cups sugar + ¼ cup juice or water

Lemon (1 medium, juiced)

- 2–3 tablespoons bottled lemon juice

Lemongrass

- Equal amounts of grated lemon zest + 1 teaspoon fresh lemon juice

Lemon Peel (1 teaspoon)

- ½ teaspoon lemon extract

Milk, whole (1 cup)

- ⅔ cup 1% milk + ⅓ cup half and half
- ¾ cup 2% milk + ¼ cup half and half
- ½ cup evaporated milk + ½ cup water

Mustard, dry (1 teaspoon)

- 1 tablespoon prepared mustard

Orange (1 large, juiced)

- ½ to ¾ cup concentrated orange juice

Pumpkin Pie Spice (1 teaspoon)

- ½ teaspoon ground cinnamon + ¼ teaspoon ground ginger + ⅛ teaspoon ground allspice + ⅛ teaspoon ground nutmeg

Sugar, Palm

- Equal parts maple sugar or brown sugar moistened with maple syrup

Sugar (Superfine) (1 cup)

- Grind 1 cup of granulated sugar in the food processor for 45 seconds

Sugar, Powdered (Confectioner's) (1 cup)

- 1 cup granulated sugar + 1 cup cornstarch. Grind in food processor.

Tahini (1 cup)

- 1 cup sesame seeds ground in a blender + 1 teaspoon sesame oil OR
- ⅓ cup peanut butter + 4 tablespoons sesame oil

Tapioca, Minute ® (1 tablespoon)

- 2 tablespoons all purpose flour

Tomato Sauce (1 cup)

- ⅓ cup tomato paste plus ½ cup water

Tomato Juice (1 cup)

- ½ cup tomato sauce plus ½ cup water

Whipped Cream

- Whip 1 cup of lowfat ricotta cheese with 3 tablespoons nonfat plain yogurt and ½ teaspoon vanilla extract

Wine (1 cup)

- 1 cup grape juice (red or white) + 1 tablespoon vinegar or lemon juice

Yogurt

- 1 cup sour cream or quark

Appendix B:

# Measurements & Conversions

| | | | | |
|---|---|---|---|---|
| Dash | = | Less than ⅛ teaspoon | | |
| 3 teaspoons | = | 1 tablespoon | = | ½ fluid ounce |
| 4 tablespoons | = | ¼ cup | = | 2 ounces |
| 5⅓ tablespoons | = | ⅓ cup | = | 2⅔ ounces |
| 8 tablespoons | = | ½ cup | = | 4 ounces |
| 12 tablespoons | = | ¾ cup | = | 6 ounces |
| 16 tablespoons | = | 1 cup | = | 8 ounces |
| 2 cups | = | 1 pint | = | 480 milliliters |
| 2 pints | = | 1 quart | = | Approximately 1 liter |
| 4 quarts | = | 1 gallon | = | 3.75 liters |
| 8 quarts | = | 1 peck | = | 8.8 liters |
| 4 pecks | = | 1 bushel | = | 35 liters |
| 1 ounce | = | 28.35 grams (rounded to 30) | | |
| 16 ounces | = | 1 pound | = | 430.59 grams (rounded to 450) |
| 1 kilogram | = | 2.2 pounds | | |

1 gallon = 4 quarts = 8 pints = 16 cups (@8 oz) = 128 ounces

1 measuring cup holds 8 ounces

1 egg white = average 2 ounces

1 lemon = 1¼ ounces of juice

1 orange = 3¾ ounces of juice

**To convert ounces and pounds to grams:**

Multiply ounces by 28.35; multiply pounds by 453.59

Temperature:

| °F | °C |
|------|-----|
| 32 | 0 |
| 150 | 66 |
| 200 | 93 |
| 250 | 121 |
| 275 | 135 |
| 300 | 149 |
| 325 | 163 |
| 350 | 177 |
| 375 | 191 |
| 400 | 204 |
| 425 | 218 |
| 450 | 232 |

**To convert Fahrenheit into Celsius:**

- Subtract 32 from the Fahrenheit number.
- Divide the answer by 9.
- Then multiply that answer by 5.

**To convert Celsius into Fahrenheit:**

- Multiplying the Celsius temperature by 9.
- Divide the answer by 5.
- Now add 32.

| Volume Conversions | | |
|---|:---:|---|
| 1 teaspoon | = | 5 milliliters |
| 1 tablespoon | = | 15 milliliters |
| 1 fluid ounce (2 T) | = | 30 milliliters |
| 2 fluid ounces (¼ cup) | = | 60 milliliters |
| 8 fluid ounces (1 cup) | = | 240 milliliters |
| 16 fluid ounces (1 pint) | = | 480 milliliters |
| 32 fluid ounces (1 quart) | = | 950 milliliters (.95 liter) |
| 128 fluid ounces (1 gallon) | = | 3.75 liters |

(NOTE: Metric values have been rounded.)

| Weight Conversions | | |
|---|:---:|---|
| ¼ ounce | = | 7 grams |
| ½ ounce | = | 14 grams |
| 1 ounce | = | 28 grams |
| 4 ounces | = | 113 grams |
| 8 ounces (½ pound) | = | 227 grams |
| 16 ounces (1 pound) | = | 454 grams |
| 32 ounces (2 pounds) | = | 908 grams |
| 40 ounces (2.2 pounds) | = | 1 kilogram |

Appendix C:

# Meat Cooking Temperatures

The most important advice I can give is to get a cooking thermometer. Learn how to calibrate it and never cook by time. Always cook by temperature!

Be sure your thermometer is not resting against a bone, which is porous and will be cooler than the meat. This can cause you to overcook the meat because you think it's not as hot as it really is.

| This chart lists minimum internal temperatures that the US Department of Agriculture considers to be "safe" temperatures for cooking the following products: | |
|---|---|
| All ground meats: (including meat, pork and fish): | 155°F (68°C) for 15 seconds |
| Injected meats: (including brined ham and any flavor injected roasts) | 155°F (68°C) for 15 seconds |
| Pork, beef, veal and lamb: | Steaks and chops should be cooked to 145°F (63°C) for 15 seconds. |
| Roast cuts of pork, beef, veal and lamb: | Roasts should be cooked to 145°F (63°C) for 4 minutes. |
| Poultry (chicken, turkey and duck, whole or ground): | 165°F (74°C) for 15 seconds |
| Fish: | 145°F (63°C) for 15 seconds |
| Eggs, poultry, fish and meat cooked in a microwave oven: | 165°F (74°C). Then let food stand for 2 minutes after cooking. |

**\*Common Cooking Temperatures used in Restaurants:** (Not to be confused with "safe" temperatures listed above.)

These are temperatures used for beef steaks, beef roasts, etc.

Rare: 120°F

Medium Rare:125-130°F

Medium: 140°F

Medium well to well done: 150°F +

**A note about "Carryover cooking"**

When you take meat out of the oven, frying pan etc., it will continue to cook for a short period of time. It will generally rise about 5°F before it starts to cool. Therefore, to account for this, take your meat away from its heat source when it reaches 5°F below your target temperature. Otherwise, your meat will be overdone.

Appendix D

# Abbreviations and Terms

Mince = Chopped very tiny

Dice = Chopped as follows:

**Small:** ¼" cubes

**Medium:** ½" cubes

**Large:** ¾" cubes

Pinch = The amount you can "pinch" between your thumb and index finger. For a small pinch, just use the tips of your fingers. For a large pinch, pinch all you can.

Fold = Carefully mixing with a folding motion. Place your spatula in the middle of the mixture and then scoop out and up the sides of the bowl. The purpose of careful folding is so that the mixture is not deflated.

Garden onion = scallion

oz. = oz.

lb. = pound

® = Registered trademark

T = tablespoon

Salt & pepper to taste: Let's say you have a casserole sitting before you that represents eight portions. Imagine that the portions are sitting side by side. Each one belongs to a person. If one was yours, how much salt and/or pepper would you want to sprinkle on each one? So sprinkle on the salt. Taste the results and decide if you need some more. Adjust or not. Then do the same with the pepper. That's it!

Sear: To brown at a high temperature.

Pepper = If no special kind of pepper is indicated, use black pepper.

Mixed pepper = any brand of mixed peppers, for example, McCormick®

An Exercise: Try this to learn how to add "Salt and pepper to taste":

Carve out some time to teach yourself the power of the three things that kick up flavor the most: **Salt, lemon\*** and **pepper**

Make some plain mashed potatoes. Divide them into cup sized portions. Then add a little of each ingredient at a time and taste carefully until you experience the "kick." Try different combinations. Move on to the next "portion" and do it again. After awhile you will be making much more educated guesses.

Take note of the First Commandment in cooking! Always taste everything before you serve it to your guests. Use salt, acid and pepper to adjust the taste to your preferences. Use just a little cayenne pepper to add an almost unrecognizable "bite" that sits on the back of your tongue and finishes off the taste experience.

\*and in other cases, other acids like wine and vinegar

Appendix D:

*Think before you throw it away!*

# What to do with Leftovers:

Common leftovers can be useful components for your next meal — adding texture, variety and flavor. Turn them into colorful garnish or use them as components for a side dish. Following is a list that should fuel your imagination for using odds and ends that you tuck away in your refrigerator. Under refrigeration, cooked foods last up to 7 days, so save and recycle your leftovers! You will also save money in the process. Remember the rule though! SEVEN DAYS AND THROW IT OUT.

Bread crusts or trimmed crusts from toast points can easily become croutons. Just dice them into the crouton size that you would like. Place in a bowl. Drizzle with clarified butter and stir to distribute the butter. Place on a baking sheet and bake at 400°F for about 7 minutes. Stir and continue to bake until crispy (usually a couple of minutes longer).

To make homemade breadcrumbs from the crusts, place leftover crusts and pieces of bread in your kitchen machine and pulverize them into crumbs. Then follow the same steps as for croutons above. If your bread has a heavy crust, you may need to trim it off in order for your kitchen machine to work properly.

Chicken or beef: Slice into small strips. Mix in BBQ sauce, salt and pepper. Spread on a toast point. Top with a thin sliver of cheese. Place on a baking sheet and bake at 350°F just until cheese melts. Garnish with fresh basil chiffonade or chopped fresh chives. Serve as an appetizer.

Chicken, beef or fish:

- Mix with horseradish mayonnaise, salt and pepper. Use to fill hard boiled egg halves.

- Use as a sandwich filling with mayonnaise or mustard, salt and pepper.

- Use as a panini filling – just add thinly sliced cheese on top. Paint outside of bread with clarified butter or olive oil and grill in a nonstick pan or Panini grill.

- Use as a filling for savory crêpes. Top crêpes with your favorite sauce.

- Shred and make nachos or use in casseroles.

- Add to a similar kind of gravy to fortify it. Cook with the liquid ingredients and then purée it using an immersion blender or food processor at the end.

Crab Cakes: Use mix as a stuffing for beef filet, ravioli or seafood.

Fresh herbs can be dried and used much later.

Fresh pasta can be dried and kept for up to 3 months. Cooked ravioli can be fried in a small amount of clarified butter or olive oil and served with eggs.

Hard boiled eggs can be kept for up to a week. They can be chopped or thinly sliced for salads or garnish. The cooked egg yolk can be pushed through a sieve to make a feathery and bright yellow garnish.

Risotto: Cut small cubes of your favorite cheese. (It has to be a cheese that will easily melt. Examples: Fontina, Cheddar, mozzarella). Using leftover risotto, form a bite-sized ball around the cheese that completely conceals it. Dip the ball in beaten egg and then in finely chopped breadcrumbs or panko (Japanese breadcrumbs). Deep fry in hot peanut or corn oil until golden brown.

Small pieces of colorful vegetables can be trimmed and cut into shapes, julienne strips, or small dice and used for garnish.

Stalk ends of asparagus or other vegetables can be made into soup. See recipe: How to make soup out of any vegetable, page 74.

Sun-dried tomatoes and olives are packed in oil. When they are gone, use these oils to flavor grilled vegetables or salad dressings or rub it into steak or fish that you plan to grill.

Vegetable peelings and leftover bits (from tomatoes, onions and other root vegetables): When you have enough to fill ⅔ of a saucepan, you can easily use them to make vegetable stock. Simply add in any root vegetables that you don't plan on using before they will spoil, cover to 2" above with cold water. Bring to a boil. Reduce heat to simmer for 1½ hours. Skim the surface. Drain off stock. Cool quickly in an ice bath and use or freeze. You can also flavor the stock to fit your purpose. For example, if you want to make carrot risotto, then add extra carrots to the mix so it will have a dominant carrot taste.

## STANDARD VEGETABLE CUTS:

For those of you who want to get into more complicated recipe cuts, here are the standard ones:

Paysanne: Means "country". Rough cuts different shapes: ½" x ½" x ⅛"

Fermiere: ⅛" to ½"

Lozenge: Diamond Shapes ½" x ½" x ⅛"

Rondelle: Circles: Use a round vegetable and slice ⅛" to ½" thick

Tourné: Approx. 2" long, with seven sides

Batonnet: ¼" x ¼" x 2"

Julienne Strips: ⅛" X ⅛" X 1"

Small dice: ¼" cubes

Medium dice: ½" cubes

Large dice: ¾" cubes

# INDEX

# INDEX *(continued)*

# INDEX *(continued)*

PASSION: "a pursuit to which one is devoted; the subject of an engrossing pursuit." (Webster's Dictionary)

As we turned the last page of the last proof of this book, the passion flower was blooming in the backyard sun.

One who shared my passion intensely was my book designer, Jon Fenlon. Thank you, Jon, for your project leadership and amazing attention to detail. You are sorely missed.

# Heartfelt Thanks...

**To my friend, Ann Manix,**
for her confidence in my project and the brainstorming
that finally set me on my way.

**To my friend, Deb Chiesa,**
who convinced me I would love cooking school,
kept me laughing all the way through
and continues to support my every endeavor.

**To my friend, Karen Rooke,**
my dearest Florence Nightingale.

**To Tod Baker of Thomson-Shore,**
for his patience and contagious enthusiasm.

**To the awesome proof reading team:**
Joan Boddie, Perry Carroll, Mary Ann Chau, Nancy Craig, Talbot Payne,
Teri Petrie, Karen Rooke, Barbara Russell and Leanette Yasuda.

**To all of my girlfriends:**
who are always there for me. I am blessed to have so many!

**To my sisters, brothers and moms:**
Michelle Bauman and Barbi Sansom, Thomas and Mark Holcomb,
Lynn and Medell Holcomb, Shirley Wilson and Ruth Miller,
for their constant and fearless support.

**To all of my students who came to cooking classes:**
You asked the questions that convinced me
to pursue the publication of this book.

Lynn Miller was an extreme hobby cook for over twenty-five years. Driven by her love of cooking, entertaining and teaching, she then earned a degree in Culinary Arts from Schoolcraft College in Livonia, Michigan.

Chef Lynn also has a BSBA in Marketing from the University of Phoenix, has lived in Germany for eight years and has attended many specialty classes, including those held at the Ritz Escoffier and the Cordon Bleu in Paris, as well as in Provence and Stuttgart, Germany.

She designs cooking classes for fun loving cooks in and near Bloomfield Hills, Michigan, where she lives with her husband and two keeshonds.

Chef Lynn is a member of the Women Chefs and Restaurateurs (WCR) and the American Culinary Federation (ACF).

For more information, please visit www.flavorsecrets.com.